THIRD EDITION

QuickBooks® ONLINE

FOR ACCOUNTING

Glenn Owen

 CENGAGE

Australia • Brazil • Mexico • Singapore • United Kingdom • United States

QuickBooks® Online For Accounting,
Third Edition
Glenn Owen

Senior Vice President, Higher Education Product Manager: Erin Joyner

Product Director: Jason Fremder

Associate Product Manager: Jonathan Gross

Content Manager: Tricia Hempel

Marketing Manager: Chris Walz

Manufacturing Planner: Doug Wilke

Production Service: Lumina Datamatics, Inc.

Senior Designer: Bethany Bourgeois

Intellectual Property

   Analyst: Reba Frederics

   Project Manager: Carly Belcher

Cover Image Credit: ©blinkblink/Shutterstock

For product information and technology assistance, contact us at **Cengage Learning Customer & Sales Support, 1-800-354-9706.**

For permission to use material from this text or product, submit all requests online at **www.cengage.com/permissions.** Further permissions questions can be emailed to **permissionrequest@cengage.com.**

Library of Congress Control Number: 2019936414

Package ISBN: 978-1-337-91134-4
Book ISBN: 978-1-337-90270-0

Cengage Learning
20 Channel Street
Boston, MA 02210
USA

Cengage Learning is a leading provider of customized learning solutions with employees residing in nearly 40 different countries and sales in more than 125 countries around the world. Find your local representative at: **www.cengage.com.**

Cengage Learning products are represented in Canada by Nelson Education, Ltd.

To learn more about Cengage platforms and services, visit **www.cengage.com.**

To register or access your online learning solution or purchase materials for your course, visit **www.cengage.com.**

Printed in the United States of America
Print Number: 01   Print Year: 2019

Brief Contents

Chapter 1 **An Introduction to QuickBooks Online**   1

Chapter 2 **Sample Company Walkthrough**   15

Chapter 3 **Setting Up a New Company**   34

Chapter 4 **Operating Activities: Sales and Cash Receipts**   60

Chapter 5 **Operating Activities: Purchases and Cash Payments**   83

Chapter 6 **Investing and Financing Activities**   108

Chapter 7 **Payroll**   126

Chapter 8 **Budgets and Bank Reconciliations**   149

Chapter 9 **Adjusting Entries**   168

Chapter 10 **Financial Statements and Reports**   184

Appendix 1 **Sales Tax**   206

Appendix 2 **Comprehensive Case Problems**   207

Appendix 3 **Overview – Do I Need to Become QuickBooks Online Certified?**   223

Index   227

Contents

Preface vi

About the Author & Dedication xi

**Note to the Student
and Instructor** xii

**Chapter 1 An Introduction to
QuickBooks Online** 1

Overview 1
What Is QBO? 1
How Is QBO Similar/Different than the
  Desktop Version QuickBooks? 2
Creating a New QBO Account 3
Providing QBO Information 4
Navigating QBO 6
Assigning an Instructor as the
  Company's "Accountant" 10
Using QBO's Help Feature 11
End Note 13
Chapter 1 Practice 14
Chapter 1 Questions 14
Chapter 1 Matching 14

**Chapter 2 Sample Company
Walkthrough** 15

Overview 15
Begin Your Sample Company Walkthrough 15
Customers, Vendors, and Employees 17
Banking Transactions 21
Sales and Expense Transactions 23
Chart of Accounts 25
Lists 27
Reports 28
Company Settings 31
End Note 32
Chapter 2 Practice 33
Chapter 2 Questions 33
Chapter 2 Matching 33

**Chapter 3 Setting Up a
New Company** 34

Overview 34
Company Settings 35
Modify the Chart of Accounts and
  Establish Beginning Balances 36

Close Opening Balance Equity and
  Create a Balance Sheet 43
Create, Print, and Export a Transaction
  Detail by Account 45
End Note 46
Chapter 3 Practice 47
Chapter 3 Questions 47
Chapter 3 Matching 47
Chapter 3 Cases 47
Case 1 48
Case 2 51
Case 3 53
Case 4 56

**Chapter 4 Operating Activities:
Sales and Cash Receipts** 60

Overview 60
Services, Products, and Customers 60
Sales Receipts and Invoices 64
Cash Receipts 67
Transaction Detail by Account 70
End Note 71
Chapter 4 Practice 72
Chapter 4 Questions 72
Chapter 4 Matching 72
Chapter 4 Cases 72
Case 1 73
Case 2 75
Case 3 77
Case 4 79

**Chapter 5 Operating Activities:
Purchases and Cash
Payments** 83

Overview 83
Vendors 83
Purchase Orders 84
Bills 87
Payment of Bills, Use of a Credit Card,
  Payments for Items Other than Bills 91
Trial Balance 94
End Note 97
Chapter 5 Practice 98
Chapter 5 Questions 98
Chapter 5 Matching 98

Chapter 5 Cases	98
Case 1	99
Case 2	101
Case 3	103
Case 4	106

Chapter 6 Investing and Financing Activities   **108**

Overview	108
Fixed Assets	109
Long-Term Investments	110
Common Stock and Dividends	112
Long-Term Debt	114
Acquisition of a Fixed Asset in Exchange for Long-Term Debt	115
End Note	116
Chapter 6 Practice	117
Chapter 6 Questions	117
Chapter 6 Matching	117
Chapter 6 Cases	117
Case 1	118
Case 2	119
Case 3	121
Case 4	123

Chapter 7 Payroll   **126**

Overview	126
Employees	126
Payroll Accounts	128
Pay Employees	129
End Note	135
Chapter 7 Practice	136
Chapter 7 Questions	136
Chapter 7 Matching	136
Chapter 7 Cases	136
Case 1	137
Case 2	139
Case 3	142
Case 4	145

Chapter 8 Budgets and Bank Reconciliations   **149**

Overview	149
Budget Creation	149
Budget Reports	151
Bank Reconciliation	155
End Note	158
Chapter 8 Practice	159
Chapter 8 Questions	159
Chapter 8 Matching	159
Chapter 8 Cases	159
Case 1	160

Case 2	162
Case 3	164
Case 4	166

Chapter 9 Adjusting Entries   **168**

Overview	168
Trial Balance	169
Adjusting Journal Entries: Prepaid Expenses	170
Adjusting Journal Entries: Accrued Expenses	173
Adjusting Journal Entries: Unearned Revenue	174
Adjusting Journal Entries: Accruing Revenue	175
Adjusting Journal Entries: Depreciation	176
End Note	178
Chapter 9 Practice	179
Chapter 9 Questions	179
Chapter 9 Matching	179
Chapter 9 Cases	179
Case 1	180
Case 2	180
Case 3	181
Case 4	182

Chapter 10 Financial Statements and Reports   **184**

Overview	184
Income Statement	185
Balance Sheet	187
Statement of Cash Flows	190
Accounts Receivable Aging Summary	192
Accounts Payable Aging Summary	194
Inventory Valuation Summary	196
Customizing and Saving Reports	198
End Note	200
Chapter 10 Practice	201
Chapter 10 Questions	201
Chapter 10 Matching	201
Chapter 10 Cases	201
Case 1	202
Case 2	203
Case 3	203
Case 4	204

Appendix 1 Sales Tax   **206**

Appendix 2 Comprehensive Case Problems   **207**

Appendix 3 Overview – Do I Need to Become QuickBooks Online Certified?   **223**

Index   **227**

Preface

Overview

Accounting has arrived in the Cloud and its time has come. *Cloud computing* is a general term for anything that involves delivering hosted services over the Internet. According to a recent study by KPMG (a global network of professional firms), businesses large, medium, and small are using the Cloud to drive cost efficiencies, better enable a mobile workforce, and improve alignment with their customers and vendors.

Imagine being able to update your business's accounting information system from anywhere on any device using any operating system. That is where the global economy is going. Are you on the path?

Is This Text for You?

This text is for you if you are an instructor who desires a self-paced, self-directed environment for your students to learn the essentials of QuickBooks Online Plus (QBO) and to review their understanding of financial accounting and reporting.

This text is for you if you are a business owner looking for a self-paced, self-directed environment for yourself to learn the essentials of QBO as well as a means to refresh your understanding of financial accounting and reporting.

This book focuses on QBO. It is not designed for users of QuickBooks Pro, Accountant, or any other desktop version of QuickBooks. In that case, my QuickBooks Accountant books are a better fit. The desktop version and online versions are different, and though you can import files created in the desktop version into the online version, significant differences exist as discussed in Chapter 1.

Instructional Design

Each chapter of this text begins with a listing of expected student learning outcomes followed by a step-by-step explanation of how to obtain those outcomes. In most chapters, the explanations utilize a Sample Company created by Intuit in which the author demonstrates how various operating, investing, and financing activities of a business are captured and then reported in QBO.

End-of-chapter questions, matching, and student cases follow these explanations. The questions help you to review the text-explained concepts and processes, while the matching section helps with terms and definitions. The student cases provide the information necessary to add data to the student's company file. Each chapter requires the student to add information to the previous chapter's rendition. Thus, for success in learning, each student must complete the previous chapter's student case before attempting the next chapter's student case.

Each copy (license) of QBO will work with one and only one company other than the sample company provided online. In the author's other QuickBooks texts, multiple cases were available for illustration and practice. However, because of Intuit's limit of one company per license, that option was absent unless the user purchased multiple licenses, which was impractical and costly.

Solutions to each chapter's student case are provided in the instructor manual.

Case #	1	2	3	4
Name	Case 01 - Student Name (ID Number)	Case 02 - Student Name (ID Number)	Case 03 - Student Name (ID Number)	Case 04 - Student Name (ID Number)
Address	811 Prospect Street, La Jolla, CA 92037	811 Prospect Street, La Jolla, CA 92037	3990 La Jolla Shores Drive, La Jolla, CA 92037	6540 Sunset Blvd., Hollywood, CA 90028
Start using QBO	01/01/18	01/01/19	01/01/20	01/01/21
Company type - tax form	Corporation	Corporation	Sole Proprietor	Corporation
Company type - Industry	Retail Shop or Online Commerce	Retail Shop or Online Commerce	Retail Shop or Online Commerce	Fitness and Recreational Sports Centers
Business	Surfboard distributor	Toy distributor	Cell phone retail	Sports Gym
Inventory products	Surfboards	Remote control toys	Cell phones	T-shirts, Yoga pants
Service business	Consulting	Repairs	Repairs	Monthly Fee, Training
Track expenses	Yes	Yes	Yes	Yes
Bill payment terms	Net 30	Net 30	Net 30	Net 30
Checking account	Yes	Yes	Yes	Yes
Accounts receivable	Yes	Yes	Yes	Yes
Fixed assets	Yes	Yes	Yes	Yes
Track depreciation	Yes	Yes	Yes	Yes
Accounts payable	Yes	Yes	Yes	Yes
Long-term liabilities	Yes	Yes	Yes	Yes
Equity	Yes	Yes	Yes	Yes
Write checks	Yes	Yes	Yes	Yes
Receive payments on account	Yes	Yes	Yes	Yes
Make payments on account	Yes	Yes	Yes	Yes
Record sales receipts	Yes	Yes	Yes	No
Record sales invoices	Yes	Yes	Yes	Yes
Record bills	Yes	Yes	Yes	Yes
Add customers	Yes	Yes	Yes	Yes

(Continued)

Case #	1	2	3	4
Add vendors	Yes	Yes	Yes	Yes
Add employees	Yes	Yes	Yes	Yes
Add inventory items	Yes	Yes	Yes	Yes
Add service items	Yes	Yes	Yes	Yes
Add/delete accounts	Yes	Yes	Yes	Yes
Use journal entries	Yes	Yes	Yes	Yes
Purchase orders	Yes	Yes	Yes	Yes
Enter beginning balances	Yes	Yes	Yes	Yes
Process manual payroll	Yes	Yes	Yes	Yes
Hourly employees	Yes	Yes	Yes	Yes
Salary employees	Yes	Yes	Yes	Yes
Export reports to Excel	Yes	Yes	Yes	No
Trial balance report	Yes	Yes	Yes	Yes
Income statement report	Yes	Yes	Yes	Yes
Balance sheet report	Yes	Yes	Yes	Yes
Transaction detail by acct. report	Yes	Yes	Yes	Yes
Sales tax	No	No	Yes (override)	Yes
Adjusting (accrual) entries	Yes	Yes	Yes	Yes

Comprehensive Problems

Additional transactions for cases 1, 2, 3, and 4 can be found in Appendix 2. Students who have successfully completed a case in the text through Chapter 10 can be assigned these comprehensive problems. Each pick up in the month following the chapter work. For example in Case 1, chapter work occurred in January 2018, thus the comprehensive problem will describe transactions occurring in February 2018. The transactions included in February are similar in nature to those described in Chapters 3–10. Students assigned Case 1 would be able to complete comprehensive Case 1. Those assigned Case 2 would only be able to complete comprehensive Case 2 etc.

Textbook Goals

This textbook takes a user and a preparer perspective by illustrating how accounting information is created and then used for making decisions. QBO is user-friendly and provides point-and-click simplicity and sophisticated accounting reporting and analysis tools. The textbook uses proven and successful instructional design (described earlier) to demonstrate the application's features and elicit student interaction.

The first and foremost goal of this text is to help students review fundamental accounting concepts and principles through the use of the QBO application and the analysis of business events. The content of this text complements the first course in accounting principles or financial accounting. Thus, this text should either be used concurrently with an accounting principles or financial accounting course or be used subsequent to completion of such a course.

A second goal of this text is to teach students how to set up QBO for a business, use it to record business events, and use it to generate financial statements and reports. Acquiring these skills will help students improve their job prospects whether the company they work for uses QuickBooks or not.

A third goal of this text is to teach students the value of a computerized accounting information system and how it can be used to communicate important information to business owners, investors, and creditors.

Date Warning

The Sample Company (created and maintained by Intuit) is used to demonstrate many aspects of QBO in this text. The author has no control over the dates used by Intuit and those dates may change depending on when you are accessing the file online. The dates that appear in the figures supplied by the author in this text may not be the dates that appear on your screen.

The student cases (Case 1, 2, 3, and 4) are set in 2018, 2019, 2020, and 2021 respectively. If transactions are entered into the student case in other than the proper period, answers will be wrong. Be careful about entering dates into QBO when you are working on this case. The default date when entering new transactions into QBO is the computer's system date that may or may not be in those years.

Update Warning

QBO is frequently upgraded by Intuit to provide new features, correct errors, or improve functionality. This book was written in late 2018 and early 2019, and all figures are based on how QBO looked at that time. If you are using this text in 2019 or later, Intuit may have made modifications in how QBO looks and feels or functions. Differences will occur, which are out of the author's control.

Accounts vs. Categories Confusion

In early 2019, Intuit decided to change some terms used in the process of classifying business transactions involving bills, expenses, checks, purchase orders, and credit card transactions. In the past, as in all the known accounting world, a chart of accounts was created separating different business transactions into different accounts. Each account was assigned a category type: asset, liability, equity, revenue, or expense as well as a detail type and name. Inventory and service items were assigned an inventory asset account, income account, and expense account. Inventory was assigned to a category depending on the nature of their business.

QBO continues to use a chart of accounts. However, now accounts are assigned an account type: asset, liability, equity, revenue, or expense as well as a detail type and name. Business transactions (bills, expenses, checks, purchase orders, and credit card transactions) are now classified has having an effect on a particular category whereas before they were classified as having an effect on an account.

Throughout this text, figures illustrating bills, expenses, checks, purchase orders, and credit card transactions will have the title Account details not Category details and the column title as Account and not Category as shown on your QBO software. Steps will also use the term Account when your QBO software will reflect the use of the term Category. Once again, this change took place after this text was completed. Call outs are used in chapters 1 through 5 to highlight these differences. In chapters 6–10 no call outs are provided as its assumed students and instructors are now aware of these differences.

Despite these changes a chart of accounts is still maintained, and inventory and service items are still assigned an inventory asset account, income account, and expense account and Inventory is still assigned to a category.

No doubt this change will cause a significant level of confusion for both the student and instructor, which is out of the control of the author. Intuit, creator of QBO, was contacted multiple times about this change and the confusion it may cause and did not offer any explanation or comment.

Instructor as Your Accountant

Your instructor may choose to have you assign him or her as your accountant so that he or she can see your work and progress at his or her convenience without having you to "send" the file. In fact, you cannot "send" your file, since all the files are on the Cloud. Instructions on how to set your instructor as your accountant are provided in Chapter 1.

Video Demonstrations

Video demonstrations, created in 2015 and updated in 2017 and 2019, are available throughout this text and are referenced by a Demonstration Icon in the margin. These demonstrations are stand-alone full-action videos with audio showing step-by-step illustrations of business processes explained in this text. Intuit may have made some changes in how QuickBooks Online looks and functions, which may not be reflected in these videos. However, the author believes the videos in their present form convey the important steps and functions and are beneficial to students.

All of these are available via the text's companion website located at http://www.cengage.com. Navigate your browser to http://www.cengage.com. Type Glenn Owen in the Search for Books or Materials text box, and then click Find. Locate and then click the QuickBooks Online text from the listing provided.

Click the Free Materials tab and then click Access Now. When you navigate your browser to the student companion site for the text, you should see Video Demonstrations. Video Demonstrations need to be downloaded from the companion site to your computer by clicking the Video Demonstrations text. Usually, these files are downloaded to a folder on your computer called Downloads. In some cases you may be asked where you want these files downloaded.

The file you download is a very large compressed zip file. When you double click the file downloaded, you'll see a list of files. All of these need to be extracted (decompressed) first before you can view them. Click Extract to a folder, and then create a folder on your computer or flash drive that you want to contain all of your demonstration files. Remember where you extracted these files so that you can find them later.

About the Author

Glenn Owen is a retired member of Allan Hancock College's Accounting and Business faculty, where he lectured on accounting and information systems from 1995 to 2016. In addition, he is a retired lecturer at the University of California at Santa Barbara, where he taught accounting and information systems courses from 1980 to 2011. His professional experience includes five years at Deloitte & Touche as well as vice president of finance positions at Westpac Resources, Inc., and Expertelligence, Inc. Mr. Owen completed his 4th edition of his Using Excel and Access in Accounting text in 2016, which gives accounting students specific, self-paced instruction on the use of spreadsheets (Excel 2016) and database applications (Access 2016) in accounting. He has also recently completed the 15th edition of his QuickBooks Accountant for Accounting 2018 text, which is also a self-paced, case-based instruction on the use of a commercial accounting application (QuickBooks 2018). QuickBooks 2018 is the most recent version of the desktop product available for educational labs even though they continue to produce a commercial desktop product. His innovative teaching style emphasizes the decision maker's perspective and encourages students to think creatively. His graduate studies in educational psychology and his 41 years of business experience yield a balanced blend of theory and practice. Mr. Owen was presented the Lifetime Achievement Award in August 2016 by the Two-Year Section of the American Accounting Association.

Dedication

I would like to thank my wife Kelly for her support and assistance during the creation of this and previous editions of this text. Though our boys are out of the house and pursuing their own interests, she continues to listen to my often crazy ideas for new cases and experiences with college students, providing an excellent sounding board and reality check. You and the boys continue to define what life is all about.

Note to the Student and Instructor

The text and related data files created for this book were constructed using QuickBooks Online. In this version of QuickBooks, Intuit continues its use of a basic payroll service but has made it more accessible by having it live on its Cloud-based system. QuickBooks Online initially comes with the current tax tables; however, these tables soon become outdated, and the payroll feature is disabled unless the user subscribes to the payroll service.

The author decided to use the manual payroll tax feature, which requires that students manually enter the tax deductions. This alleviates the discrepancies between the solutions manual and the students' data entry and removes the burden of having to purchase the tax table service for each copy of QuickBooks Online used. Instructions on how to set up payroll for manual calculation of payroll taxes are provided in the text. For more information, see your QuickBooks Online documentation.

All reports have a default feature that identifies the basis in which the report was created (e.g., accrual or cash) and the date and time the report was printed. The date and time shown on your report will, of course, be different from that shown in this text.

An Introduction to QuickBooks Online

Upon completion of this chapter, the students will be able to do the following:

- Identify the basic features of QuickBooks Online Plus (QBO)
- Explain how QBO is similar and differs from the desktop version of QuickBooks
- Create a new QBO account using codes provided with this text
- Provide information to QBO about your company
- Successfully navigate the QBO Dashboard
- Assign their instructor as their "Accountant"
- Use QBO's help feature

Overview

The focus of this chapter is to introduce you to QuickBooks Online Plus (QBO) and get your account and company established. A description of QBO will be provided along with a brief comparison of how QBO differs from its desktop version. This text includes codes, which will allow you to create your own personal account with Intuit and create one and only one company. You will assign your company a name that includes your name for identification purposes. Welcome to the journey.

What Is QBO?

QBO is an online version of the popular QuickBooks accounting software developed by Intuit. The software is designed to capture common business events like purchases from and payments to vendors, sales to and collections from customers, payments and receipts to/from other operating, investing, and financing activities, period end accrual adjustments, and reports. Reports include the standard financial statements, including the income statement, statement of stockholders' equity, balance sheet, statement of cash flows, and other useful reports like accounts receivable aging. All interaction with QBO is done via an Internet connection. In other words, if you have not connected to the Internet, you will have no QBO. In other words QBO cannot work offline.

All interaction with QBO is done online, there are no files to maintain on a computer and everything is saved online. Thus, there is no need for backup files. The monthly fee for using QBO covers one and only one company. This text includes access codes for the user to create one company online for a limited amount of time.

How Is QBO Similar/Different than the Desktop Version QuickBooks?

Even though these two products share the name "QuickBooks," they are unrelated. QBO isn't a copy of QuickBooks that has been web enabled. They are different products with different database structures and approaches to solving problems even though both were developed in-house by Intuit to capture and report on accounting events.

Not all features available in QBO are available in the Windows desktop version of QuickBooks Accountant (QBDT). Likewise, not all features of QBDT are available in QBO. QBO requires an Internet connection. QBDT requires installation of software on to a computer. QBO requires a monthly fee. QBDT requires a one-time purchase and no monthly fees.

A key difference is that because QBO is online, it works on multiple operating systems (Windows, Apple, etc.) and multiple devices (desktops, laptops, smart phones, or tablets). The same cannot be said for QBDT. Intuit requires different software for QBDT to run on a Windows-based or an Apple-based computer. In this text, QBDT will always mean the Windows version of QuickBooks Accountant.

Some additional notable differences are the following:

- QBDT can be used for an unlimited number of companies; QBO limits you to one company per license fee. Need to manage more than one company using QuickBooks? Each will cost you another monthly fee.

- QBO can automatically download bank transactions for no additional cost.

- QBDT can track inventory purchases and sales based on an average cost assumption or a first-in-first-out assumption.

- QBO can track inventory purchases and sales based only on a first-in-first-out assumption.

- QBDT can account for the receipt of inventory items (receive items function) based on a purchase order; QBO cannot and calls inventory products and services.

- QBO can automatically schedule and send invoices whereas QBDT cannot.

- QBDT can perform manual payroll without paying Intuit a monthly payroll processing fee. QBO encourages you to sign up for its payroll service and makes manually processing payroll difficult.

- QBO can be accessed from anywhere in the world where you have access to the Internet. QBDT requires a computer with the QuickBooks application and data files installed.

- QBDT provides for profit and loss as well as balance sheet budgeting. QBO only provides for profit and loss budgeting.

- QBO operates irrespective of platform (desktop, laptop, mobile device, or tablet) or operating system (Microsoft Windows or Apple iOS). QBDT does have a version of QuickBooks for both of those operating systems, but they are different and require two separate application purchases.

- QBDT includes a fixed asset management, which will calculate depreciation and maintain detailed fixed asset records by individual asset, whereas QBO does not calculate depreciation and does not maintain detailed records of fixed assets.

- QBO provides automatic upgrades; this is a good and a bad feature. With QuickBooks Online, you are almost always running the most current version (whether you want to or not).

Creating a New QBO Account

Before getting started, you will need to establish your account with QBO. This text includes access codes for one user. Once you use the codes, they will not work again.

To launch QBO and create a new account, do the following:

1 Open your Internet browser.

2 Type **https://quickbooks.intuit.com/signup/retail** into your browser's address text box.

3 Type your license number and product number (provided with the text) shown in Figure 1.1.

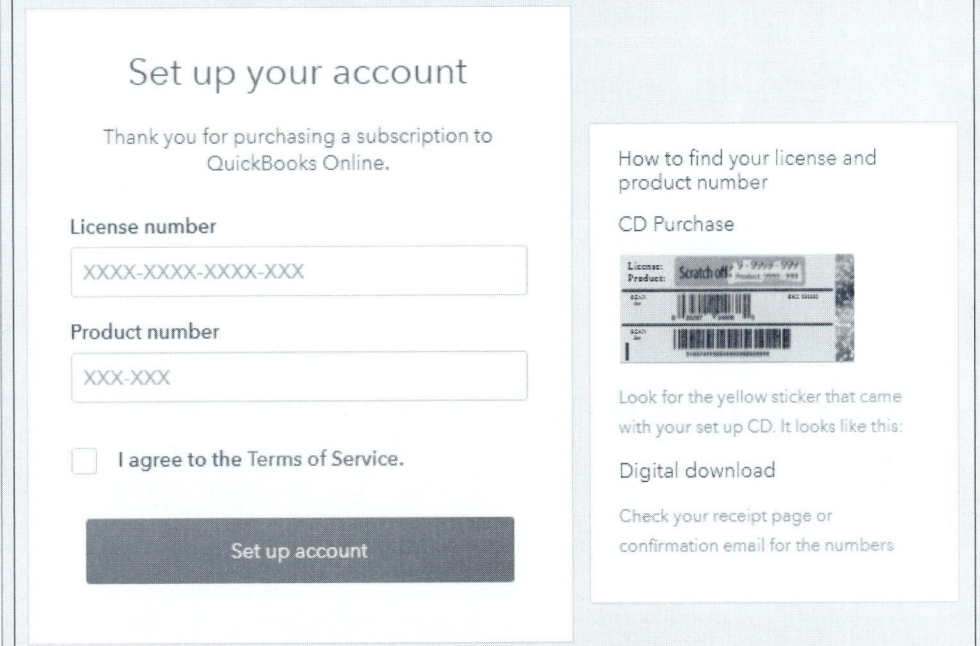

Figure 1.1

Set Up Your Account window

4 Click the **I agree to the Terms of Service** check box and then click **Set Up Account**.

5   Enter information about you as shown in Figure 1.2, changing all the information to your first and last name, your email address (user id), and password, then click **Create Account**.

Figure 1.2

Setting Up Your Account

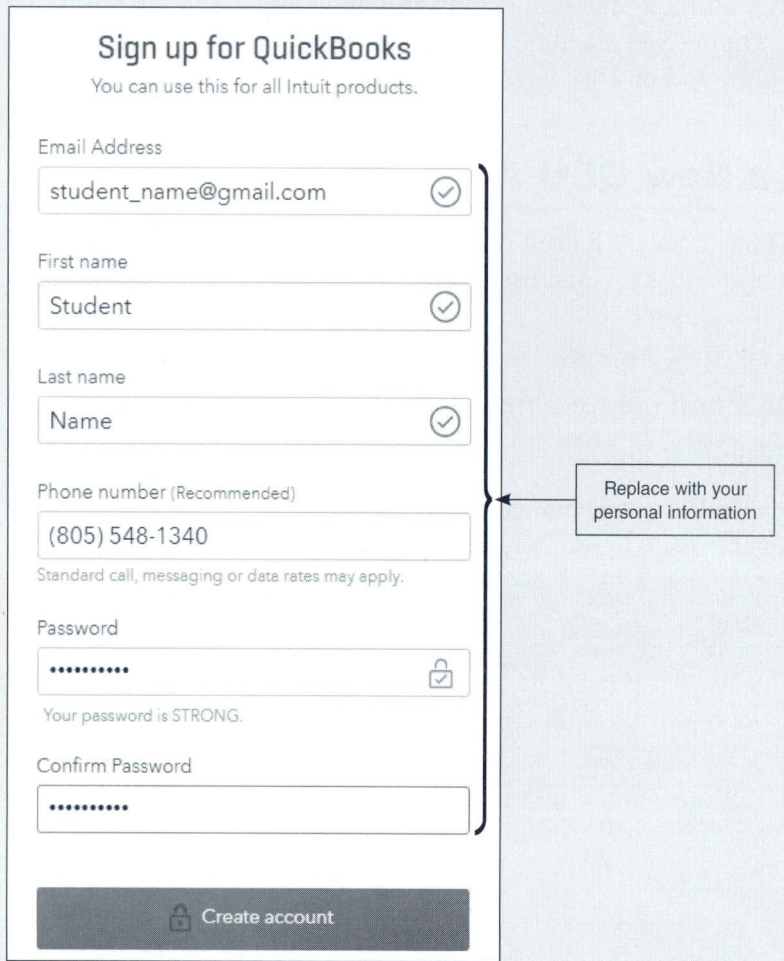

Providing QBO Information

To continue, QBO requires additional information, such as the industry your company operates, the types or products you sell, etc.

To provide QBO additional information (continuing from above), do the following:

1   Type your name and your identification number as specified by your instructor to answer the question "What is your business called?". Then select **Less than one year** to answer the question "How long have you been in business?". Then click **Next**.

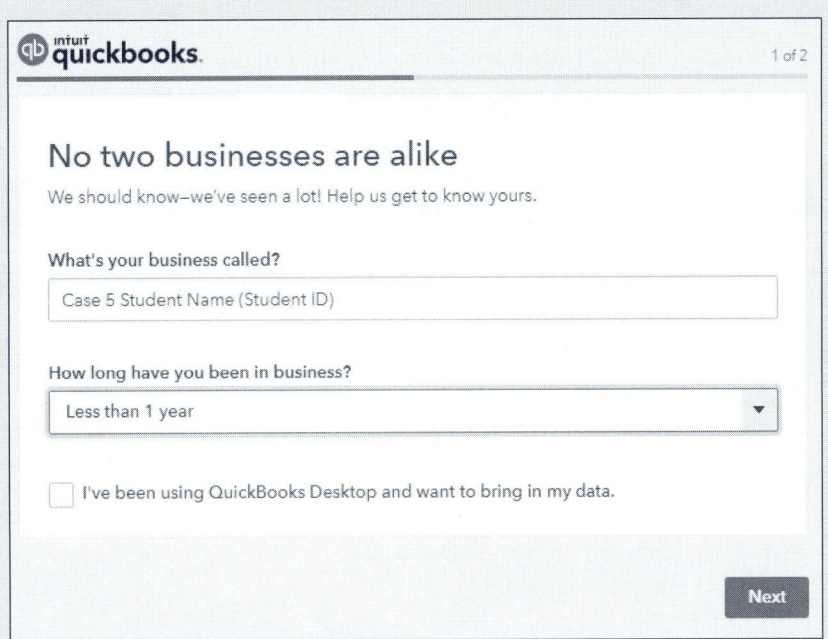

Figure 1.3

Basic Info window

2 Select all buttons as shown in Figure 1.4 then click **Next**.

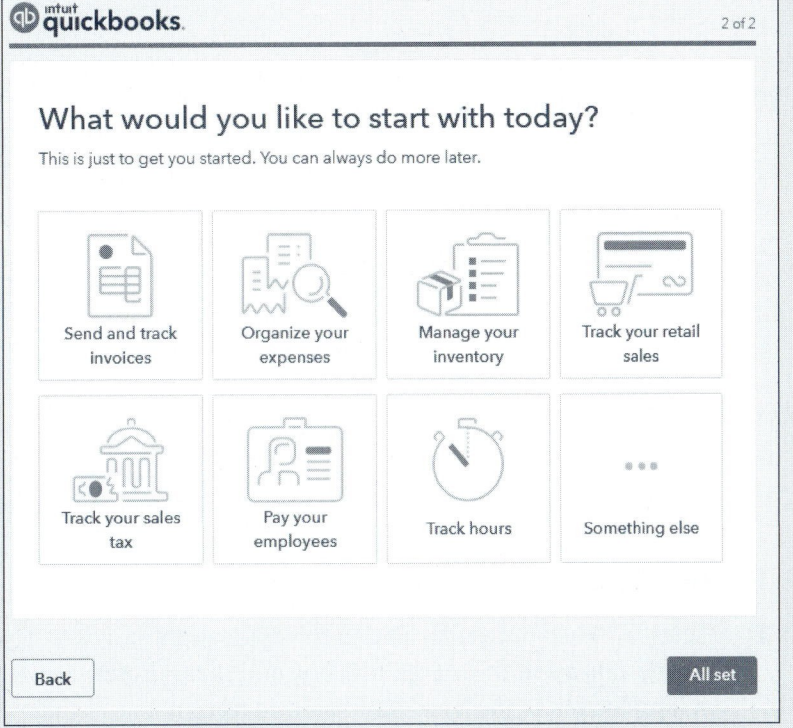

Figure 1.4

Choose Options in QBO

3 The Dashboard should now look somewhat like Figure 1.5. (Note: Your window may reflect more items depending on its size. Resize the window to see how your screen appears.)

Figure 1.5

Dashboard (partial view)

Navigating QBO

The Dashboard provides links to various tasks and resources. The Customers window provides access to adding new customers, viewing existing balances, and highlighting overdue accounts. The Vendors window provides access to adding new vendors, viewing existing balances, and highlighting overdue accounts. The Employees window provides access to adding new employees and viewing payroll information. The Transactions and Reports links will be addressed later in this text. To begin, you should access QBO's help features.

To use QBO help:

1 Click the **? Help** button located in the upper-right portion of your window. Type **dashboard** in the search text box and press [**Enter**]. Click the text **An introduction to the home dashboard** to open a window shown in Figure 1.6.

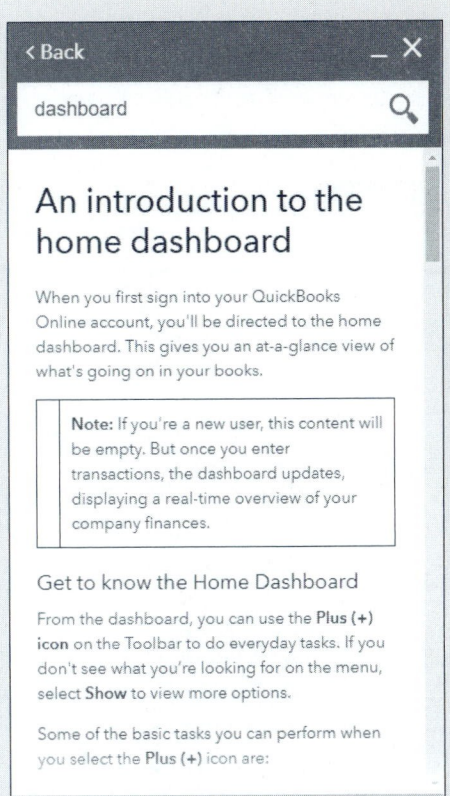

Figure 1.6

Home Dashboard Overview

2 Type **Plus** (+) into the search text box and then press [**Enter**] to view Figure 1.7.

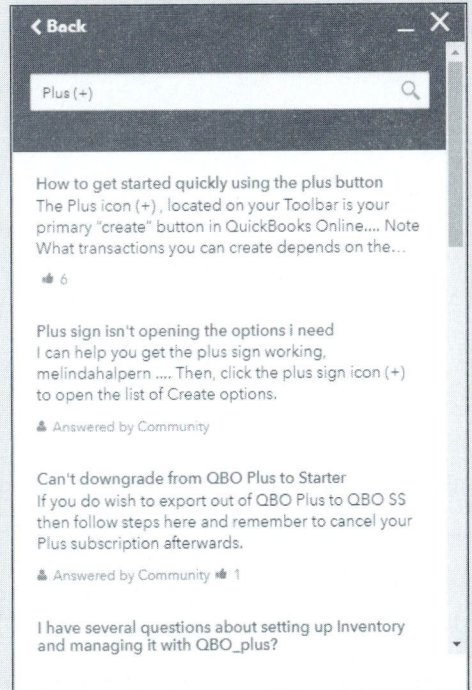

Figure 1.7

Help using the Plus icon (+) button

3 Close the help window, and then click the **Plus (+)** icon button at the top of the Dashboard to view the full create menu items available as shown in Figure 1.8.

Figure 1.8

The Plus (+) menu

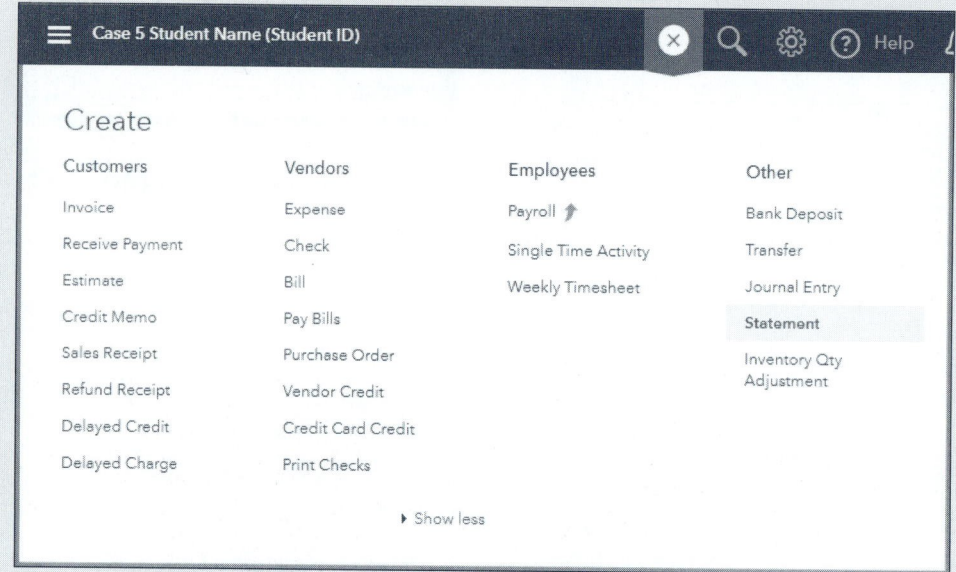

4 Click the (**X**) icon to close the Plus (+) menu then click **Sales** from the navigation bar and then click **Customers** to view Figure 1.9. Since you have not yet entered any customers, QBO will ask you to add your first customer. You will do this later in Chapter 3. Remember QBO is an online application and Intuit will change it often. Thus the figures in this text may differ from what you see in QBO online.

Figure 1.9

Customers window

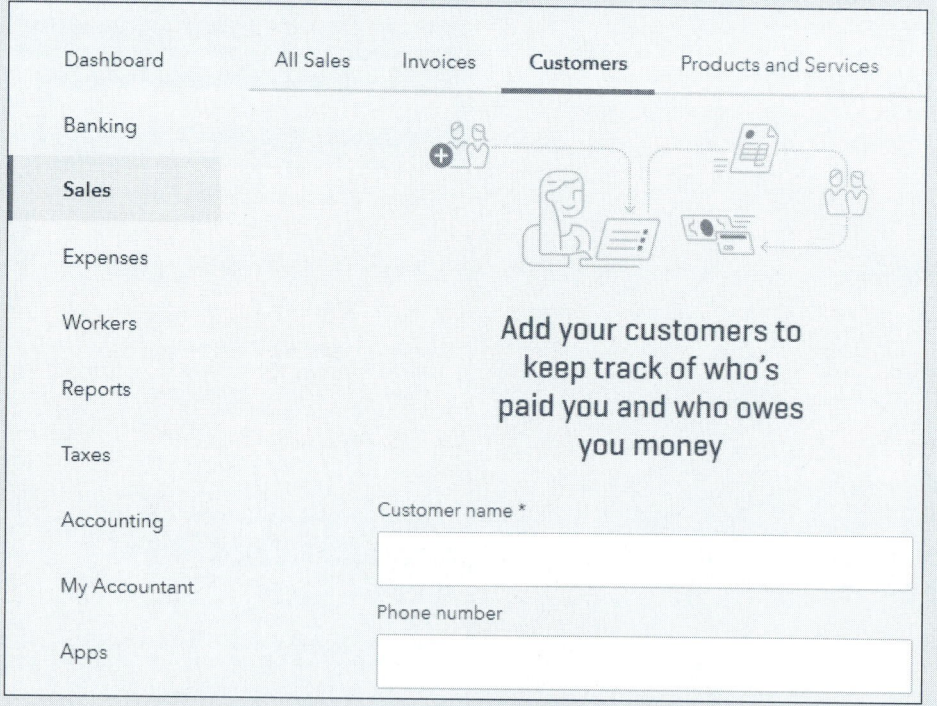

5 Click **Expenses** from the navigation bar and then click **Vendors** to view Figure 1.10.

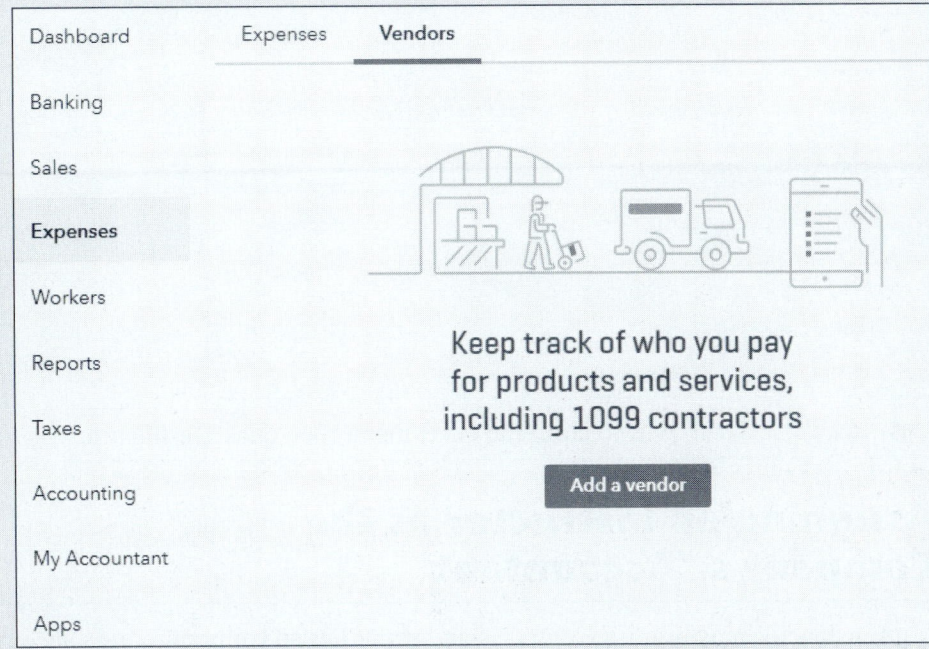

Figure 1.10

Vendors window

6 Click **Workers** from the navigation bar and then click **Employees** to view Figure 1.11.

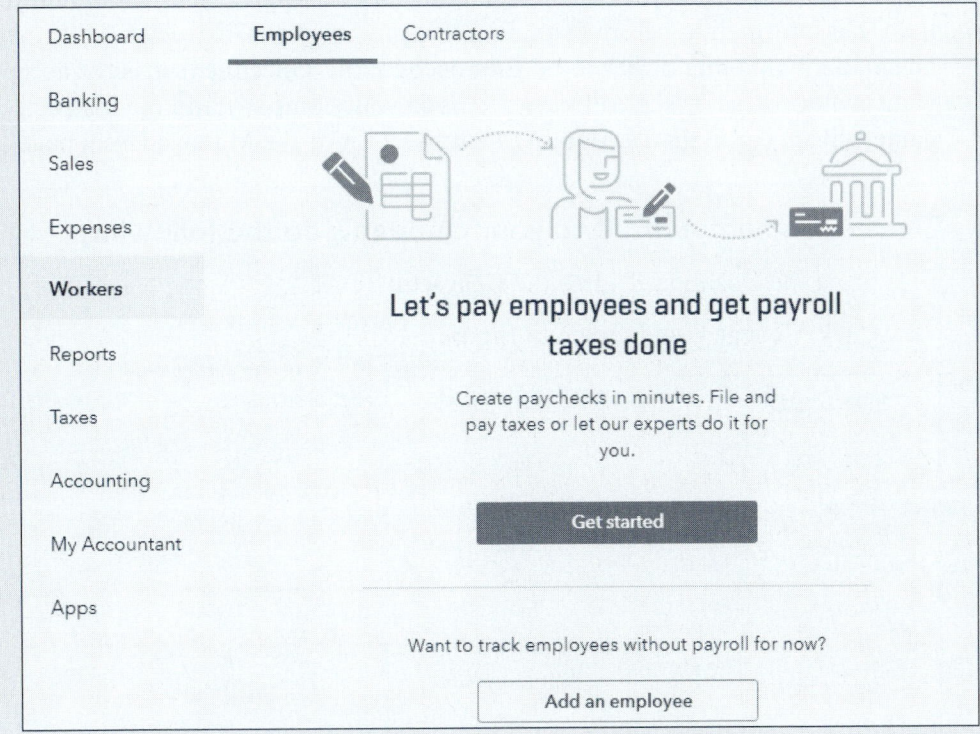

Figure 1.11

Employees window

7 Click the **Gear** icon located in the upper-right corner to view Figure 1.12.

Figure 1.12

Gear window

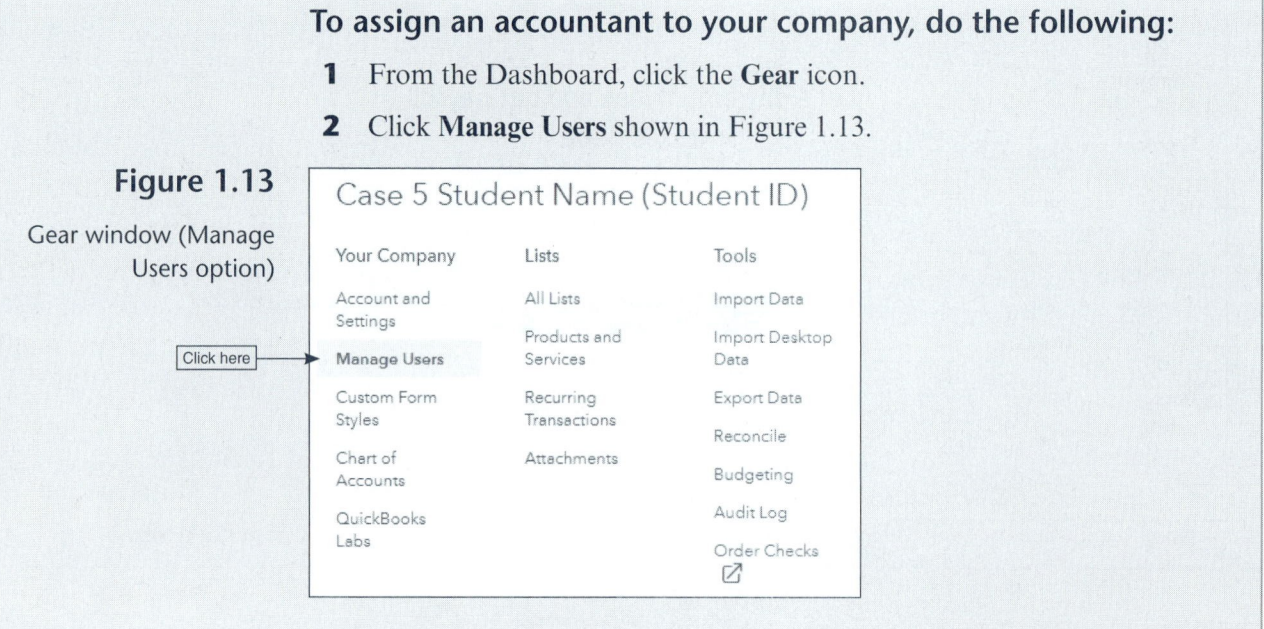

Case 5 Student Name (Student ID)

Your Company	Lists	Tools	
Account and Settings	All Lists	Import Data	User Profile
Manage Users	Products and Services	Import Desktop Data	Feedback
Custom Form Styles	Recurring Transactions	Export Data	Refer a Friend
Chart of Accounts	Attachments	Reconcile	Privacy
QuickBooks Labs		Budgeting	
		Audit Log	🔓 Sign Out
		Order Checks ↗	

8 Click the **Gear** icon to close the Gear menu then click **Dashboard**.

Assigning an Instructor as the Company's "Accountant"

Your instructor may require you to assign him or her as your company's accountant. You do this so he or she, as your accountant, will always have access to your company files for grading and evaluation purposes. This will also assist the instructor in answering questions you may have about your company. The process of assigning an accountant to your company involves a brief interview in which you will provide your instructor's email address and name. Make sure you have that information before beginning this process. Your instructor will receive an email inviting him or her to be your accountant. Once the instructor accepts your invitation, he or she will have access to your company and the instructor's name will appear in the Accounting Firms section of the Manage Users page.

To assign an accountant to your company, do the following:

1 From the Dashboard, click the **Gear** icon.

2 Click **Manage Users** shown in Figure 1.13.

Figure 1.13

Gear window (Manage Users option)

Case 5 Student Name (Student ID)

Your Company	Lists	Tools
Account and Settings	All Lists	Import Data
Manage Users ← Click here	Products and Services	Import Desktop Data
Custom Form Styles	Recurring Transactions	Export Data
Chart of Accounts	Attachments	Reconcile
QuickBooks Labs		Budgeting
		Audit Log
		Order Checks ↗

3 Click the **Accountants** tab and then type your instructor's email address in the space provided as shown in Figure 1.14.

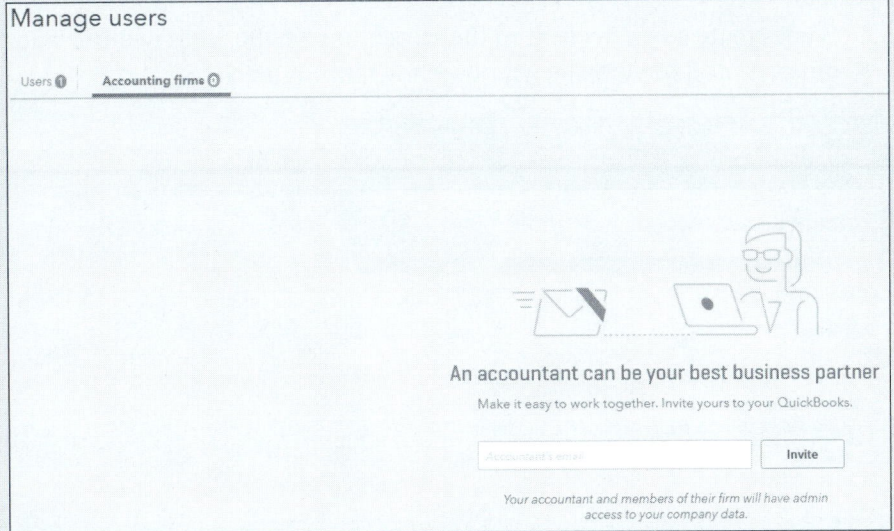

Figure 1.14

Manage Users window (inviting instructor as accountant)

4 Click the **Invite** button.

5 Click **Dashboard** to exit from the Manage Users window.

Using QBO's Help Feature

QBO provides help with a handy search feature. Help comes in two forms: built-in from Intuit and dynamic help from the QuickBooks Community.

To access Help from within QBO, do the following:

1 Click **?**

2 Type **create a new account** in the search box of the Help window and then press [**Enter**] to view the window shown in Figure 1.15.

Figure 1.15

Help window
(create a new account)

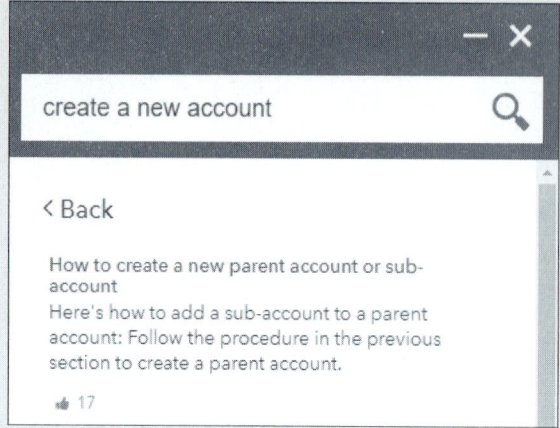

3 Click the text **How do I create a new parent account or subaccount?** to view Figure 1.16.

Figure 1.16

Help window
(creating a new account or
subaccount in QuickBooks)

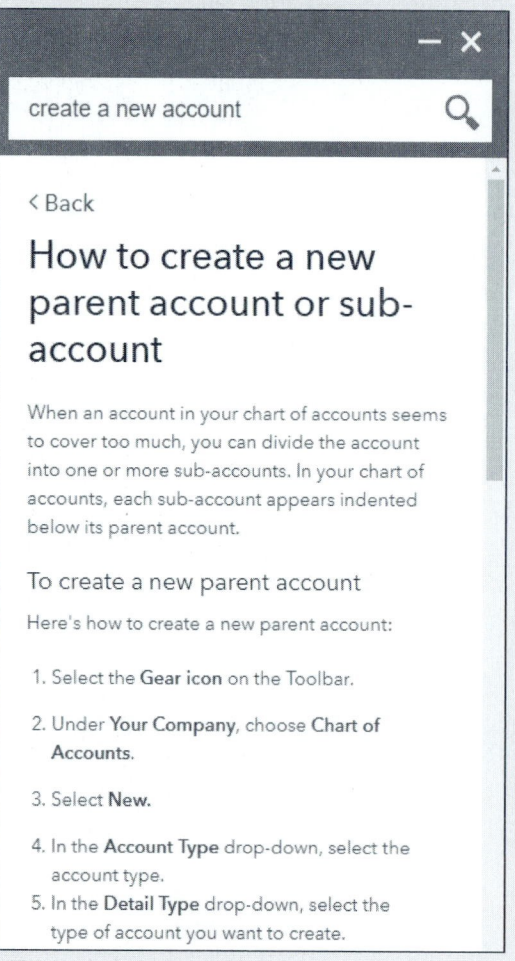

End Note

You have now been introduced to QBO, its basic features, and how it is similar to but not the same as QBDT. You created your Intuit account and provided basic information about your company and learned how to navigate around the QBO application. After assigning your instructor as your accountant and learning more about the help features in **QBO**, you are ready to learn more about the application by exploring a sample company provided by Intuit in Chapter 2. Don't worry because you will be back to your company in Chapter 3.

1

Chapter 1 Questions

1 How are QBO and QBDT different in the number of companies they can manage per license?

2 Does QBO work offline, without an Internet connection?

3 Do you need to back up QBO files?

4 How are QBO and QBDT similar?

5 What information do you need to supply to assign your instructor as the company's accountant?

Chapter 1 Matching

a. QBO	_____	Click to access help
b. QBDT	_____	Click to find past transactions
c. Gear icon	_____	Click to access QBO employee information
d. Workers	_____	Online version of QuickBooks
e. Navigation bar	_____	Click to add your instructor as your accountant
f. + icon	_____	Provides links to QBO tasks and resources
g. Magnifying Glass	_____	Windows Desktop version of QuickBooks
h. Help (?) icon	_____	Click to add any transaction
i. Manage Users	_____	Click to manage your subscription, users, and settings
j. Dashboard	_____	On the left of the Dashboard, it shows a menu of items

Sample Company Walkthrough

Student Learning Outcomes

Upon completion of this chapter, the student will be able to do the following:

- Open the Sample Company provided by Intuit to explore QBO
- Access customer, vendor, and employee information
- Explore banking transactions
- Explore sales and expense transactions
- Explore the chart of accounts
- Explore lists
- Access reports
- Use the Gear icon to view company settings

Overview

Intuit has provided a Sample Company online to provide new users a test drive of its QBO product. You will open this Sample Company and explore various features of QBO. In this chapter, you will be viewing the Sample Company looking at customer, vendor, and employee information. You will also be viewing banking, sales, and expense transactions and will be looking at the chart of accounts, lists, reports, and company settings. You will not be making any changes, such as adding a customer, invoice, check, etc. That will occur in the next chapter.

The author has no control over the dates used by Intuit, and those dates may change, depending on when you are accessing the file online. The dates that appear in the figures supplied by the author in this text may not be the dates that appear on your screen.

Throughout this text, figures illustrating bills, expenses, checks, purchase orders, and credit card transactions will have the title Account details not Category details and the column title as Account and not Category as shown on your QBO software. Once again this change took place after this text was completed. See the Preface of this text for a complete discussion of the confusion this change created.

Begin Your Sample Company Walkthrough

You can use this Sample Company to explore QBO as often as you like. No matter what you do to modify this Sample Company, you will be unable to save it. When you leave and later return, it will look the same as it did initially. Each time you open this Sample Company, it will retrieve your current system date (the actual date you are working on your computer) and place that date under the company name on the home page.

To open the Sample Company, do the following:

1   Open your Internet browser.

2   Type **https://qbo.intuit.com/redir/testdrive** into your browser's address text box, and press [**Enter**] to view the Sample Company Dashboard shown in Figure 2.1. You may be asked to provide security information before proceeding. Click **Hide** to close the Setup Guide like you did in Chapter 1 and then click **X** to close the Bring it back anytime window. Transaction dates may differ on your screen from the figures shown throughout this text.

Figure 2.1

Sample Company Dashboard

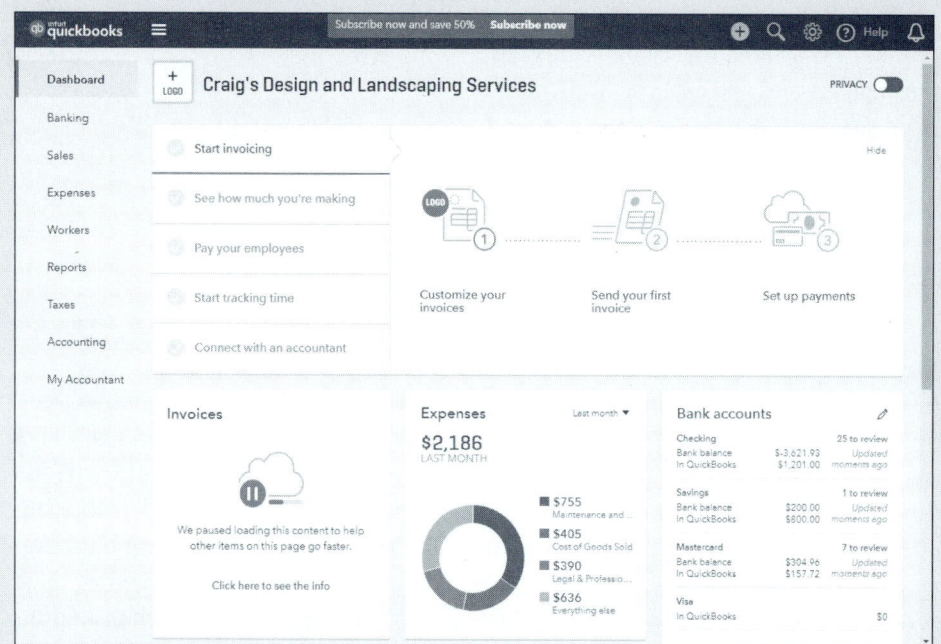

In Chapter 1, you were introduced to the Plus (+) icon that provided you a menu of items you could create as shown in Figure 2.2 as a reminder.

Figure 2.2

Create menu

Create

Customers	Vendors	Employees	Other
Invoice	Expense	Payroll 🔼	Bank Deposit
Receive Payment	Check	Single Time Activity	Transfer
Estimate	Bill	Weekly Timesheet	Journal Entry
Credit Memo	Pay Bills		Statement
Sales Receipt	Purchase Order		Inventory Qty Adjustment
Refund Receipt	Vendor Credit		
Delayed Credit	Credit Card Credit		
Delayed Charge	Print Checks		

Customers, Vendors, and Employees

QBO provides easy access to customer information using the navigation bar. In this section, you will open the Customers section in a new tab and drill down to a specific customer, and specific transactions relate to that customer.

To access customer information, do the following:

1 Click **Sales** and then click **Customers** from the navigation bar as shown in Figure 2.3.

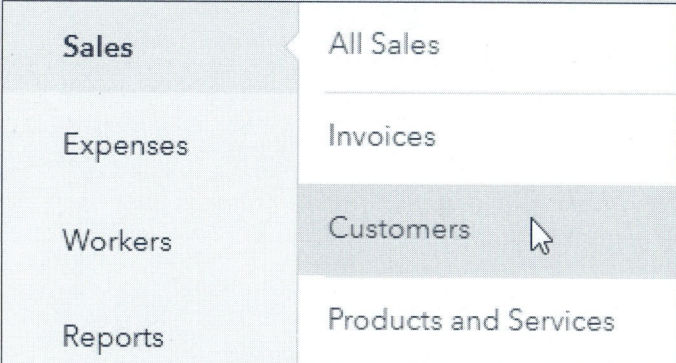

Figure 2.3

Dashboard (right click to view Customers in a new tab)

2 The resulting Customers window is then revealed as shown in Figure 2.4.

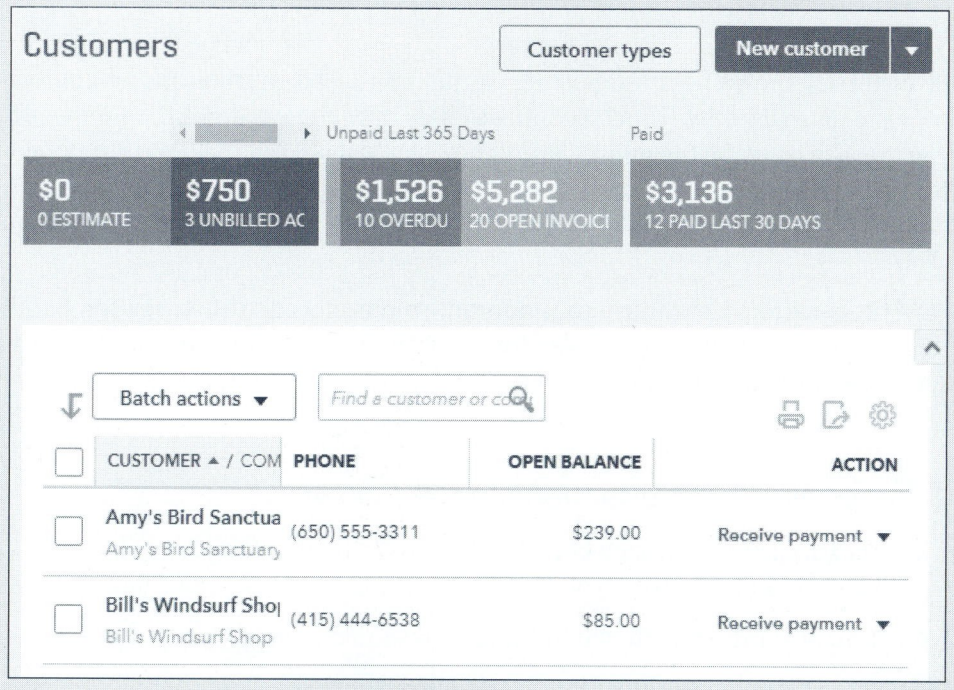

Figure 2.4

Customers window

3 Click on the text **Amy's Bird Sanctuary** to view detail transactions related to that particular customer shown in Figure 2.5

Figure 2.5

Amy's Bird Sanctuary

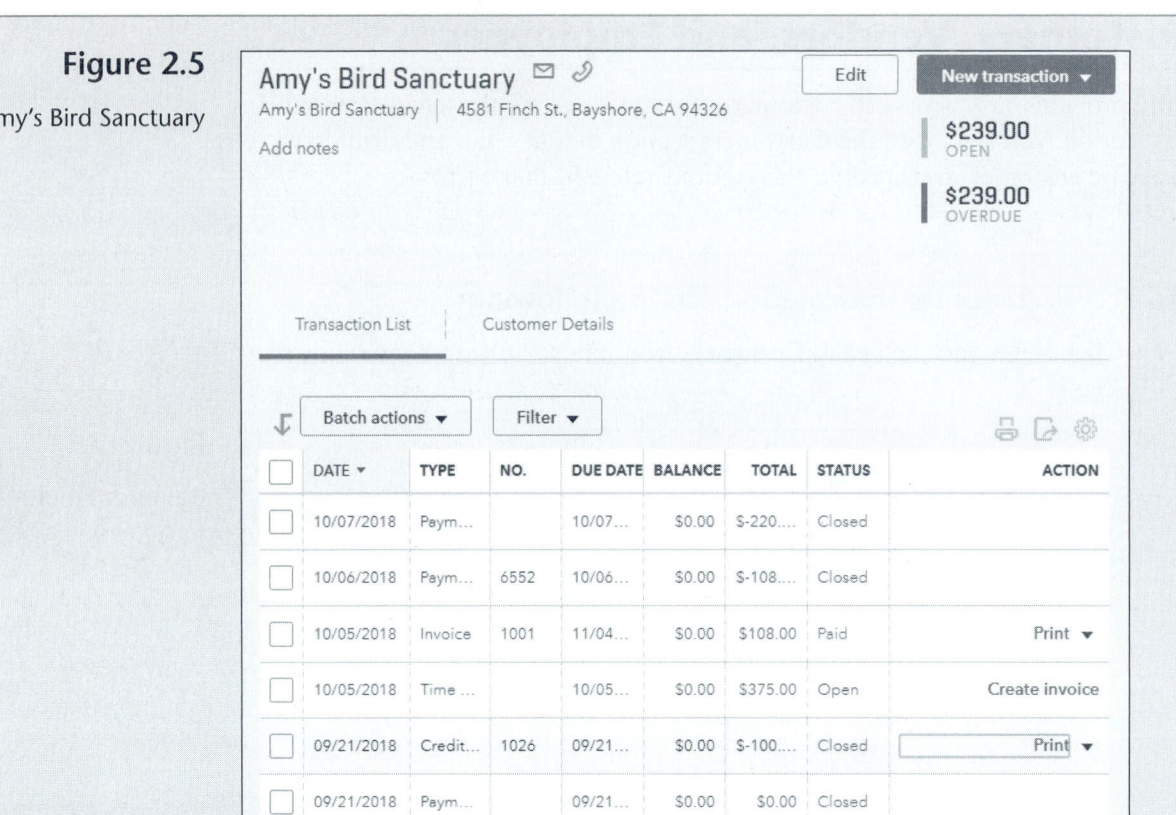

The $239.00 overdue balance noted at the top of the window correlates to invoice 1021 shown near the bottom of the figure. (The author has no control over the dates used by Intuit, and those dates may change depending on when you are accessing the file online. The dates, which appear in the figures supplied by the author in this text, may not match the dates that appear on your screen.)

QBO provides easy access to vendor information using the navigation bar. In this section, you will open the Vendors section in a new tab and drill down to a specific vendor and specific transactions related to that vendor.

To access vendor information, do the following:

1   Click **Expenses** and then click **Vendors** from the navigation bar (in a manner similar to what you just did for Sales and Customers above).

2   A Vendor listing as shown in Figure 2.6 should appear.

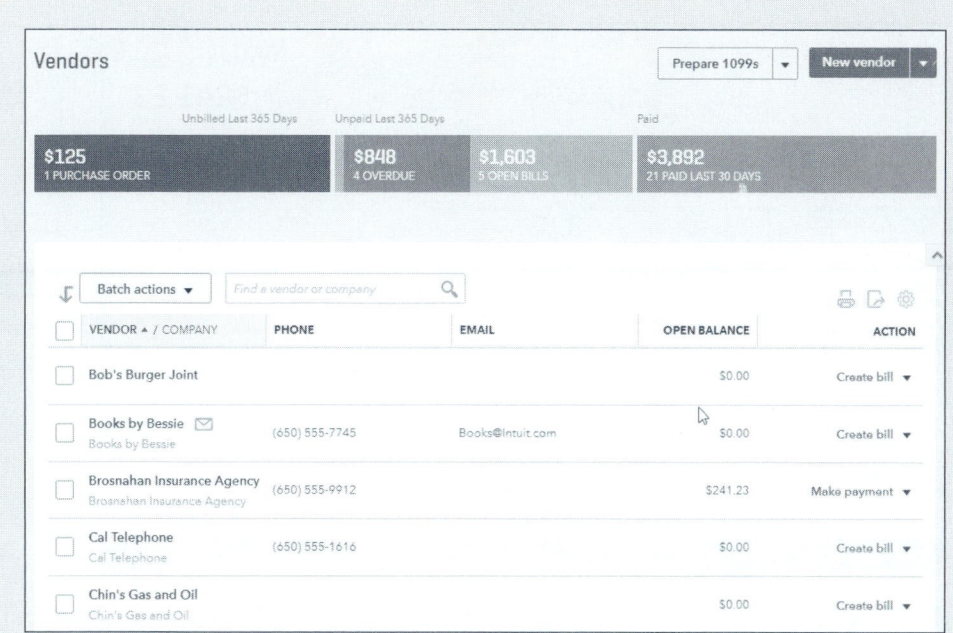

Figure 2.6

Vendors information

3 Click on the text **Brosnahan Insurance Agency** to view detail transactions related to that particular vendor shown in Figure 2.7

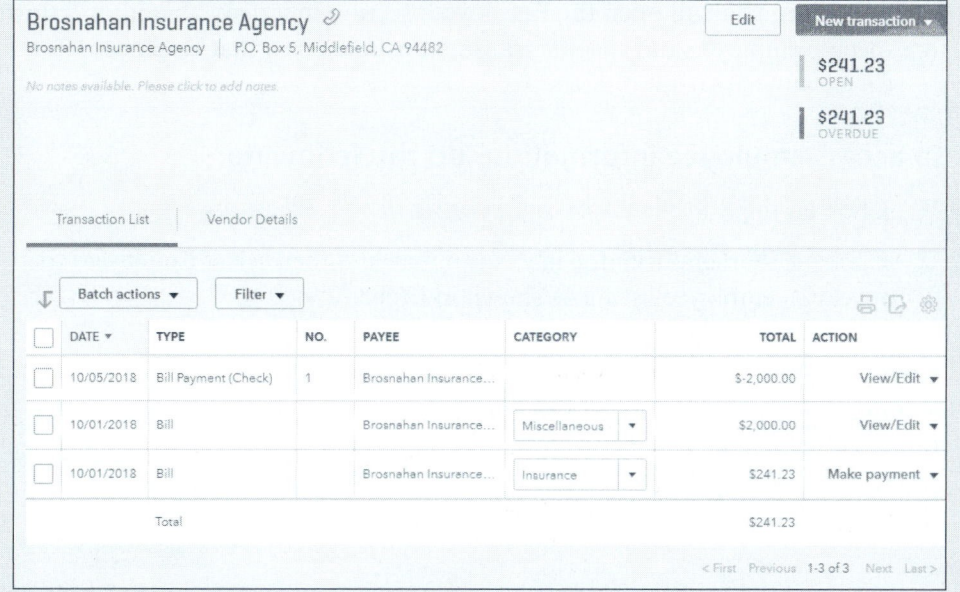

Figure 2.7

Brosnahan Insurance Agency

4 Double click on the **$241.23** balance to view the bill received as shown in Figure 2.8.

Figure 2.8

Bill from Brosnahan
Insurance Agency

Note that your screen has the title Category details not Account details and the column title is Category and not Account as shown here. Once again this change took place after this text was completed. See the Preface of this text for a complete discussion of the confusion this change created.

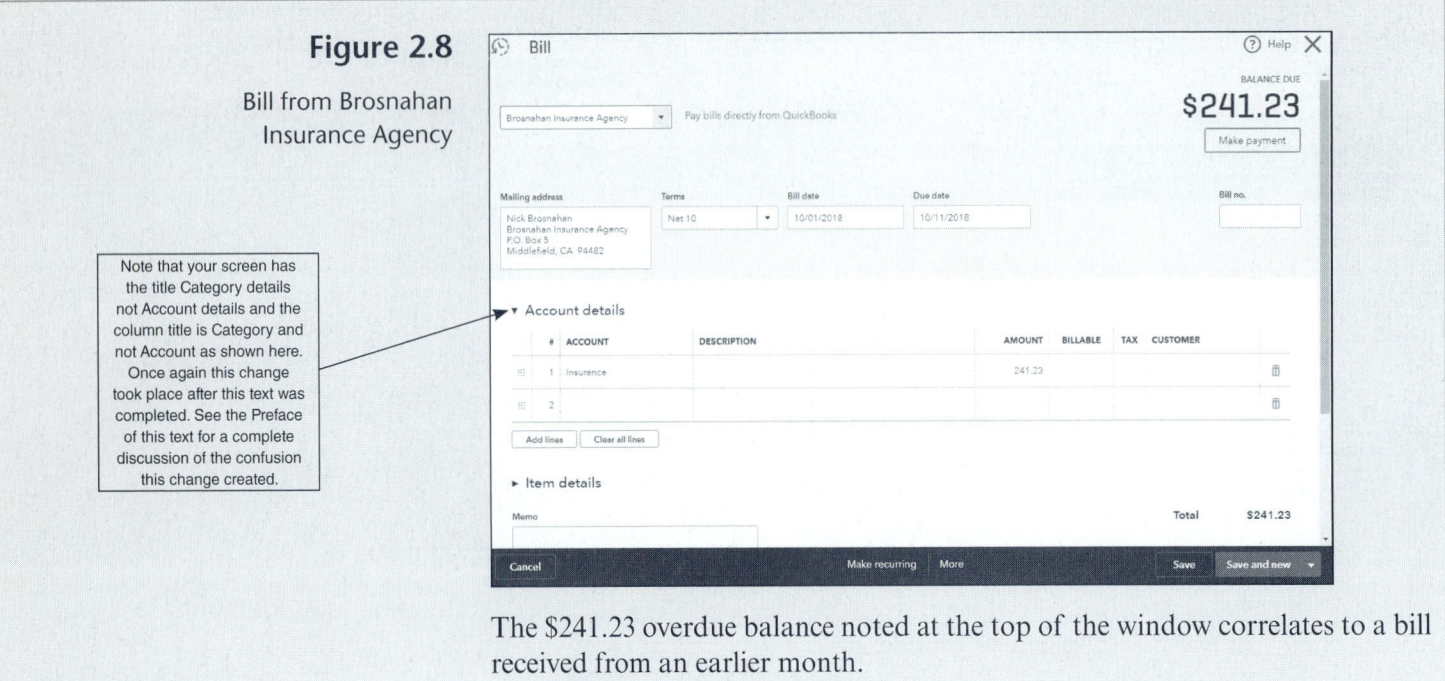

The $241.23 overdue balance noted at the top of the window correlates to a bill received from an earlier month.

QBO provides easy access to employee information using the navigation bar. In this section, you will open the Employees section in a new tab and drill down to a specific employee and specific transactions related to that employee.

To access employee information, do the following:

1 Click on the **X** in the upper-right corner of the Bill to close it.

2 Click on **Workers** from the navigation bar and then select **Employees** to reveal an employee listing as shown in Figure 2.9.

Figure 2.9

Employees information

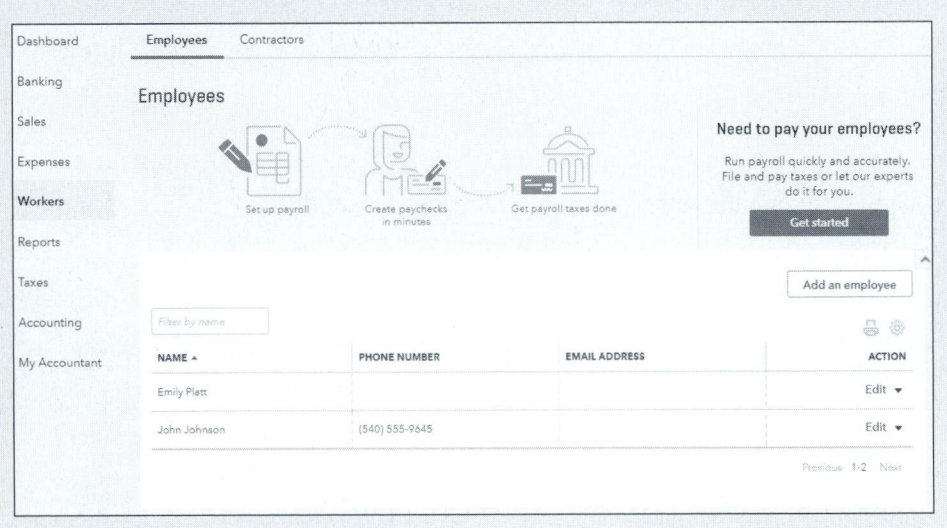

1   Click on the text **Edit** for John Johnson to view employee information for John Johnson shown in Figure 2.10.

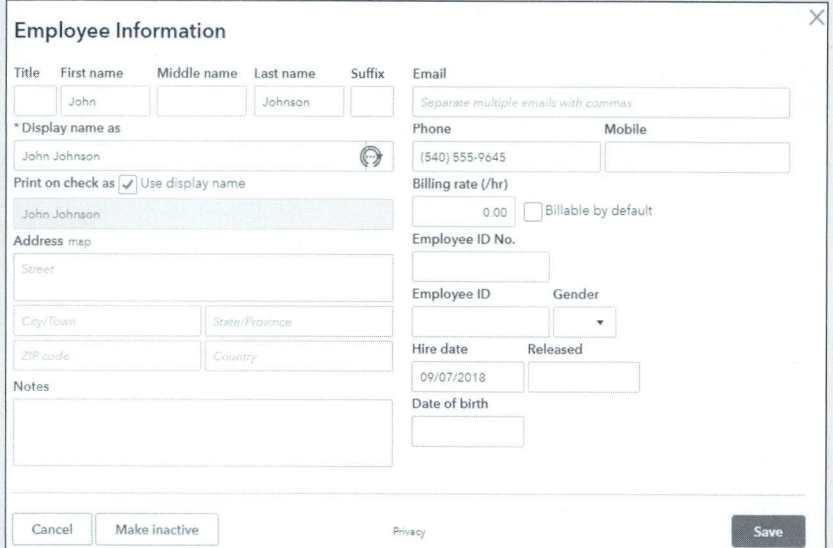

Figure 2.10

Employee Information for John Johnson

2   Click **Cancel** to close this window.

3   Click the **Gear** icon, and click **Sign Out** to close the Sample Company.

Banking Transactions

QBO has an online banking feature that lets you automatically connect to your bank and download banking-related transactions. The application automatically matches the banking transaction with a previously recorded QBO transaction. QBO calls this "Recognizing." This feature is briefly reviewed since this text is academically based and no "real" bank account is linked to this sample and no "real" bank account will be linked to your student company.

To view banking transactions, do the following:

1   Open your Internet browser.

2   Type **https://qbo.intuit.com/redir/testdrive** into your browser's address text box and then press [**Enter**] to view the Sample Company Home page shown in Figure 2.1. You may be asked to provide security information before proceeding. Click **Continue**.

3   Click **Banking** from the navigation bar on the Dashboard to view the **Bank and Credit Cards** page of the Sample Company.

4 Select **Checking** from the drop-down menu at the top of the window (if it is not already selected) to view the window shown in Figure 2.11.

Figure 2.11

Bank and Credit Cards (partial view)

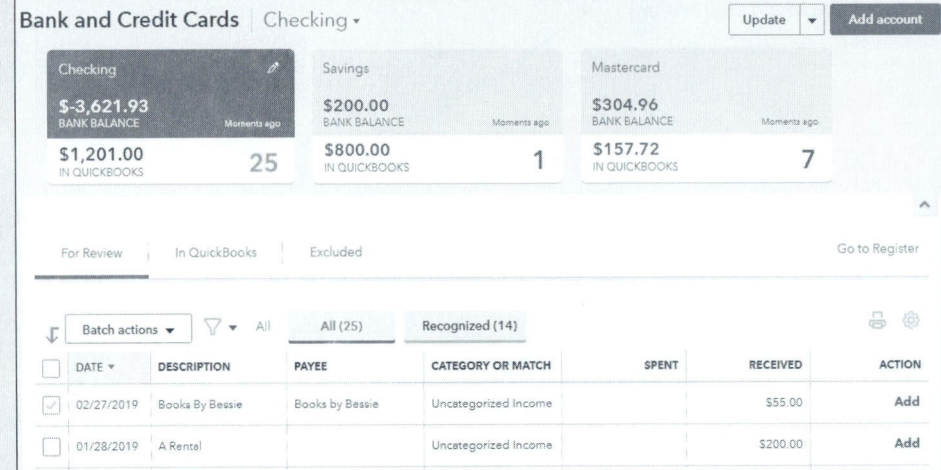

5 Click the **Recognized** (14) tab to view the listing of only those banking transactions recognized by QBO shown in Figure 2.12.

Figure 2.12

Bank and Credit Cards (recognized banking transactions: partial view)

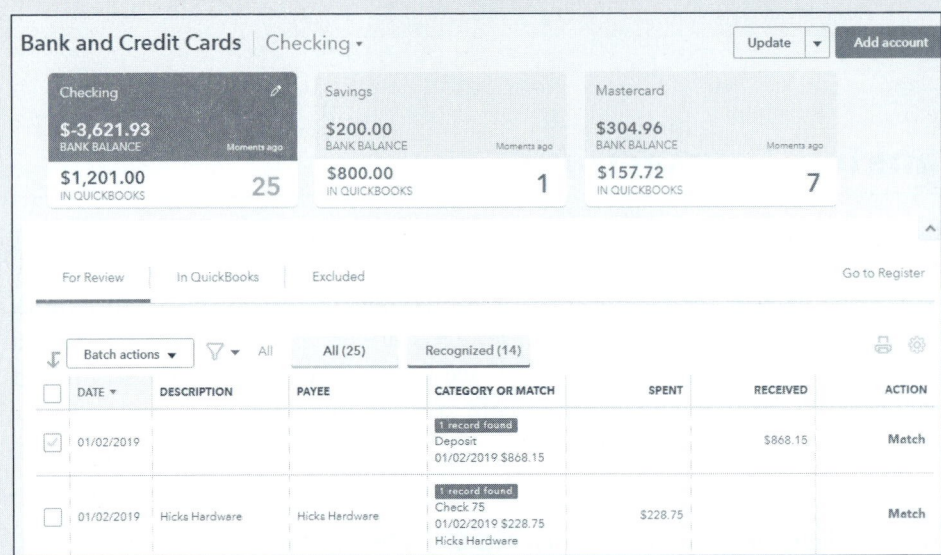

6 Click **Go to Register** on the right to view the traditional checking account register listing each QBO recorded check, deposit, or cash transaction affecting the checking account shown in Figure 2.13. Close any messages that may appear. You may have to enlarge your window to view the Deposit and Balance columns.

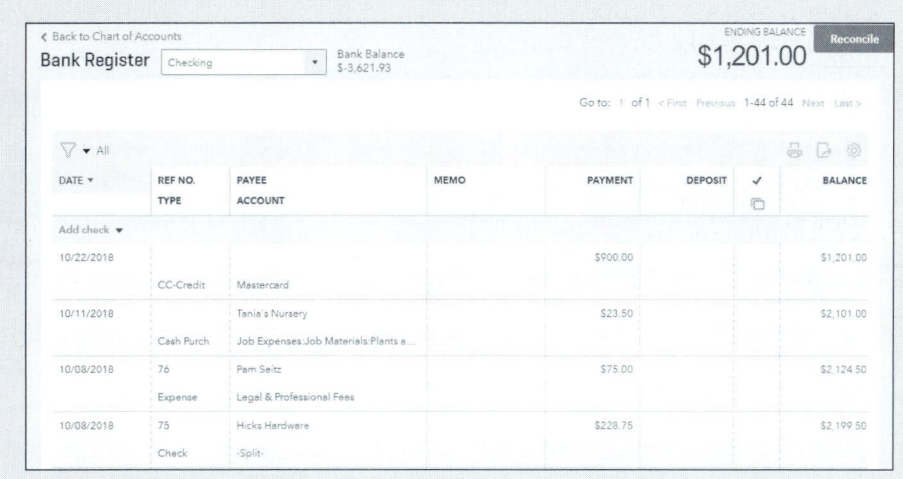

Figure 2.13

Bank Register (partial view)

Bank deposits, which have not been recorded in QBO, are not recognized and are temporarily classified as Uncategorized Income. Bank charges that have not been recorded in QBO are not recognized and are temporarily classified as Uncategorized Expense.

The Register seen in Figure 2.13 is similar to the general ledger account concept seen in traditional accounting without the debits and credits. The balance is shown after every increase or decrease in the account. In a bank account, increases are deposits and decreases are payments. Registers exist for all asset, liabilities, and equity accounts and are a great way to identify and/or correct errors if they occur.

Sales and Expense Transactions

The next two choices in the navigation bar are sales and expenses transactions. The sales transaction section will provide a listing of recent sales invoices and payments: Some are closed and others are open, meaning payment has not been received. Thus, the action of receiving payment is listed for all open invoices. This screen also highlights unbilled activity, open balances, overdue balances, and those invoices paid in the last 30 days across the top. You can decide to drill down to view a particular invoice.

To view sales and expenses transactions, do the following:

1 Click **Sales** and then click **All Sales** from the navigation bar to view the Sales section shown in Figure 2.14.

Figure 2.14

Sales Transactions (partial view)

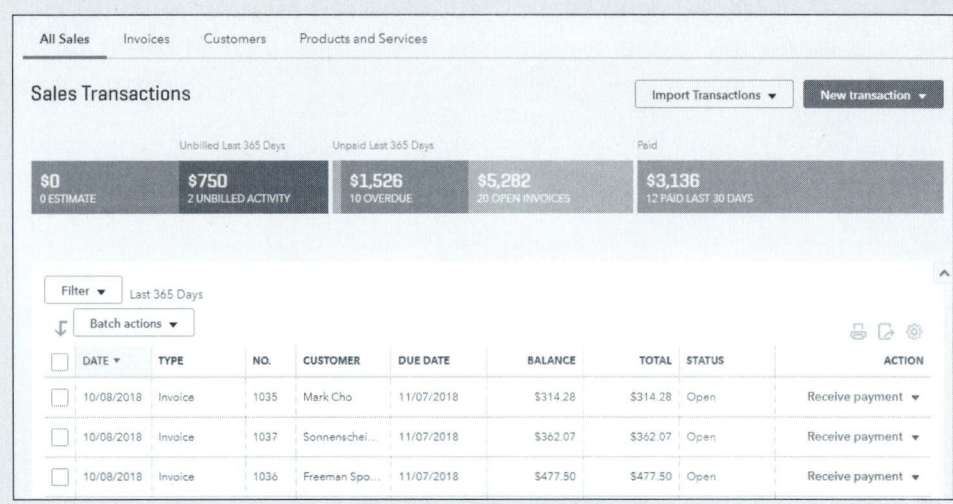

2 Double click on Invoice No. **1035** to reveal the invoice shown in Figure 2.15.

Figure 2.15

Invoice # 1035

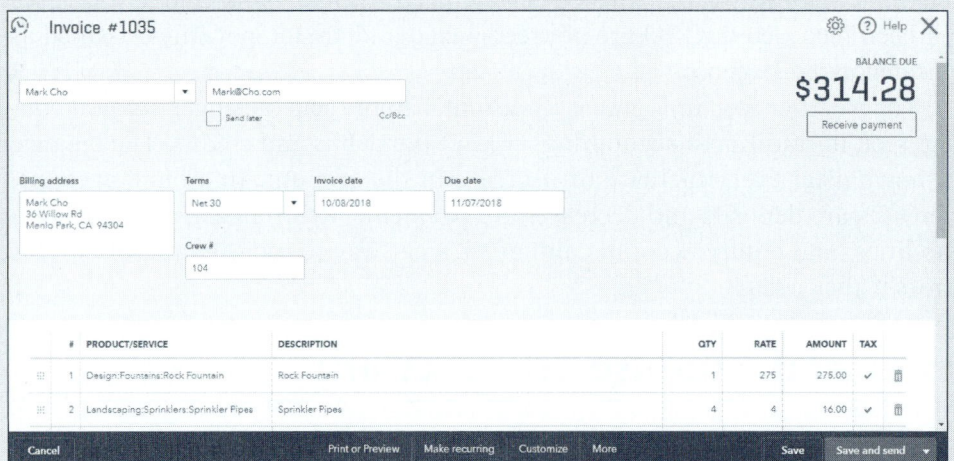

3 Click **Cancel** to close Invoice No. 1035.

The expenses section will provide a listing of recent credit card transactions, bills, expenses, purchase orders, checks, bill payments, and cash transactions. You can decide to drill down to view a particular credit card transaction.

4 Click **Expenses** and then click **Expenses** again from the navigation bar to view the Expense Transactions section shown in Figure 2.16.

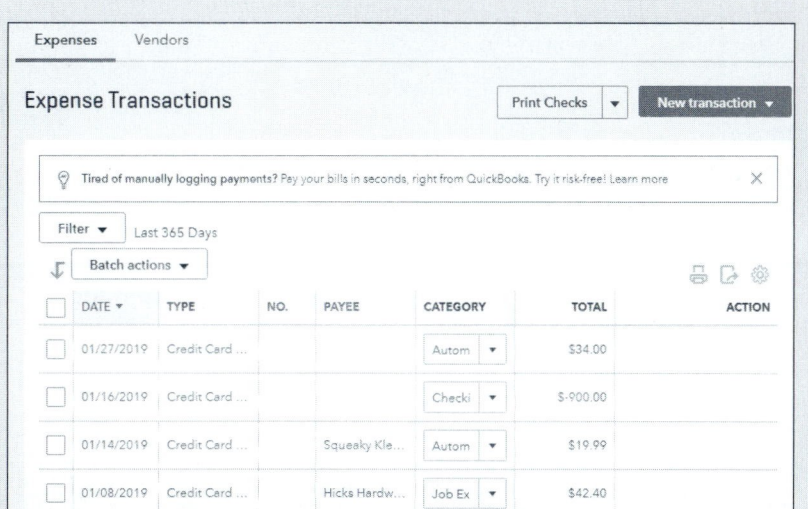

Figure 2.16

Expense Transactions (partial view)

5 Double click the Credit Card Expense for $19.99 with payee **Squeaky Kleen Car Wash** to reveal the charge shown in Figure 2.17.

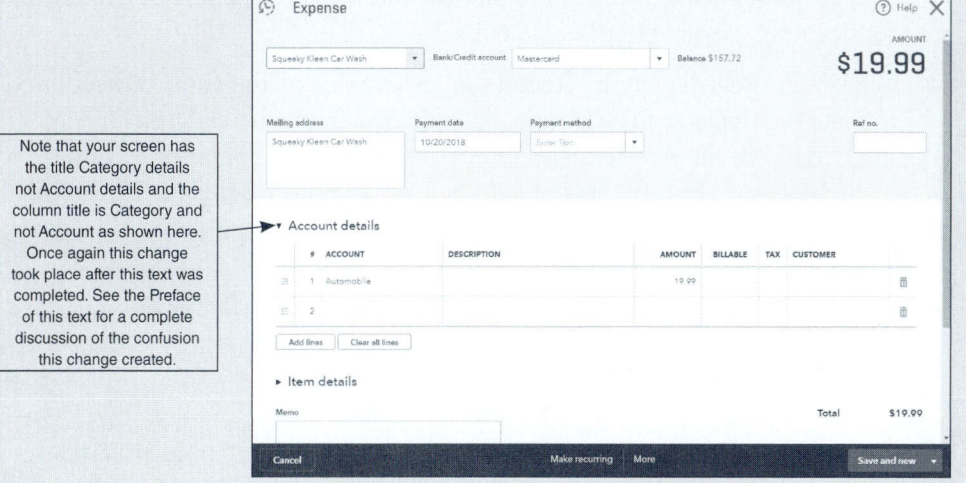

Figure 2.17

Expense window (credit card charge for $19.99)

Note that your screen has the title Category details not Account details and the column title is Category and not Account as shown here. Once again this change took place after this text was completed. See the Preface of this text for a complete discussion of the confusion this change created.

6 Click **Cancel** to close the credit card charge window.

Chart of Accounts

A chart of accounts is a listing of all accounts available. Each account is assigned a type and a detailed type. The Sample Company's chart of accounts has been modified from the default chart of accounts and tailored to this company's needs. Not all companies need these particular accounts, and some will need additional accounts.

To view the Sample Company's chart of accounts, do the following:

1 Click **Gear** icon and then click **Chart of Accounts** to view the Chart of Accounts section. Then click **See your Chart of Accounts** shown in Figure 2.18.

Figure 2.18

Chart of Accounts (partial view)

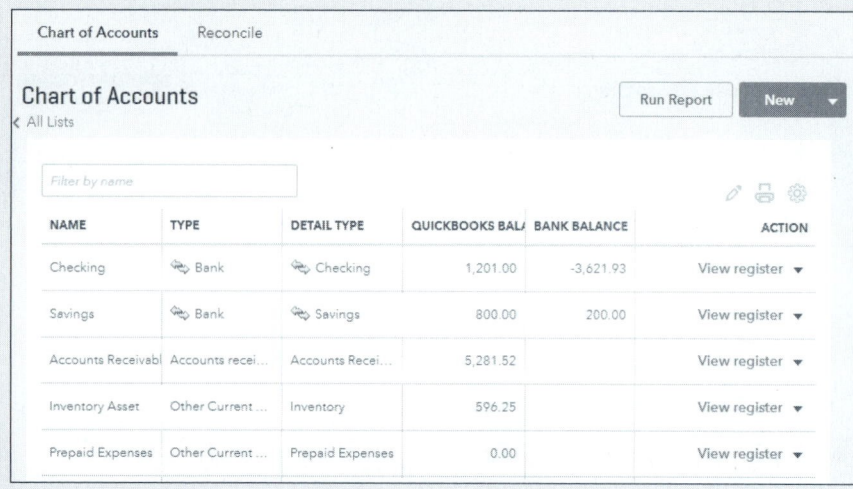

2 Scroll down the chart of accounts. Each asset, liability, and equity account has a View Register action item listed.

3 As you scroll down, you will see that the balance in the chart of accounts for accounts payable (A/P) is $1,602.67.

4 Click **View Register** on the Accounts Payable line of the chart of accounts to view the Register for accounts payable shown in Figure 2.19. The ending balance in the A/P Register matches the $1,602.67 balance specified in the chart of accounts listing. (Remember to ignore dates in this Sample problem.)

Figure 2.19

A/P Register

5 Click **Back to Chart of Accounts** located at the top of the A/P Register.

6 Scroll down the chart of accounts to see that each revenue and expense account has a Run Report action item listed. Click on **Run Report** on the Landscaping Service account line to view an Account Quickreport for the Landscaping Services account.

7 Scroll to the top of this Account QuickReport report. Click in the Report period drop-down list and select **This Year-to-date,** and then click **Run Report** to view the report shown in Figure 2.20.

Figure 2.20

Account Quickreport

Lists

Lists in QBO provide you with an easy and quick way to view a collection of common items. Some of the more common lists include the chart of accounts, products and services, and terms. You can decide to view a summary of all the lists available in QBO and explore the list of terms.

To view a list of lists and the list of terms, do the following:

1 Click the **Gear** icon and then click **All Lists** to view a list of lists shown in Figure 2.21.

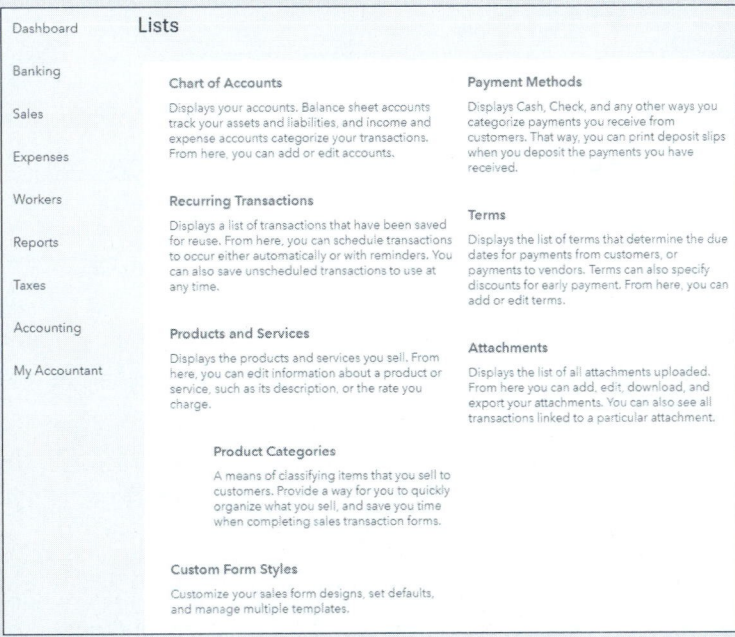

Figure 2.21

Lists

2 Click **Terms** to view the list shown in Figure 2.22.

Figure 2.22

Terms

Reports

QBO comes with many predesigned reports for use in business, all of which you can customize for your particular needs. For instance, you can decide to focus on the common financial statement reports: the Income Statement (known in QBO as the Profit and Loss report), Balance Sheet, and Statement of Cash Flows.

1 Click **Reports** from the navigation bar.

2 Click **Standard**.

3 Scroll down the page to see Business Overview report options shown in Figure 2.23.

Figure 2.23

Business Overview reports

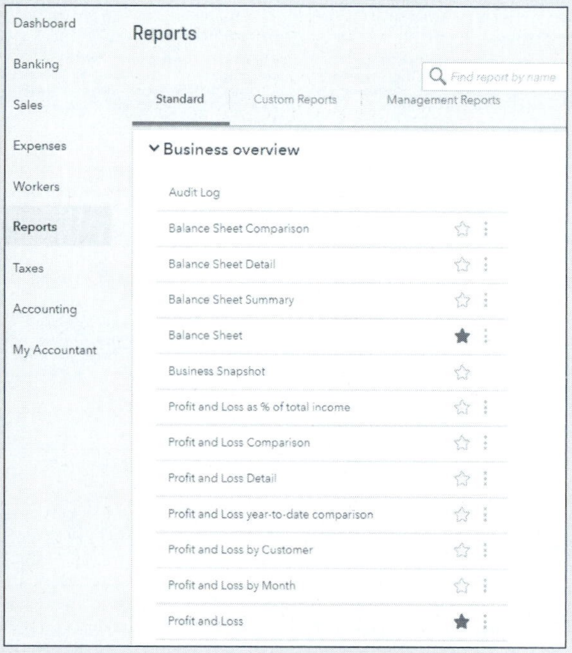

5 Click **Profit and Loss**. Click **Collapse** and then scroll to the top of the report to view the top part of the Profit and Loss report shown in Figure 2.24. (If you view the entire report you would note that clicking the **Collapse** text summarizes details under a heading. For example, Landscaping Services is shown as one number when Collapse is selected. Clicking **Expand** would show more detail. You will learn more about customizing and creating other reports in Chapter 10. Remember, the dates on your screen may differ from those shown in the figure.)

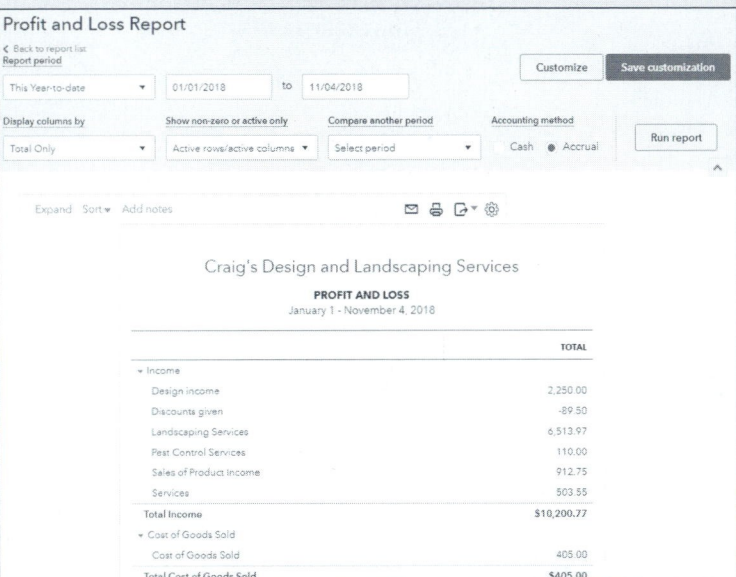

Figure 2.24

Profit and Loss report

6 Click **Reports** and then scroll down to find and click **Balance Sheet** and then scroll to the top of the report to view the top part of the Balance Sheet report shown in Figure 2.25.

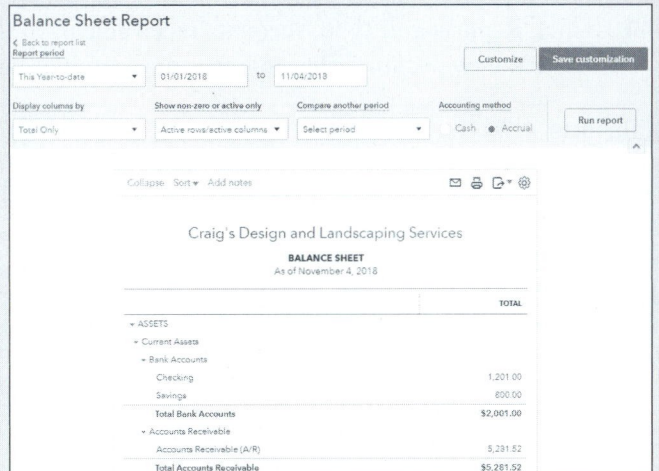

Figure 2.25

Balance Sheet (partial view)

7 Click **Reports** and then scroll down to find and click **Statement of Cash Flows** and then scroll to the top of the report to view the top part of the Statement of Cash Flows report shown in Figure 2.26.

Figure 2.26

Statement of Cash Flows

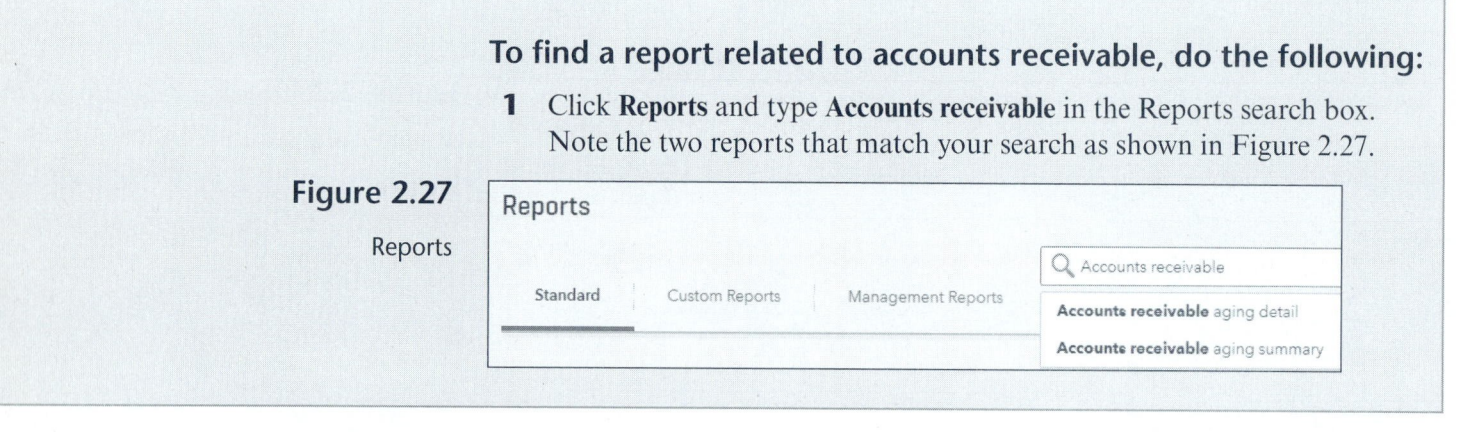

Alternatively, you can easily find a report if you know its name or part of its name. For example, if you wanted to access a report dealing with accounts receivable (A/R), you would type Accounts receivable into the report search box located in the Reports section.

To find a report related to accounts receivable, do the following:

1 Click **Reports** and type **Accounts receivable** in the Reports search box. Note the two reports that match your search as shown in Figure 2.27.

Figure 2.27

Reports

Company Settings

Four tabs are in the Settings section of QBO: Company, Sales, Expenses, and Advanced. You can edit these by clicking on the Pencil icon to the right of each section. The settings for the Sample Company have been modified from the default settings provided when QBO first creates a company. These options in the Settings section change the way QBO appears to the user. For example, in the Advanced section, if time tracking is turned off, no time tracking features will be available in QBO. Also, if purchase orders are turned off in the Expenses section, no purchase orders will be available in QBO. You can decide to view each of these sections to learn more about what options you are given in QBO.

1 Click the **Gear** icon and then click **Account and Settings** and click the **Company** tab to view the company settings section shown in Figure 2.28.

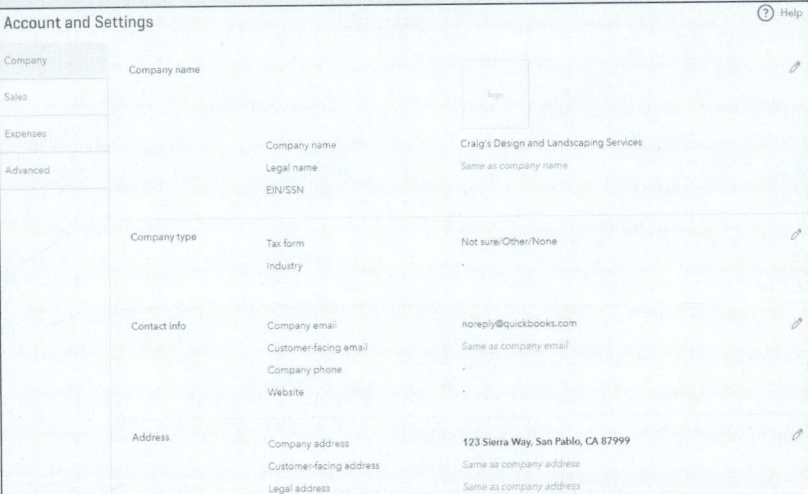

Figure 2.28

Company settings

2 Click the **Sales** tab in the **Account and Settings** window to view options provided shown in Figure 2.29.

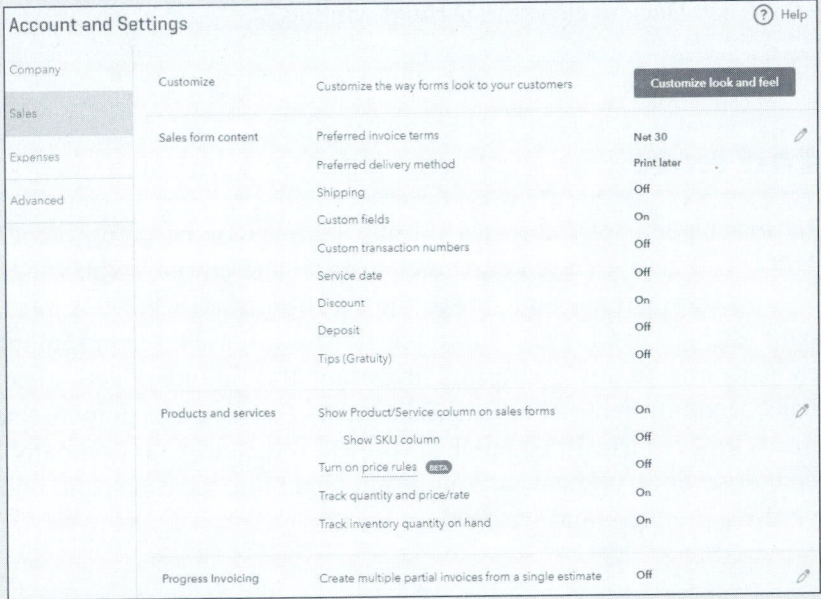

Figure 2.29

Sales settings

3 Click the **Expenses** tab in the **Account and Settings** window to view options provided shown in Figure 2.30.

Figure 2.30

Expenses settings

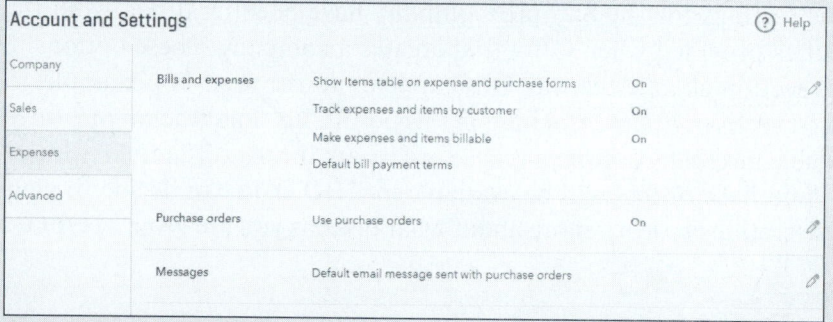

4 Click the **Advanced** tab in the **Account and Settings** window to view options provided shown in Figure 2.31.

Figure 2.31

Advanced settings

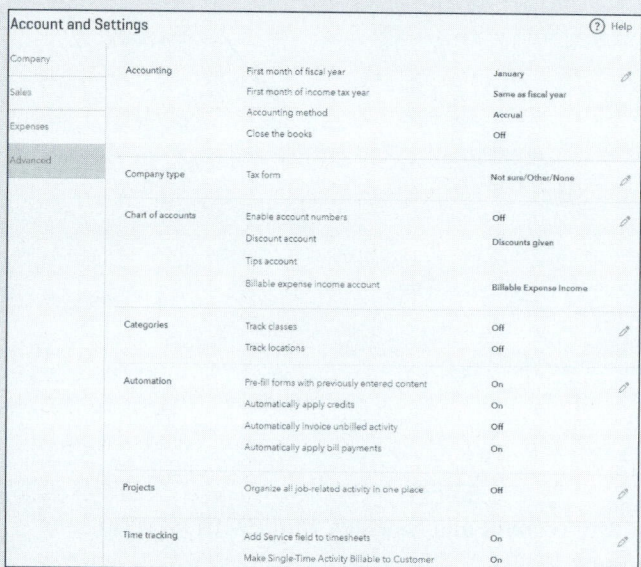

5 Click **Done** to close the **Settings** window.

End Note

In this chapter, you have used Intuit's Sample Company to practice navigating QBO. You have accessed customer, vendor, and employee information; viewed various transactions; and viewed the chart of accounts, lists, reports, and company settings. In Chapters 4 through 10, you will use the same Sample Company to learn how to add operating, investing, and financing activities; reconcile a bank account; create a budget; add adjusting entries; and prepare financial statements and reports. In Chapter 3, you will return to your company and modify default settings; add new accounts and beginning balances; and add customers, vendors, products, and services.

Chapter 2 Questions

1 What steps do you take to view customer information in a new tab?

2 What steps do you take to view detail transactions related to a particular customer?

3 What steps do you take to view a specific bill from a specific vendor?

4 What steps do you take to view a specific employee's information?

5 How are bank deposits, which have not been recorded in QBO, classified?

6 How are bank charges, which have not been recorded in QBO, classified?

7 Opening the sales transaction section of QBO will provide a listing of _____.

8 Opening the expense transaction section of QBO will provide a listing of _____.

9 What lists are available in QBO?

10 What steps do you take to view all reports related to accounts payable (A/P)?

Chapter 2 Matching

a. Navigation bar   _____ An employee in the Sample Company

b. Amy's Bird Sanctuary   _____ Bank deposits not yet recognized

c. Brosnahan Insurance Agency   _____ Exist for all asset, liability, and equity accounts

d. Recognizing   _____ Specify due dates for payment to/from vendors/customers

e. Uncategorized Income   _____ Used to access a list of sales and expense transactions

f. Uncategorized Expense   _____ A vendor in the Sample Company

g. Registers   _____ A listing of all accounts available

h. John Johnson   _____ Bank charges not yet recognized

i. Terms   _____ A customer in the Sample Company

j. Chart of accounts   _____ Matching a banking transaction with a QBO transaction

3

Setting Up a New Company

Student Learning Outcomes

Upon completion of this chapter, the student will be able to do the following:

- Log into their account
- Change company settings
- Modify the chart of accounts; establish beginning balances; and create new customers, vendors, products, and services
- Close opening balance equity and create a balance sheet
- Create, print, and export a transaction detail by account report

Overview

You began this process in Chapter 1 when you created your account and provided basic information about your company including the company name, address, industry, type, etc. Now it's time to continue that process.

First off, however, you're going to revisit the sample company you worked on in Chapter 2. Each of the following chapters will work the same way. To begin, you will navigate your browser to the Intuit Sample Company. The text will demonstrate how to do certain tasks, such as modify defaults, add a new account, add a new transaction, etc. These demonstrations will occur in the Sample Company. Remember, you can modify the Sample Company throughout each session, but once you close your browser window, QBO will not remember any of your activity in the Sample Company. When you navigate your browser back to the sample company, it will appear as it first did.

Each section of every chapter will begin with a demonstration using the Sample Company. That is followed by you logging back into QBO with the user name and password you created in Chapter 1 to complete an end of chapter case. In the case, you will be asked to perform tasks similar to those demonstrated in the Sample Company but now in your company. The tasks you accomplish on your company, named "Student Name (ID Number)," are permanent and will be there even after you close your QBO browser window. There is no Save File or Save File As command in QBO. Everything is saved for you.

The dates used in this text for the sample company (Craig's Design and Landscaping Services) coincide with the dates this edition was written (November/December 2018). When you access this sample company (in September of 2019, for example), the transaction dates will be different. Thus the figures in this text and the instructions given specifying dates (like 9/30/2018) will be different than what you see on your screen. The transactions themselves will be the same but their corresponding dates will be different.

Throughout this text, figures illustrating bills, expenses, checks, purchase orders, and credit card transactions will have the title Account details not Category details and the column title as Account and not Category as shown on your QBO software. Once again this change took place after this text was completed. See the Preface of this text for a complete discussion of the confusion this change created.

Company Settings

You can use this Sample Company to explore QBO as often as you would like. No matter what you do to modify this Sample Company, you will not be able to save it. When you leave and later return, it will look the same as it did initially.

To modify Sample Company settings, do the following:

1   Open your Internet browser.

2   Type **https://qbo.intuit.com/redir/testdrive** into your browser's address text box, and press [**Enter**] to view the Sample Company Dashboard.

3   From the Sample Company home page, click the **Gear** icon to manage your settings shown in Figure 3.1.

Figure 3.1

Settings

4   Click **Account and Settings**. The first screen shown is the Sample Company information shown in Figure 3.2. Scroll down this page to view information provided and then close this window.

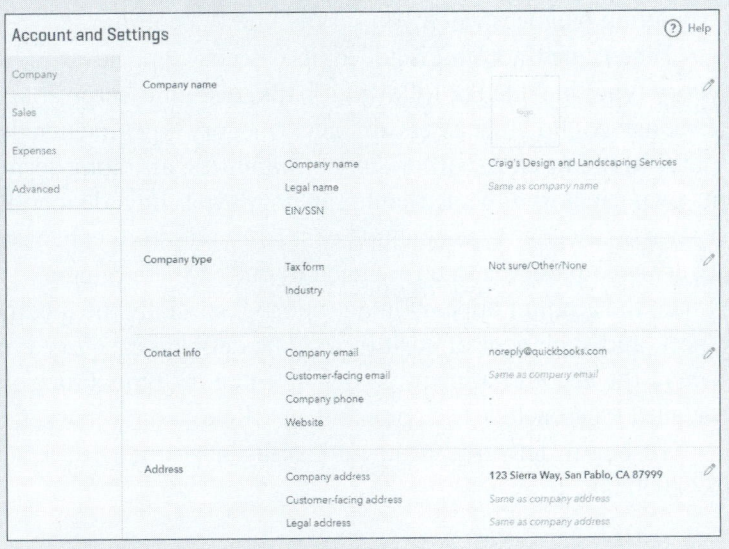

Figure 3.2

Company settings

When you modify the settings of your company, you will visit this section of QBO to make changes and start by selecting the Pencil icon to edit each individual section. You reviewed the four sections of the Company Settings window: Company, Sales, Expenses, and Advanced in Chapter 2. The most common changes to Company Settings involve turning on inventory, tracking of quantities on hand, tracking expenses by customer, making expenses and items billable, establishing default bill payment terms, using purchase orders, and time tracking.

Once you have modified the company settings, it is time to modify the chart of accounts.

Modify the Chart of Accounts and Establish Beginning Balances

You will continue your use of the Sample Company to learn the process of creating, modifying, and deleting accounts and of establishing beginning balances. If you are continuing from above, you will not need to open the Sample Company again. If not, follow the steps above to view the Sample Company. You should complete this entire section in one sitting so you do not lose your work. If you do leave and return, the cumulative balances will be inaccurate as your work will not have been saved while working in the Sample Problem.

Creating accounts and related beginning balances only occurs when you are utilizing QBO for the first time and your business has been in operation for some time. The transition to QBO from a previous accounting system will indicate business events and balances occurred prior to the first date of QBO use.

In this section, you will be adding new checking, inventory, prepaid rent, long-term debt, and common stock accounts to the Sample Company. You will also be establishing beginning balances for checking, accounts receivable, prepaid rent, inventory, and accounts payable. Every time you add a beginning balance, an equal and opposite amount is recorded to the Opening Balance Equity account (to keep debits and credits in balance).

QBO lets you establish a beginning amount for all of these accounts using basic journal entries. We will do that for some accounts, accounts receivable, accounts payable, and common stock. For the other accounts, such as checking, inventory, prepaid rent, long-term debt, and common stock, you will set some beginning balances when you set up a new account.

When a new account is added, its category type needs to be specified. Asset category types include the following: bank, accounts receivable, other current assets, fixed assets, and other assets. Liability category types include the following: accounts payable, credit cards, other current liabilities, and long-term liabilities. Equity is its own category type. Revenue category types include income and other income. Expense category types include cost of goods sold, expenses, and other expense. Every account needs to be assigned to one of these category types. This will dictate where the account appears in all reports, especially the income statement, balance sheet, and statement of cash flows. The detailed category type will further define where the account appears under its category type. Examples of bank category detailed types include cash on hand, checking, money market, and savings.

To begin, let's add a new checking account with a beginning balance of $20,000.00.

To add a new checking account to the chart of accounts and establish a beginning balance, do the following:

1   Click the **Gear** icon and then click **Chart of Accounts**.

2   Click the **See your Chart of Accounts** button.

3   Click the **New** button in the upper-right corner of the chart of accounts.

4   Click anywhere in the Account Type text box and select **Bank** shown in Figure 3.3.

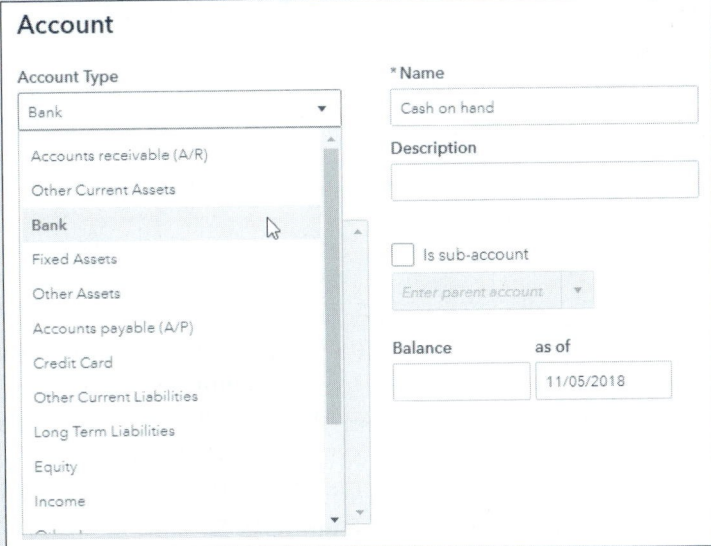

Figure 3.3

Account (adding a new bank account)

5   Select **Checking** from the Detail Type list and type **Checking BOA** in the Name text box.

6   Type **20000** in the Balance text box and type **11/1/2018** in the as of text box shown in Figure 3.4 and then press [**Tab**].

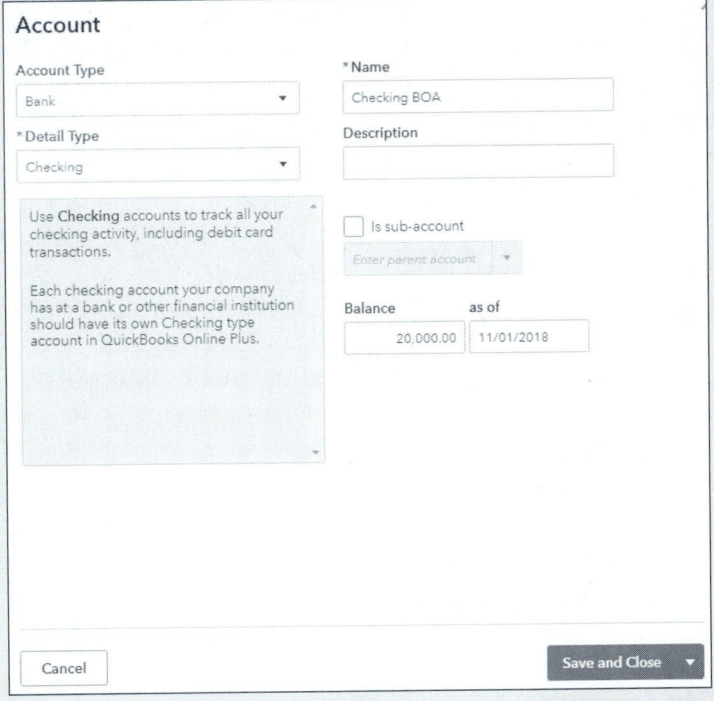

Figure 3.4

Account (completing the addition of a new checking account)

7 Click the **Save and Close** button to view the modified chart of accounts shown in Figure 3.5, which now includes a new checking account with a balance of $20,000.00.

Figure 3.5

Chart of Accounts (modified with the new checking BOA account)

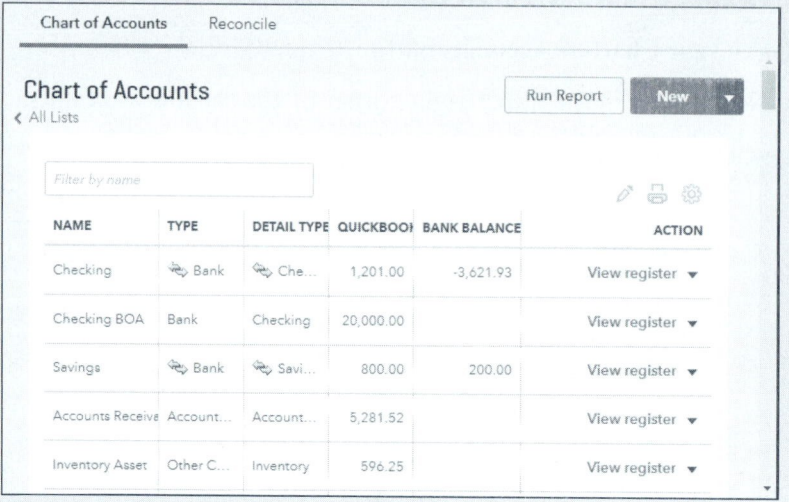

So far, we have added a $20,000 increase to the assets to the Sample Company as of 11/1/18. The Opening Balance Equity account has also increased as the result of this adjustment. To continue, let's add a new product. In QBO, products are merchandise a company purchases from a vendor, maintains in inventory, and then sells to customers. Services are efforts made by a company to add value to a customer. In the Sample Company, an inventory account exists. If you create a new company, an inventory account may not exist. However, when you add a new product, a new inventory account, called inventory asset, will automatically be created.

To add a new product and service, do the following:

1 View the chart of accounts and note the Inventory Asset account with a QuickBooks balance of $596.25.

2 Click the **Gear** icon and click **Products and Services** from the Lists column.

3 Click **New**.

4 Select **Inventory** from the **Select a Type** list.

5 Type **Stone Tile** as the new product in the Name text box.

6 Select **Landscaping** from the Category drop-down list.

7 Type **500** in the Initial quantity on hand text box and **11/1/2018** in the As of date text box.

8 Leave **Inventory Asset** as the Inventory asset account.

9 Type **Stone Tile** as the description for the Sales and Purchasing information text boxes.

10 Type **2.50** in the Sales price/rate text box and **1.25** in the Cost text box.

11 Leave **Sales of Product Income** as the Income account and **Cost of Goods Sold** as the Expense account.

12 Check the **Is taxable** check box. Your window should look like Figure 3.6.

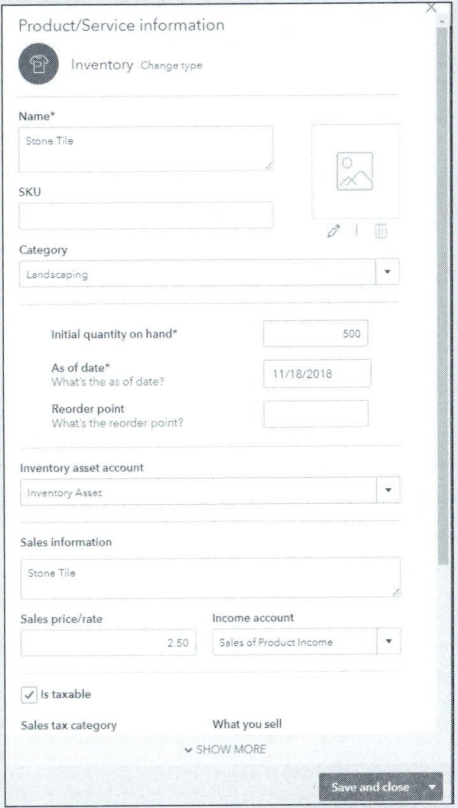

Figure 3.6

Partial view of Product/Service information window

13 Click the down arrow in the **Save and close** button and then select **Save and new**.

14 Click the **Change type** text next to the word Inventory at the top of the window. Click **Service**.

15 Type **Estimates** as the name of a new service.

16 Check the **I sell this product/service to my customers** check box and then uncheck the **I purchase this product/service from a vendor** check box.

17 Type **Estimates** as the description in the Sales information text box and then select **Design** from the Category drop-down list.

18 Type **50** in the Sales price/rate text box.

19 Uncheck the **Is taxable** check box.

20 Click the **Save and Close** button.

21 Scroll down the list of products and services. Note the addition of the new Stone Tile product, with a quantity of 500, and the new Estimates service added.

> 22 Click the **Gear** icon and then **Chart of Accounts** and note the new balance in the Inventory Asset account of $1,221.25, which equals the previous balance of 596.25 plus the addition of $625.00 (500 units at the rate of $1.25).

So far, we have added a $20,625 (20,000.00 + 625.00) net increase to the assets to the Sample Company as of 11/1/2018. The Opening Balance Equity account has increased as the result of this adjustment. To continue, let's add prepaid rent, long-term debt, and common stock accounts.

To add additional accounts, do the following:

1 Click the **New** button in the upper-right corner of the chart of accounts.

2 Click anywhere in the Account Type text box, and select **Other Current Assets**.

3 Select **Prepaid Expenses** as the Detail Type, and type **Prepaid Rent** as the name.

4 Type **4000** in the Balance text box and **11/1/2018** in the as of text box.

5 Click the down arrow in the **Save and Close** button, and select **Save and New**.

6 Click anywhere in the Account Type text box, and select **Long Term Liabilities**.

7 Select **Notes Payable** as the Detail Type, and type **Notes Payable Chase** as the name.

8 Type **9000** in the Unpaid balance text box and **11/1/2018** in the as of text box.

9 Click **Save and New**.

10 Click anywhere in the Account Type text box, and select **Equity**.

11 Select **Common Stock** as the Detail Type, and type **Common Stock** as the name.

12 Type **1000** in the Balance text box and **11/1/2018** in the as of text box.

13 Click the down arrow in the **Save and New** button, and select **Save and Close**.

14 Scroll down the chart of accounts. Note the addition of the new Prepaid Rent account with a balance of $4,000.00.

15 Continue scrolling down the chart of accounts. Note the addition of the new Notes Payable Chase account with a balance of $9,000.00.

16 Continue scrolling down the chart of accounts. Note the addition of the new Common Stock account with a balance of $1,000.00.

So far, we have added a $14,625 (20,000 + 625.00 + 4,000.00 − 9,000.00 − 1,000.00) net increase to the assets to the Sample Company as of 11/1/2018. The Opening Balance Equity account is automatically increased as the result of this adjustment.

Lastly, we will set up beginning balances in accounts receivable and accounts payable by using journal entries and add a new customer and vendor at the same time. Journal entries are commonly used to adjust accounts. A customer is an entity to whom you sell products or provide a service. A vendor is an entity from whom you purchase products or services.

To journalize accounts receivable and payable beginning balances, do the following:

1   Before you leave the chart of accounts, note the Opening Balance Equity account that has a balance of $5,287.50.

2   Click the + icon, and click on **Journal Entry** from the Other column.

3   Type **11/1/2018** in the Journal date text box.

4   Click in the **Category** column and then click the drop-down arrow.

5   Select **Accounts Receivable (A/R)** as the first account, and type **775** in the Debits column.

6   Click in the **Name** column, click the drop-down arrow, and select + **Add New** to add a new customer related to this balance shown in Figure 3.7.

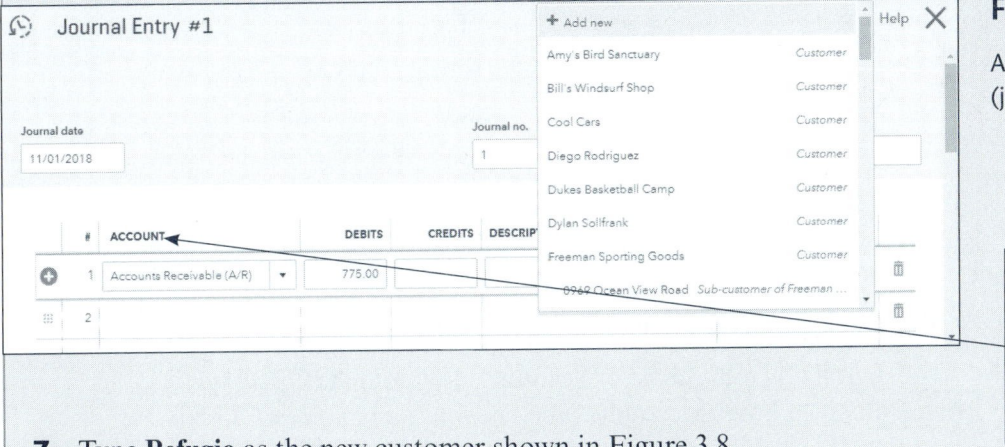

Figure 3.7

Accounts Receivable and Payable (journalizing beginning balances)

> Note that your screen has the title Category details not Account details as shown here. Once again this change took place after this text was completed. See the Preface of this text for a complete discussion of the confusion this change created.

7   Type **Refugio** as the new customer shown in Figure 3.8.

Figure 3.8

New Name (adding a new customer name)

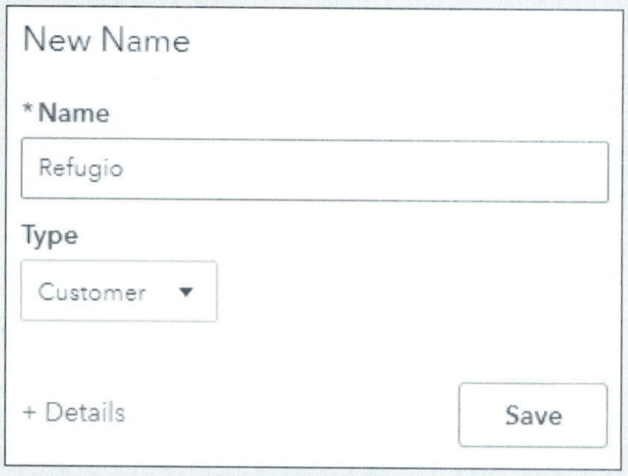

New Name

* Name

Refugio

Type

Customer   ▾

+ Details   Save

8 Click **Save** in the New Name box.

9 Select **Accounts Payable (A/P)** as the second account, and type **500** in the Credits column.

10 Click in the **Name** column, click the drop-down arrow, and select + **Add New** to add a new vendor.

11 Type **Rockster** as the Name, change the Type to **Vendor,** and click **Save**.

12 Select **Opening Balance Equity** as the Category on line 3, and accept 275.00 in the credit column. Your journal entry should look like Figure 3.9.

Figure 3.9

Journal Entry to Set Up A/R and A/P

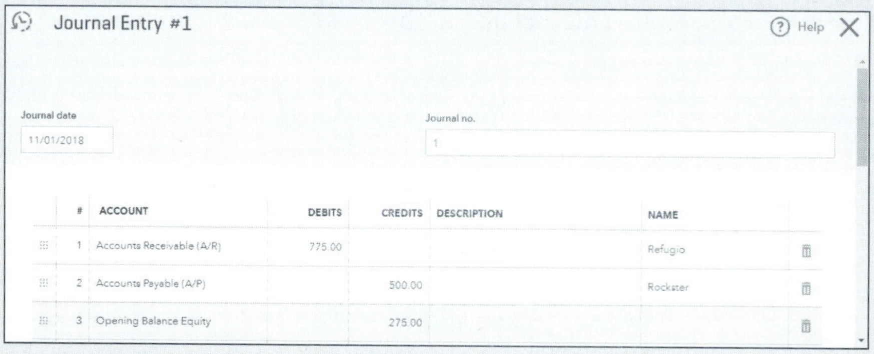

Journal Entry #1   ⑦ Help ✕

Journal date					Journal no.	
11/01/2018					1	

	#	ACCOUNT	DEBITS	CREDITS	DESCRIPTION	NAME	
⊞	1	Accounts Receivable (A/R)	775.00			Refugio	🗑
⊞	2	Accounts Payable (A/P)		500.00		Rockster	🗑
⊞	3	Opening Balance Equity		275.00			🗑

13 Click **Save and Close** to save your work.

14 Scroll down the chart of accounts, and note the Opening Balance Equity account, which now has a balance of $5,562.50 (5,287.50 + 775.00 − 500.00).

So far, we have added a $14,900 (20,000.00 + 625.00 + 4,000.00 − 9,000.00 − 1,000.00 + 775.00 − 500.00) net increase to the Sample Company as of 11/1/2018. The Opening Balance Equity account has increased as the result of this adjustment. Additional adjustments were made when Intuit first set this company up. The balance as of 11/1/2018 in the Opening Balance Equity account is $5,562.50.

Close Opening Balance Equity and Create a Balance Sheet

The final step in establishing beginning balances in QBO is to close out the Opening Balance Equity account as of 11/1/2018 of $5,562.50. Since we established a common stock account, the only account left in a corporation's equity accounts is retained earnings. Retained earnings are the earnings generated from prior years less dividends. You will need to create a trial balance, which lists the debit or credit balance in all accounts as of a specific date. Your instructor may ask you to customize, print, or export the trial balance to Excel, so you may do that as well.

To close opening balance equity and create, customize, save, print, and export a balance sheet, do the following:

1 Click the **+** icon, and click on **Journal Entry** from the Other column.

2 Type **11/1/2018** in the Journal date text box.

3 Select **Opening Balance Equity** as the first category, and type **5562.50** in the Debits column.

4 Select **Retained Earnings** as the second category, and type **5562.50** in the Credits column. Note: Retained Earnings was used since this company is a corporation. If this company was a sole proprietorship you would use Owner's Equity. Your journal entry should look like Figure 3.10.

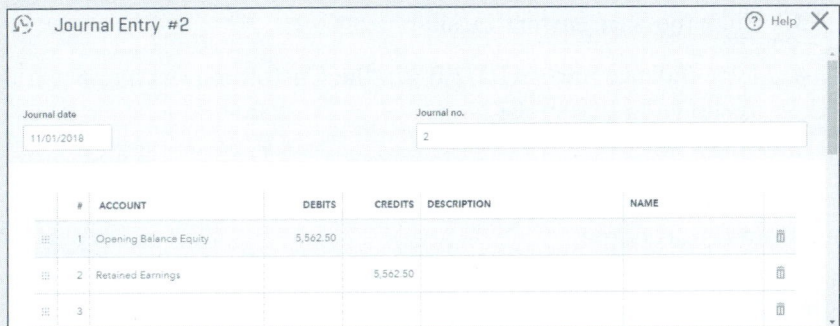

Figure 3.10

Journal Entry #2 (for closing Opening Balance Equity)

5 Click **Save and close**.

6 Click **Reports** in the navigation bar.

7 Type **Balance Sheet** into the Find report by name search text box, and then select **Balance Sheet** from the list provided from your search.

8 Select **Custom** from the drop-down list in the Report period text box.

9 Press [**Tab**] and then type your current system date in the from text box, and press [**Tab**].

10 Type your current system date in the to text box, and press [**Tab**].

11 Click the **Run Report** button. Scroll to the top of the Balance Sheet report and your screen should look similar to Figure 3.11 with different dates.

12 Click the **printer** icon at the top of the report and follow instructions to print your report as either a PDF file or printed document and then close the Print window.

Figure 3.11

Balance Sheet (as of 11/1/2018)

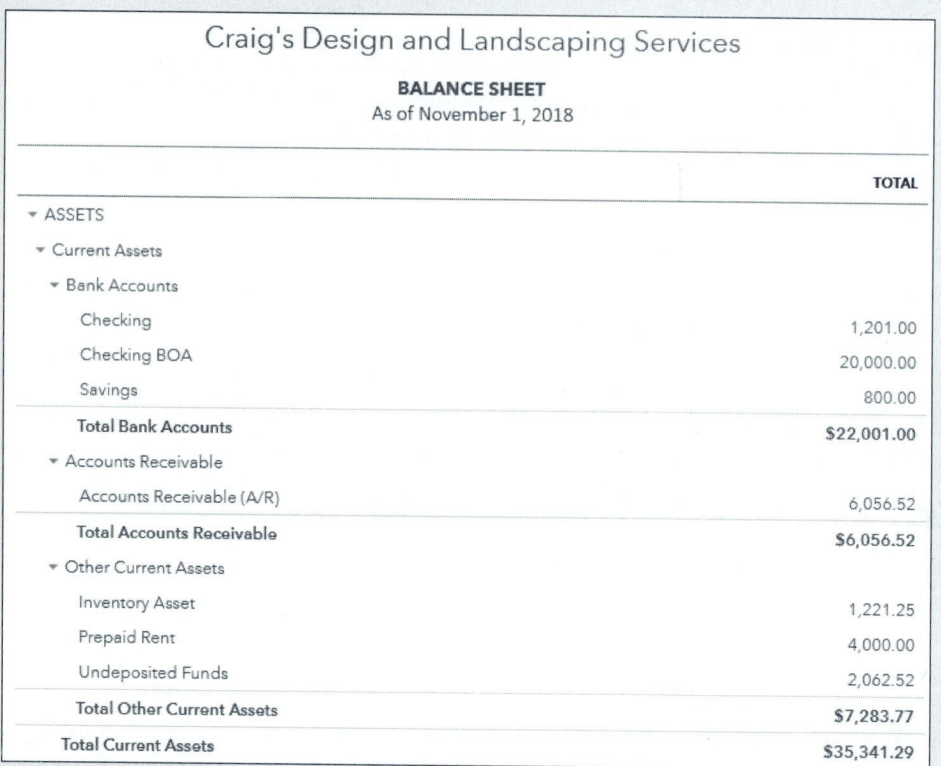

Craig's Design and Landscaping Services

BALANCE SHEET
As of November 1, 2018

	TOTAL
▾ ASSETS	
▾ Current Assets	
▾ Bank Accounts	
Checking	1,201.00
Checking BOA	20,000.00
Savings	800.00
Total Bank Accounts	**$22,001.00**
▾ Accounts Receivable	
Accounts Receivable (A/R)	6,056.52
Total Accounts Receivable	**$6,056.52**
▾ Other Current Assets	
Inventory Asset	1,221.25
Prepaid Rent	4,000.00
Undeposited Funds	2,062.52
Total Other Current Assets	**$7,283.77**
Total Current Assets	**$35,341.29**

13   Click the **Save customization** button.

14   Type **Balance Sheet 11/1/2018** in the Custom report name text box as shown in Figure 3.12.

Figure 3.12

Save Report Customizations

Custom report name

Balance Sheet 11/1/2018

Add this report to a group

None ▾

Add new group

Share with

None ▾

Save

15   Click **Save**.

16   Click the **Export** icon shown next to the Printer icon at the top of the report and then select **Export to Excel** from the drop-down list to begin the export to Excel process.

17   Select **Save File** and click **OK**. Type **Balance Sheet** as the file name in the Save As window and then click **Save** after you have navigated to a place on your computer to save this file.

18   Open Excel and then open the file you just saved.

19   After viewing your newly created Excel file, close Excel.

Create, Print, and Export a Transaction Detail by Account

Often, you will want to investigate a detailed list of transactions you have recorded for a specific period. In your end of chapter cases, a usual explanation for an incorrect report is recording a transaction in the incorrect period. To explore this option, you will create a transaction detail by account report for a specific period. You can create such a report for a large period to see if your transactions were recorded in the proper period and to see where you may have entered a wrong amount or account.

To create, print, and export a transaction detail by account report for the period 1/1/2010 to 12/31/2020, do the following:

1   Click **Reports** from the navigation bar.

2   Type **Transaction** in the Find a report by name text box.

3   Select **Transaction Detail by Account**.

4   Scroll to the top of the report window and then select **Custom** from the Report period drop-down text box and then press [**Tab**].

5   Type **1/1/2010** in the text box and then press [**Tab**].

6   Type **12/31/2020** in the text box and then press [**Tab**].

7   Click **Run Report**. While the transactions shown in this report should match yours, the dates will be different. The top of the report is shown in Figure 3.13.

Figure 3.13

Transaction Detail by Account report (top section)

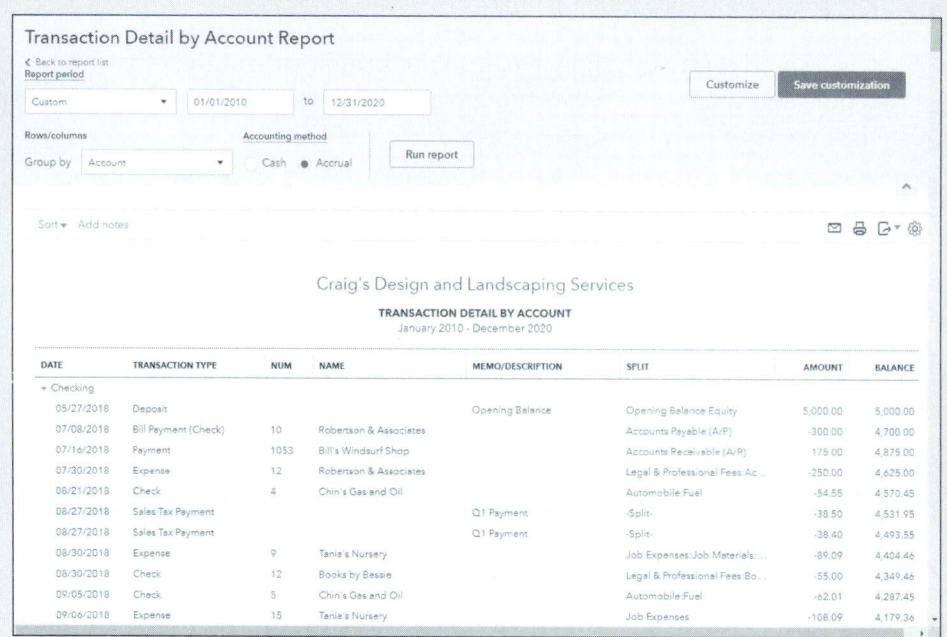

8   Click on **10** to view the Bill Payment (check) written to Robertson & Associates.

9   Close this window, scroll down the report, and investigate other transactions.

10 Scroll back to the top of this report, and click **Save customization**.

11 Click **Save**. Export this report like you exported the Balance Sheet earlier in this chapter.

12 Click the **Print** button to set this report up for printing; however, do not print this report since it is too long and unnecessary. Click **Cancel**.

13 Click the **Gear** icon and then click **Sign Out**. Note that once you sign out all of your work on the Sample Company is gone. If you were to reopen the Sample Company, none of your changes made in this chapter would appear.

End Note

In this chapter, you have logged into your account with QBO, modified company settings, added new accounts to the chart of accounts, and added beginning balances where appropriate. You have added customers, vendors, products, and services, and closed the Opening Balance Equity account. You are ready to add operating activities like sales receipts, invoices, and cash receipts.

Chapter 3 Questions

1   How do you access Company Settings?

2   When is it appropriate to add beginning balances to accounts?

3   What steps need to be followed to add an account to the chart of accounts?

4   When you add a beginning balance to an account, what other account is affected?

5   What information is required when adding a new product to QBO?

6   What additional information is required when you add beginning balance amounts to the accounts receivable account?

7   What additional information is required when you add beginning balance amounts to the accounts payable account?

8   Which additional account is used when you close Opening Balance Equity?

9   How do you access the Balance Sheet report?

10 How can you review a Transactions Report for any account when you are viewing the Balance Sheet?

Chapter 3 Matching

a. Transactions report	E.	Entity to whom you sell products/services
b. Trial balance	D.	Account used to offset beginning balances adjustments
c. Journal entry	G.	Merchandise a company purchases from a vendor
d. Opening Balance Equity	H.	Efforts made by a company to add value to a customer
e. Customer	B.	A listing of the debit or credit balances as of a specific date
f. Vendor	I.	Dictates where an account appears in all reports
g. Product	A.	Transactions for an account for a specified period
h. Service	F.	Entity from whom you purchase products/services
i. Category Type	J.	Checking
j. Detailed type example	C.	Commonly used to adjust accounts

Chapter 3 Cases

The following cases require you to open the company you created in Chapter 1. Each of the following cases continues throughout the text in a sequential manner. For example, if you are assigned Case 01, you will use the file you modified in this chapter in all of the following chapters. Each of the following cases is similar in concepts assessed but differs in amounts and transactions. See the preface to this text for a matrix of each student case and its attributes.

To reopen your company, do the following:

1   Open your Internet browser.

2   Type **https://qbo.intuit.com** into your browser's address text box.

3   Type your User ID and Password into the text boxes as shown in Figure 3.14.

Figure 3.14

Sign In Window (for logging in)

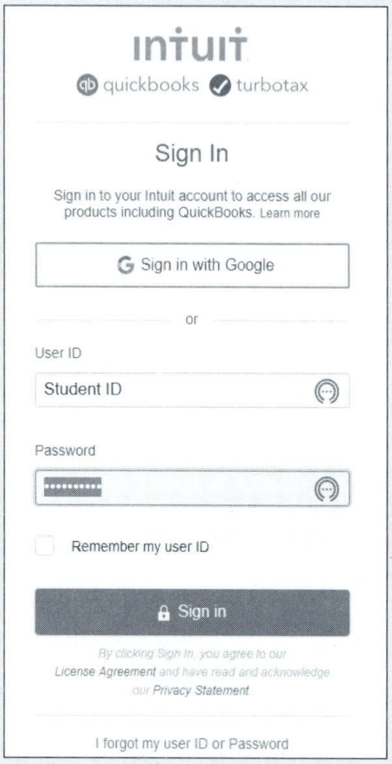

Case 1

Your company is a distributor of surfboards located in La Jolla, California. The company does not collect sales tax since all of its customers are resellers. They began business in 2017 and want to use QBO starting January 1, 2018. Beginning balances as of 12/31/2017 have been provided below.

You must make changes to your company. Based on what you learned in the text using the Sample Company, you are to make the following changes to the company you created in Chapter 1:

1   Modify settings as follows:

   a.   Company –
      i)   Company name – Modify the company name to Case 01 – Student Name (ID Number) replacing Student Name with your name and ID Number with the number your instructor indicated.
      ii) Company type – Modify the Tax form by selecting **Form 1120** from the drop-down list of forms. Then type Retail Shop or Online Commerce in the Industry text box, then click **Save**.

b. Sales – Turn on – Track quantity on hand. (This will automatically show items table on expense and purchase forms.)

c. Expenses –
   i) Turn on – Track expenses and items by customer.
   ii) Turn on – Make expenses and items billable (no markup, track billable expenses and items as income in a single account, no sales tax charged).
   iii) Default bill payment terms net 30.
   iv) Turn on – Use purchase orders (no custom fields).

d. Payments – no changes

e. Advanced
   i) Time tracking
      (1) Turn on – Add Service field to timesheets.
      (2) Turn on – Add Customer field to timesheets.

2 Create new accounts and related beginning balances as follows:

Category Type	Detail Type	Name	Balance	As of
Bank	Checking	Checking	25,000.00	12/31/17
Fixed Assets*	Furniture & Fixtures	Original cost	40,000.00	12/31/17
Fixed Assets*	Furniture & Fixtures	Depreciation	10,000.00	12/31/17
Long-Term Liabilities	Notes Payable	Notes Payable	60,000.00	12/31/17
Equity	Common Stock	Common Stock	1,000.00	12/31/17

*When entering a new fixed asset, place a check in the **Track depreciation of this asset** check box to reveal Original cost and Depreciation text boxes. Enter amounts from above as positive numbers.

3 Create two new products and one new service item as follows:

a. Products –
   i) Name/Description – Rook 15, track quantity, initial quantity 12/31/17 – 10, inventory asset account – Inventory Asset (this account will automatically be created in the chart of accounts when you add this product), price – $650, cost – $400, income account – Sales, expense account – Cost of Goods Sold.
   ii) Name/Description – The Water Hog, track quantity, initial quantity 12/31/17 – 8, inventory asset account – Inventory Asset, price – $860, cost — $500, income account – Sales, expense account – Cost of Goods Sold.

b. Service – Name/Description – Consulting, rate – $25, income account – Services

c. Make changes to the following accounts via journal entry 1 as of 12/31/17 with an offset to Opening Balance Equity:

Account	Amount	Name
Accounts Receivable	5,000.00	Blondie's Boards (new customer)
Prepaid Expenses	3,000.00	
Accounts Payable	4,500.00	Channel Islands (new vendor)

4 Close the Opening Balance Equity account to Retained Earnings via journal entry 2 as of 12/31/17.

5 Prepare and print a Trial Balance report as of 12/31/17 (Click **Reports**, then scroll down the page to the For my accountant section and click **Trial Balance**. Then select **Custom** as the report period and type **1/1/17** and **12/31/17** as the from to dates.), save it as a customized report named Trial Balance 12/31/17, and share it with all users. Your report should look like Figure 3.15.

6 If your trial balance differs from what is in Figure 3.15, do the following:

   a. Make sure all of your changes were dated 12/31/17.

   b. Click on the debit or credit balance to view a transactions report for each account, and investigate why your answer is different.

   c. Ask your instructor for assistance.

   d. Be sure your company matches the above since, in the following chapter, you will be adding additional business events.

Figure 3.15

Trial Balance (as of 12/31/17)

Case 1
TRIAL BALANCE
As of December 31, 2017

	DEBIT	CREDIT
Checking	25,000.00	
Accounts Receivable	5,000.00	
Inventory Asset	8,000.00	
Prepaid Expenses	3,000.00	
Furniture & Fixtures:Depreciation		10,000.00
Furniture & Fixtures:Original cost	40,000.00	
Accounts Payable		4,500.00
Notes Payable		60,000.00
Common Stock		1,000.00
Opening Balance Equity		0.00
Retained Earnings		5,500.00
TOTAL	**$81,000.00**	**$81,000.00**

7 Export your Trial Balance report to Excel, and save it with the file name: Student Name (replace with your name) Ch 03 Case 01 Trial Balance.xlsx.

8 Prepare and print a Transaction Detail by Account report for transactions between 1/1/2010 and 12/31/2020, save it as a customized report named Transaction Detail by Account, and share it with all users. If asked, indicate that your business is accrual based.

9 Use your Transaction Detail by Account report to locate any differences in your Trial Balance report created above.

   a. Make sure that all of your changes were dated 12/31/17.

   b. Click on the line that does not match to view the transaction for that account, and investigate why your answer differs.

    c. Ask your instructor for assistance.

    d. Be sure your company matches the above since, in the following chapter, you will be adding additional business events.

10 Export your Transactions Detail by Account report to Excel, and save it with the file name: Student Name (replace with your name) Ch 03 Case 01 Transaction Detail by Account.xlsx.

11 Sign out of your company.

Case 2

Your company is a distributor of remote control toys located in La Jolla, California. The company does not collect sales tax since all of its customers are resellers. They began business in 2018 and want to use QBO starting January 1, 2019. Beginning balances as of 12/31/2018 have been provided below.

You must make changes to your company. Based on what you learned in the text using the Sample Company, you are to make the following changes to the company you created in Chapter 1:

1 Modify settings as follows:

    a. Company – Company name – Modify the company name to Case 02 – Student Name (ID Number) replacing Student Name with your name and ID Number with the number your instructor indicated.

    b. Sales – Turn on – Track quantity on hand. (This will automatically show items table on expense and purchase forms.)

    c. Expenses –
        i) Turn on – Track expenses and items by customer.
        ii) Turn on – Make expenses and items billable (no markup, track billable expenses and items as income in a single account, no sales tax charged).
        iii) Default bill payment terms net 30.
        iv) Turn on – Use purchase orders (no custom fields).

    d. Payments – no changes

    e. Advanced
        i) Time tracking
            (1) Turn on – Add Service field to timesheets.
            (2) Turn on – Add Customer field to timesheets.

2 Create new accounts and related beginning balances as follows:

Category Type	Detail Type	Name	Balance	As of
Bank	Checking	Checking	5,000.00	12/31/18
Fixed Assets*	Machinery & Equipment	Original cost	10,000.00	12/31/18
Fixed Assets*	Machinery & Equipment	Depreciation	1,000.00	12/31/18
Long-Term Liabilities	Notes Payable	Notes Payable	12,000.00	12/31/18
Equity	Common Stock	Common Stock	100.00	12/31/18

*When entering a new fixed asset, place a check in the **Track depreciation of this asset** check box to reveal Original cost and Depreciation text boxes. Enter amounts from above as positive numbers.

3   Create two new products and one new service item:

   a.   Products –

      i)   Name/Description – Broon F830 Ride, track quantity, initial quantity 12/31/18 – 4, inventory asset account – Inventory Asset (note: this account will automatically be created in the chart of accounts when you add this product), price – $1,500, cost – $800, income account – Sales, expense account – Cost of Goods Sold.

      ii)   Name/Description – Sea Wind Carbon Sailboat, track quantity, initial quantity 12/31/18 – 3, inventory asset account – Inventory Asset, price – $1,200, cost – $620, income account – Sales, expense account – Cost of Goods Sold.

   b.   Service – Name/Description – Repairs, rate – $45, income account – Services.

   c.   Make changes to the following accounts via journal entry 1 as of 12/31/18 with an offset to Opening Balance Equity:

Account	Amount	Name
Accounts Receivable	925.00	Benson's RC (new customer)
Prepaid Expenses	2,400.00	
Accounts Payable	1,900.00	Kyosho (new vendor)

4   Close the Opening Balance Equity account to Retained Earnings via journal entry 2 as of 12/31/18.

5   Prepare and print a Trial Balance report as of 12/31/18 (Click **Reports** then scroll down the page to the For my accountant section and click **Trial Balance**. Then select **Custom** as the report period and type **1/1/18** and **12/31/18** as the from to dates.), save it as a customized report named Trial Balance 12/31/18, and share it with all users. Your report should look like Figure 3.16.

Figure 3.16

Trial Balance (as of 12/31/18)

Case 2
TRIAL BALANCE
As of December 31, 2018

	DEBIT	CREDIT
Checking	5,000.00	
Accounts Receivable	925.00	
Inventory Asset	5,060.00	
Prepaid Expenses	2,400.00	
Machinery & Equipment:Depreciation		1,000.00
Machinery & Equipment:Original cost	10,000.00	
Accounts Payable		1,900.00
Notes Payable		12,000.00
Common Stock		100.00
Opening Balance Equity		0.00
Retained Earnings		8,385.00
TOTAL	**$23,385.00**	**$23,385.00**

6 If your trial balance is different from what is in Figure 3.16, do the following:

   a. Make sure all of your changes were dated 12/31/18.

   b. Click on the debit or credit balance to view a transactions report for each account, and investigate why your answer is different.

   c. Ask your instructor for assistance.

   d. Be sure your company matches the above since, in the following chapter, you will be adding additional business events.

7 Export your Trial Balance report to Excel, and save it with the file name: Student Name (replace with your name) Ch 03 Case 02 Trial Balance.xlsx.

8 Prepare and print a Transaction Detail by Account report for all transactions between 1/1/2010 and 12/31/2020, save it as a customized report named Transaction Detail by Account, and share it with all users. If asked, indicate that your business is accrual based.

9 Use your Transaction Detail by Account report to locate any differences in your Trial Balance report created above.

   a. Make sure all of your changes were dated 12/31/18.

   b. Click on the line that does not match to view the transaction for that account, and investigate why your answer differs.

   c. Ask your instructor for assistance.

   d. Be sure your company matches the above since, in the following chapter, you will be adding additional business events.

10 Export your Transactions Detail by Account report to Excel and save it with the file name: Student Name (replace with your name) Ch 03 Case 02 Transaction Detail by Account.xlsx.

11 Sign out of your company.

Case 3

Your company sells and services cell phones. They are located in La Jolla, California. The company does collect sales tax since all of its customers are consumers (See Appendix 1 for directions on how to add a sales tax to a company file.) They began business in 2019 and want to use QBO starting January 1, 2020. Beginning balances as of 12/31/2019 have been provided below.

    You must make changes to your company. Based on what you learned in the text using the Sample Company, you are to make the following changes to the company you created in Chapter 1:

1 Modify settings as follows:

   a. Company – Company name – Modify the company name to Case 03 – Student Name (ID Number) replacing Student Name with your name and ID Number with the number your instructor indicated. Use 3990 La Jolla Shores Drive, La Jolla, CA 92037 as the company's address.

   b. SSN – Add 987-65-4321 as your business social security number as you are a sole proprietor.

   c. Sales – Make sure that Track inventory quantity on hand is on. (This will automatically show items table on expense and purchase forms.)

d. Expenses –

  i)   Turn on – Track expenses and items by customer.

  ii) Turn on – Make expenses and items billable (no markup, track billable expenses and items as income in a single account, charge sales tax).

  iii) Set Default bill payment terms to Due on receipt.

  iv) Turn on – Use purchase orders (no custom fields).

e. Payments – no changes

f. Advanced

  i)   Time tracking.

  ii) Turn on – Add Service field to timesheets.

  iii) Turn on – Make Single-Time Activity Billable to Customer.

2 Follow steps provided in Appendix 1 to add sales tax paid annually beginning 1/1/20.

3 Create new accounts and related beginning balances (Category Type, Detail Type, Name, Balance as of 12/31/19) as follows:

a. Bank, Checking, Checking, $12,000

b. Fixed Assets, Machinery & Equipment, Original cost, $15,000

  Note: When entering a new fixed asset, place a check in the Track depreciation of this asset check box to reveal Original cost and Depreciation text boxes. Enter amounts from above as positive numbers.

c. Fixed Assets, Machinery & Equipment, Depreciation, $2,000

d. Long-Term Liabilities, Notes Payable, Notes Payable, $23,000

e. Equity, Owner's Equity, Owner's Equity, 0

4 Create two new products (Name/Description, initial quantity 12/31/19, inventory asset account, price, cost, income account, expense account):

a. Apple iPhone 7, track quantity, 10, Inventory Asset (Note: This account will automatically be created in the chart of accounts when you add this product), $750, $500, Sales of Product Income, Cost of Goods Sold, taxable.

b. Pixel, track quantity, 3, Inventory Asset, $650, $400, Sales of Product Income, Cost of Goods Sold, taxable.

5 Create two new service items (Name/Description, rate, income account):

a. Apple Repairs, $45, Services, not taxable. (Note: You'll need to add Services as an account like you did in the chapter.)

b. Pixel Repairs, $40, Services, not taxable.

6 Add new Accounts Receivable, Prepaid Expenses, and Accounts Payable accounts, then make changes to the following accounts via journal entry 1 as of 12/31/19 with an offset to Opening Balance Equity:

Account	Amount	Name
Accounts Receivable (A/R)	4,125.00	GHO Marketing (new customer)
Prepaid Expenses	2,750.00	
Accounts Payable (A/P)	5,000.00	Apple Inc. (new vendor)

7 Close the Opening Balance Equity account (which should have a balance of $10,075) to Owner's Equity via journal entry 2 as of 12/31/19. (Note: Use Owner's Equity since this company is a sole proprietorship. Retained Earnings would have been used if this company had been a corporation.)

8 Prepare and print a Trial Balance report as of 12/31/19 (Click **Reports** then scroll down the page to the For my accountant section and click **Trial Balance**. Then select **Custom** as the report period and type **1/1/19** and **12/31/19** as the from to dates.), click the Run report button and then save it as a customized report named Trial Balance 12/31/19, and share it with all users. Your report should look like Figure 3.17.

Figure 3.17

Trial Balance

Case 3 - Student Name (ID number)

TRIAL BALANCE

As of December 31, 2019

	DEBIT	CREDIT
Checking	12,000.00	
Accounts Receivable (A/R)	4,125.00	
Inventory Asset	6,200.00	
Prepaid Expenses	2,750.00	
Machinery & Equipment:Depreciation		2,000.00
Machinery & Equipment:Original cost	15,000.00	
Accounts Payable (A/P)		5,000.00
Notes Payable		23,000.00
Opening Balance Equity		0.00
Owner's Equity		10,075.00
TOTAL	$40,075.00	$40,075.00

9 If your trial balance differs from what is in Figure 3.17, do the following:

a. Make sure all of your changes were dated 12/31/19.

b. Click on the debit or credit balance to view a transactions report for each account, and investigate why your answer is different.

c. Ask your instructor for assistance.

d. Be sure your company matches the above since, in the following chapter, you will be adding additional business events.

10 Export your Trial Balance report to Excel, and save it with the file name: Student Name (replace with your name) Ch 03 Case 03 Trial Balance.xlsx.

11   Prepare and print a Transaction Detail by Account report for all transactions between 1/1/2010 and 12/31/2022, save it as a customized report named Transaction Detail by Account, and share it with all users. If asked, indicate that your business is accrual based.

12   Use your Transaction Detail by Account report to locate any differences in your Trial Balance report created above.

   a.   Make sure all of your changes were dated 12/31/19.

   b.   Click on the line that does not match to view the transaction for that account, and investigate why your answer differs.

   c.   Ask your instructor for assistance.

   d.   Be sure your company matches the above since, in the following chapter, you will be adding additional business events.

13   Export your Transactions Detail by Account report to Excel and save it with the file name: Student Name (replace with your name) Ch 03 Case 03 Transaction Detail by Account.xlsx.

14   Sign out of your company.

Case 4

Your company is a Sports Gym serving the Hollywood area in California. They sell month-to-month memberships to individuals and businesses as well as T-shirts, yoga pants, and other sports-related accessories. They began their business in 2020 and want to use QBO starting January 1, 2021. Beginning balances as of 12/31/2020 have been provided below.

Based on what you learned in the text using the Sample Company, you are to make the following changes to the company you created in Chapter 1.

1   Modify settings as follows (Click the **Gear** icon and then click **Account and Settings**):

   a.   Company –
      i)   Name – Case 04 – Student Name (ID Number)
      ii)   EIN – 98-9875461
      iii)   Tax form – Form 1120
      iv)   Industry – Fitness and Recreational Sports Centers
      v)   Email – your e-mail address
      vi)   Address – 6540 Sunset Blvd., Hollywood, CA 90028

   b.   Sales (turn the following on, all others turn off or leave off) –
      i)   Preferred invoice terms – Net 30
      ii)   Custom transaction numbers
      iii)   Show Product/Service column on sales form
      iv)   Track quantity and price/rate
      v)   Track inventory quantity on hand
      vi)   Show aging table at the bottom of the statement

   c.   Expenses (turn the following on, all others turn off or leave off) –
      i)   Show items table on expense and purchase forms
      ii)   Use purchase orders

   d. Payments – no changes

   e. Advanced – no changes

2 Add sales tax that is payable to the California State Board of Equalization. (Follow the steps provided in Appendix 1.)

3 Create new accounts and related beginning balances where appropriate. (Click the **Gear** icon and then click **Chart of Accounts**.)

   a. First account –
- i) Account Type – Bank
- ii) Detail Type – Checking
- iii) Name – Checking
- iv) Balance as of 12/31/2020 – $27,000

   b. Second account –
- i) Account Type – Accounts Receivable (A/R)
- ii) Detail Type – Accounts Receivable (A/R)
- iii) Name – Accounts Receivable (A/R)
- iv) Balance as of 12/31/2020 – n/a

   c. Third account –
- i) Account Type – Other Current Assets
- ii) Detail Type – Prepaid Expenses
- iii) Name – Prepaid Expenses
- iv) Balance as of 12/31/2020 – $12,000

   d. Fourth and fifth accounts (Note: When entering a new fixed asset place a check in the **Track depreciation of this asset** check box to reveal Original cost and Depreciation text boxes. Enter both amounts from above as positive numbers.) –
- i) Account Type – Fixed Asset
- ii) Detail Type – Fixed Asset Furniture
- iii) Name – Furniture
- iv) Original cost – $65,000 as of 12/31/2020
- v) Depreciation – $10,000 as of 12/31/2020

   e. Sixth and seventh accounts (see note above) –
- i) Account Type – Fixed Asset
- ii) Detail Type – Machinery & Equipment
- iii) Name – Machinery & Equipment
- iv) Original cost – $115,000 as of 12/31/2020
- v) Depreciation – $6,500 as of 12/31/2020

   f. Eighth account –
- i) Account Type – Accounts Payable (A/P)
- ii) Detail Type – Accounts Payable (A/P)
- iii) Name – Accounts Payable (A/P)
- iv) Balance as of 12/31/2020 – n/a

   g. Ninth account –
- i) Account Type – Long-Term Liabilities
- ii) Detail Type – Notes Payable
- iii) Name – Notes Payable
- iv) Balance as of 12/31/2020 – $82,000

    h.   Tenth account –
        i)   Account Type – Equity
        ii)   Detail Type – Common Stock
        iii)   Name – Common Stock
        iv)   Balance as of 12/31/2020 – $1,000

4   Create two new Inventory products as follows:

    a.   First product –
        i)   Name – T-shirts
        ii)   Initial quantity on hand – 250
        iii)   As of date – 12/31/2020
        iv)   Inventory asset account – Inventory Asset
        v)   Sales information – T-shirts
        vi)   Sales price/rate – $25
        vii)   Income account – Sales of Product Income
        viii) Is taxable – Yes
        ix)   Purchasing information – T-shirts
        x)   Cost – $12
        xi)   Expense account – Cost of Goods Sold

    b.   Second product –
        i)   Name – Yoga pants
        ii)   Initial quantity on hand – 125
        iii)   As of date – 12/31/2020
        iv)   Inventory asset account – Inventory Asset
        v)   Sales information – Yoga pants
        vi)   Sales price/rate – $45
        vii)   Income account – Sales of Product Income
        viii) Is taxable – Yes
        ix)   Purchasing information – Yoga pants
        x)   Cost – $20
        xi)   Expense account – Cost of Goods Sold

5   Create two new service items as follows:

    a.   First service –
        i)   Name – Monthly Fee
        ii)   Sales information – Yes you do sell this service to customers. "Monthly Fee"
        iii)   Sales price/rate – $150
        iv)   Income account – Sales
        v)   Is taxable – No
        vi)   Purchase information – No you don't purchase this service from a vendor

    b.   Second service –
        i)   Name – Training
        ii)   Sales information – Yes you do sell this service to customers. "Training"
        iii)   Sales price/rate – $75
        iv)   Income account – Sales

v) Is taxable – No

vi) Purchase information – No you don't purchase this service from a vendor

6 Prepare journal entry 1 as of 12/31/2020 with an offset to Opening Balance Equity to record the following beginning balances:

a. Accounts Receivable (A/R) – Debit $8,500 – Disney (new customer)

b. Accounts Payable (A/P) – Credit $18,000 – Precor (new vendor)

7 Prepare journal entry 2 as of 12/31/2020 to close the Opening Balance Equity to Retained Earnings ($115,500).

8 Prepare and print a Trial Balance report with a custom reporting period of 1/1/2020 to 12/31/20, then save it as a customized report named Trial Balance 12/31/2020. Your report should look like Figure 3.18.

Figure 3.18

Trial Balance

Case 4 Student Name (Student ID)

TRIAL BALANCE
As of December 31, 2020

	DEBIT	CREDIT
Checking	27,000.00	
Accounts Receivable (A/R)	8,500.00	
Inventory Asset	5,500.00	
Prepaid Expenses	12,000.00	
Furniture:Depreciation		10,000.00
Furniture:Original cost	65,000.00	
Machinery & Equipment:Depreciation		6,500.00
Machinery & Equipment:Original cost	115,000.00	
Accounts Payable (A/P)		18,000.00
Notes Payable		82,000.00
Common Stock		1,000.00
Opening Balance Equity		0.00
Retained Earnings		115,500.00
TOTAL	**$233,000.00**	**$233,000.00**

9 Prepare and print a Transaction Detail by Account report for all transactions between 1/1/2010 and 12/31/2022, save it as a customized report named Transaction Detail by Account. If asked, indicate that your business is accrual-based.

10 Use your Transaction Detail by Account report to locate any differences in your Trial Balance report created above.

a Make sure all your changes were dated 12/31/20.

b. Click on the line that does not match to view the transaction for that account and investigate why your answer differs.

c. Ask your instructor for assistance.

d. Be sure your company matches the above since, in the following chapter, you will be adding additional business events.

4

Operating Activities: Sales and Cash Receipts

Upon completion of this chapter, the student will be able to do the following:

- Create a new service, product, and customer
- Record a sales receipt
- Record an invoice for services rendered on account
- Record an invoice for products sold on account
- Record cash receipts (payments received on account)
- Deposit payments received on account
- Prepare a Transaction Detail by Account report

Overview

Intuit has provided a Sample Company online to provide new users a test drive of its QBO product. In this chapter, you will open this Sample Company and practice various features of QBO. You will be recording operating activities, such as adding new services, new products, new customers, new sales receipts, new invoices, and new cash receipts to the Sample Company file. Remember, if you stop in the middle of this work, none of your work will be saved. So, when you return, the same Sample Company, without your work, will appear. In the end of chapter, you will perform the same tasks completed on the Sample Company on your Student Company. That work of course will be saved. Your system date will differ from the date shown under the company name QBO. Transaction dates on your screen may also differ from the figures shown throughout this text.

Throughout this text, figures illustrating bills, expenses, checks, purchase orders, and credit card transactions will have the title Account details not Category details and the column title as Account and not Category as shown on your QBO software. Once again this change took place after this text was completed. See the Preface of this text for a complete discussion of the confusion this change created.

Services, Products, and Customers

In this section, you will add new services, products, and customers. To add new services and products, you will access the Company section using the **Gear** icon. To add customers, you will use the Customers menu item in the navigation bar.

To add new services, products, and customers to the Sample Company, do the following:

1 Open your Internet browser.

2 Type **https://qbo.intuit.com/redir/testdrive** into your browser's address text box and the press [**Enter**] to view the Sample Company Dashboard. If asked, provide security information before proceeding.

   Your system date will differ from the date shown under the company name in the following figure. Transaction dates on your screen may also differ from the figures shown throughout this text.

3 Click the **Gear** icon, and click **Products and Services** as shown in Figure 4.1.

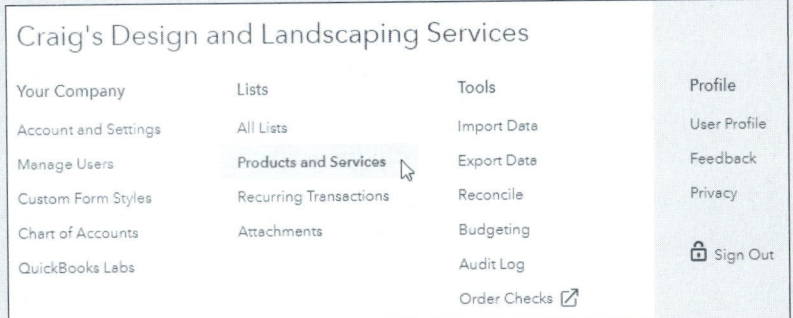

Figure 4.1

List of Products and Services

4 Click **New** in the upper right corner of the **Products and Services** list.

5 Click **Service**.

6 Type **Rose Consulting** in the Name text box and the Sales information text boxes.

7 Select **Landscaping** from the Category drop-down text box and then check the **Sales Information** check box, and then type **45** in the Sales price/rate text box.

8 Scroll down the window and accept Services as the Income account and then uncheck the **Is taxable** check box, both of which are shown in Figure 4.2.

Figure 4.2

Adding a new Service (partial view)

9 Click on the drop-down arrow to the right of the **Save and Close** button, and select **Save and New**.

10 Click **Change type** and then select **Inventory**.

11 Type **Roses** in the Name text box and then click the drop-down arrow in the Category text box and select **Landscaping**.

12 Type **0** in the Initial Quantity On Hand text box and type today's date in the As Of Date text box.

13 Select **Inventory Asset** as the Inventory Asset Account.

14 Type **Roses** in the Sale Information and in Purchasing Information text boxes.

15 Type **25** in the Sales price/rate text box and **15** in the Cost text box.

16 Select **Sales of Product Income** from the Income account drop-down list and **Cost of Goods Sold** from the Expense account drop-down list.

17 Check the **Is taxable** check box. A partial view of the Product or Service Information window should look like Figure 4.3.

Figure 4.3

Adding a New Product
(partial view)

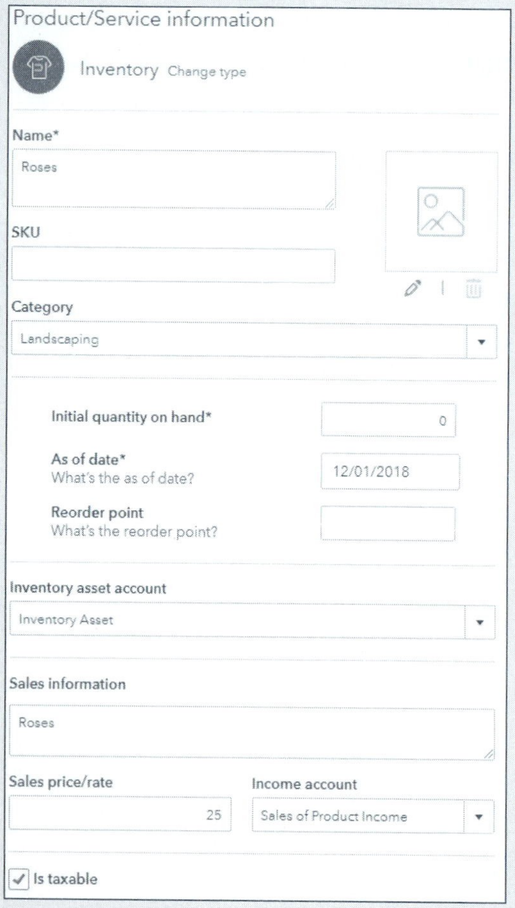

18 Click on the drop-down arrow to the right of the **Save and New** button, and select **Save and Close**.

19 Scroll down the revised list of Products and Service to see the service and product you entered shown in Figure 4.4.

	NAME ▲	SKU	TYPE	SALES DESCRIPTION	SALES PRICE	COST	TAXABLE	QTY ON HAND
☐	Rose Consulting		Service	Rose Consulting	45			
☐	Roses		Inventory	Roses	25	15	✓	0

Figure 4.4

Updated List of Products and Services (partial view)

20 Click **Sales** from the navigation bar, then click **Customers**, and then click the **New Customer** button.

21 Type **Roxy Corporation** in the Company text box.

22 Type **James** in the First name text box and **Roxy** in the Last name text box.

23 Select the Address tab, and type **101 Ocean View, La Jolla, CA, 92130** in the appropriate text boxes. Select **Roxy Corporation** from the Display name as drop-down text box. Click **Save** and then click **Edit** to view the data you just entered. A partial view of the Customer Information window is shown in Figure 4.5.

Customer information

Company	Email
Roxy Corporation	*Separate multiple emails with commas*

Title	First name	Middle name	Last name	Suffix		Phone	Mobile	Fax
	James		Roxy					

*Display name as

Roxy Corporation ▼

Other	Website

Print on check as ☑ Use display name   ☐ Is sub-customer

Roxy Corporation   Enter parent customer ▼   Bill with parent ▼

Address | Notes | Tax info | Payment and billing | Attachments | Additional Info

Billing address map

| 101 Ocean View |
| La Jolla | CA |
| 92130 | Country |

Shipping address map ☑ Same as billing address

| Street |
| City/Town | State/Province |
| ZIP code | Country |

Cancel | Make inactive   Privacy   **Save**

Figure 4.5

Customer Information window (partial view)

24 Select the **Payment and billing** tab, and select **Net 30** from the Terms text box.

25 Click **Save**.

26 The Roxy Corporation customer window appears as shown in Figure 4.6.

Figure 4.6

Roxy Corporation customer window

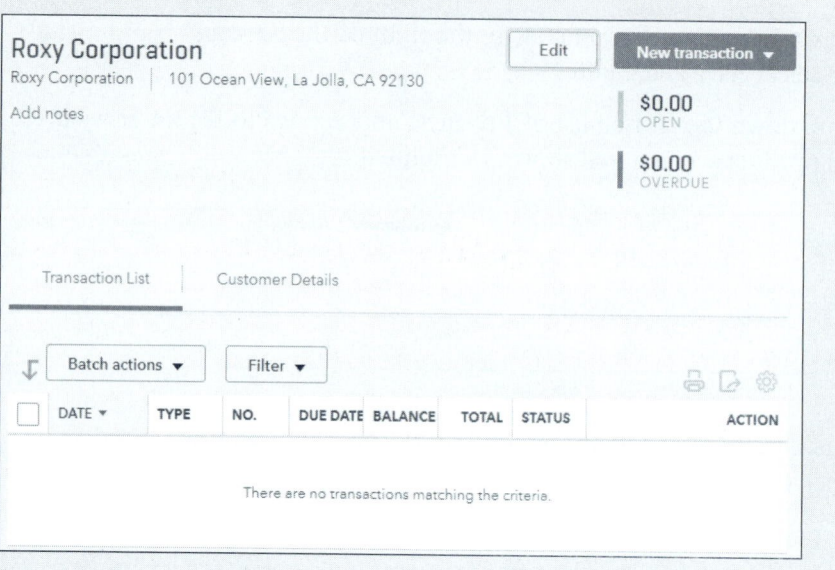

You have now added a new service, a new product, and a new customer. Next up, adding sales receipts to record cash sales and invoices to record credit sales.

Sales Receipts and Invoices

A business uses sales receipts to record sales transactions on a daily basis where payment is received at the same time as a product or service is delivered. Sales invoices are used to record sales transactions where customers are granted credit terms and given some time to pay after a product or service is delivered. In either case, sales are recorded when the product is sold or service is rendered.

To add sales receipts and invoices to the Sample Company, do the following:

1   Continue from where you left off. If you closed the Sample Company, follow the steps to reopen it found at the beginning of this chapter. Keep in mind that if you close the Sample Company, all of your work thus far in this chapter is lost as it has reset itself.

2   Click the **+** icon, and select **Sales Receipt** shown in Figure 4.7.

Figure 4.7

Create window (adding a sales receipt)

Create

Customers	Vendors	Employees	Other
Invoice	Expense	Payroll 🏃	Bank Deposit
Receive Payment	Check	Single Time Activity	Transfer
Estimate	Bill	Weekly Timesheet	Journal Entry
Credit Memo	Pay Bills		Statement
Sales Receipt	Purchase Order		Inventory Qty Adjustment
Refund Receipt	Vendor Credit		
Delayed Credit	Credit Card Credit		
Delayed Charge	Print Checks		

▸ Show less

3   Select **Bill's Windsurf Shop** from the Choose a customer drop-down list in the upper left corner of the Sales Receipt window.

4   Your computer's system date has been entered as the Sales Receipt date.

5   Select **Check** from the drop-down list of Payment methods.

6   Select **Undeposited Funds** from the Deposit to drop-down text box. The check will be recorded in the Undeposited Funds account since deposits for this company are made every other day.

7   On line 1 of the sales receipt, select **Pump P461-17** in the PRODUCT/SERVICE column.

8   Type **2** in the QTY (Quantity) column.

9   On line 2 of the sales receipt, select **Rock Fountain R154-88** in the PRODUCT/SERVICE column.

10 Type **2** in the QTY (Quantity) column and then press [**Tab**]. The sales receipt should look like Figure 4.8.

Figure 4.8

Sales Receipt before Sales Tax (partial view)

11 Scroll down the sales receipt, and select **California 8%** from the drop-down list in the Select a sales tax rate text box. The lower half of your sales receipt should look like Figure 4.9 with the $46.40 tax amount added.

Figure 4.9

Sales Receipt after Sales Tax (partial view)

12 Click **Save and close**.

13 Click **Sales** and then click **Customers** from the navigation bar, and click **Bill's Windsurf Shop**. A listing of recent transactions affecting that customer is shown, including the recorded sales receipt shown in Figure 4.10.

Figure 4.10

Bill's Windsurf Shop (recent transactions)

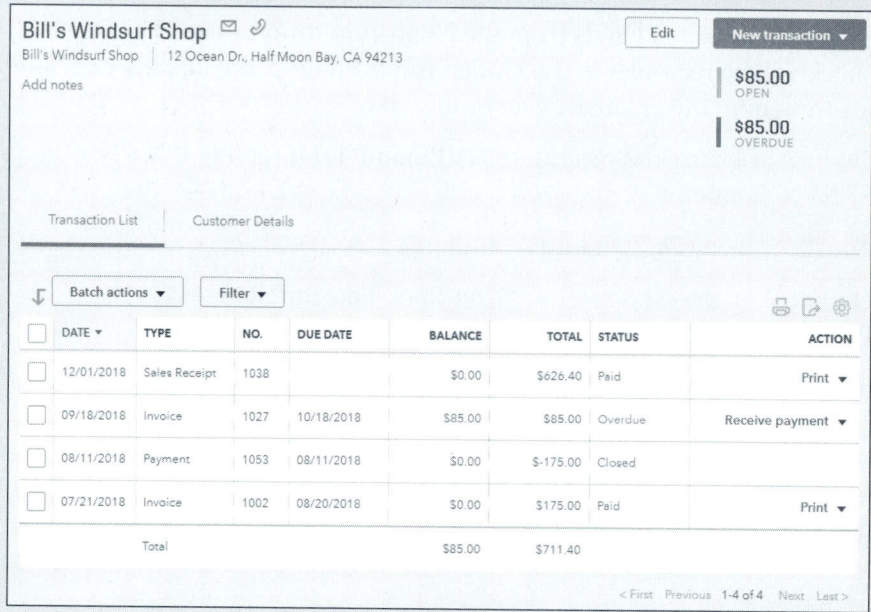

14 Click the **+** icon, and select **Invoice** shown in Figure 4.11.

Figure 4.11

Adding an invoice

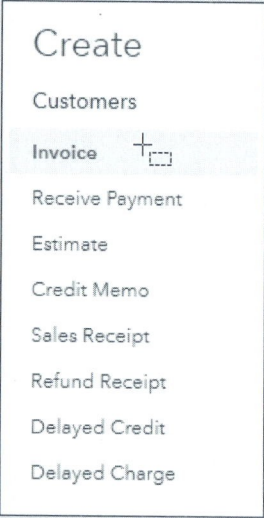

15 Select **Cool Cars** from the Choose a customer drop-down list in the upper left corner of the Invoice window.

16 Your computer's system date has been entered as the Invoice date, and the default terms for this customer are in the appropriate text boxes.

17 On line 1 of the invoice, select **Trimming** as the service provided.

18 Type **5** as the quantity.

19 On line 2 of the invoice, select **Pest Control** as the service provided.

20 Type **3** as the quantity and then press [**Tab**]. The invoice should look like Figure 4.12.

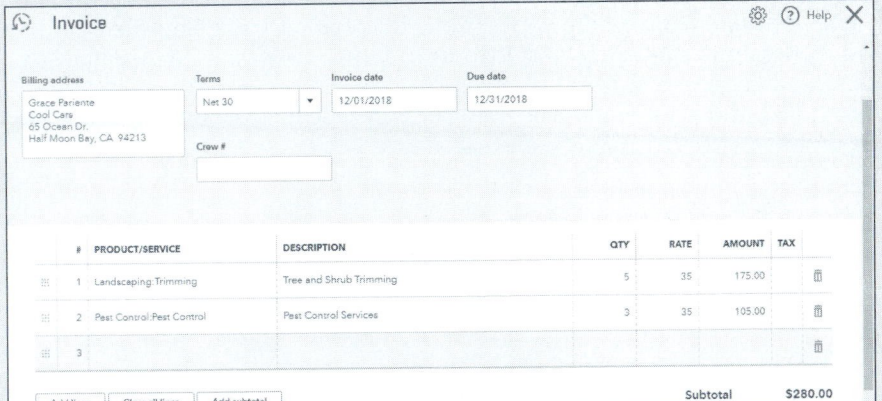

Figure 4.12

Invoice (partial view)

21 Scroll down the invoice and select **California 8%** from Select a sales tax rate text box. Even though a rate is selected, no sales tax is applied. Both services are not taxable, and thus, no sales tax is added.

22 Click **Save and Close**.

23 Click **Sales** and then select **Customers** menu item from the navigation bar and then click **Cool Cars**. A listing of recent transactions affecting that customer is shown, including the recorded invoice shown in Figure 4.13.

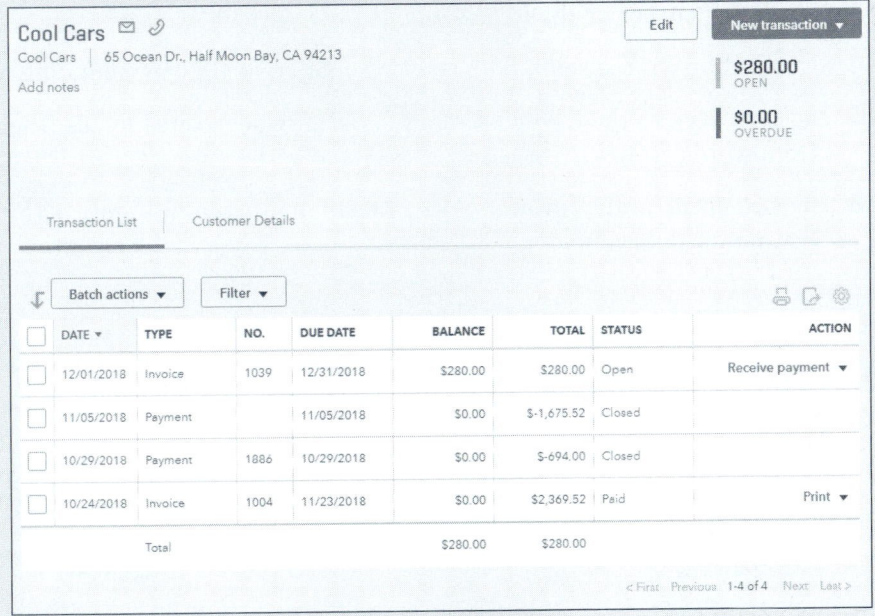

Figure 4.13

Cool Cars (recent transactions)

Cash Receipts

In QBO, the concept of cash receipts is referred to as receiving payments. Thus, to record the receipt of payment from a customer, you can use the Receive Payment item in the **Create menu** to record the transaction, or you can use Receive Payment from the Action column in a customer's list of transactions. Once a payment is received, it must be deposited into your bank account. This is a separate but important process in QBO.

To record the receipt of a payment to the Sample Company from a customer, do the following:

1   Continue from where you left off. If you closed the Sample Company, follow the steps to reopen it found at the beginning of this chapter.

2   Click the **+** icon, and select **Receive Payment** shown in Figure 4.14.

Figure 4.14

Receive payment (recording the receipt of a customer payment)

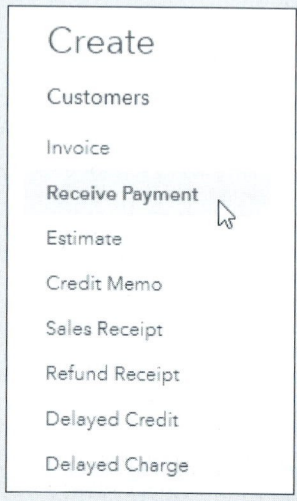

3   Select **Jeff's Jalopies** from the Choose a customer drop-down list in the upper left corner of the Receive Payment window.

4   Your computer's system date has been entered as the Payment date.

5   Select **Check** as the Payment method. Select **Undeposited Funds** from the Deposit to text box.

6   Place a check in the **Invoice # 1022** check box shown in Figure 4.15 (Do not click Save.)

Figure 4.15

Receive Payment window

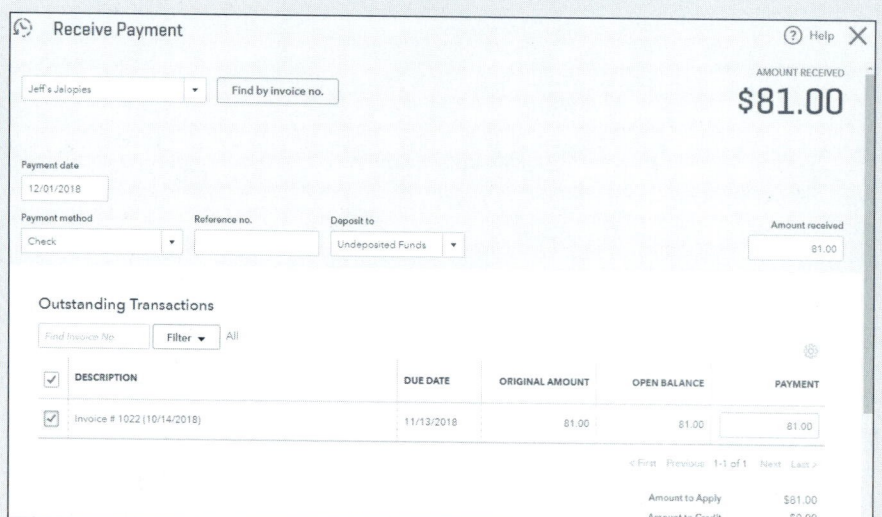

7   Click **Cancel** so you can explore the other means of recording this transaction. Click **Yes** when asked if you want to leave without saving.

8   Click Sales and then click **Customers** from the navigation bar, and click **Jeff's Jalopies**. A listing of recent transactions affecting that customer is shown including invoice # 1022 shown in Figure 4.16.

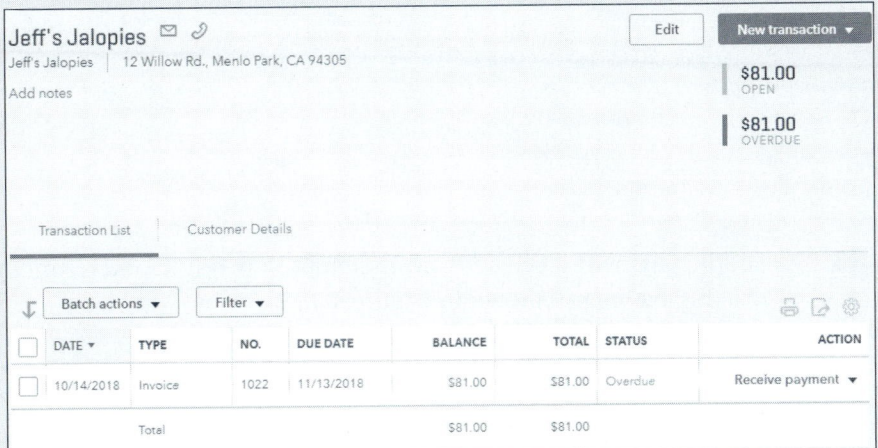

Figure 4.16

Jeff's Jalopies Recent Transactions

9   Click **Receive payment** in the Action column next to invoice # 1022.

10   The same Receive Payment window you saw earlier reappears. Thus, you have two ways of accessing and recording the receipt of payments from a customer. Enter the same information you did earlier as shown in Figure 4.15, and click **Save and Close**.

11   In the Jeff's Jalopies window, the transactions and payment are shown, and the balance is $0.00 shown in Figure 4.17.

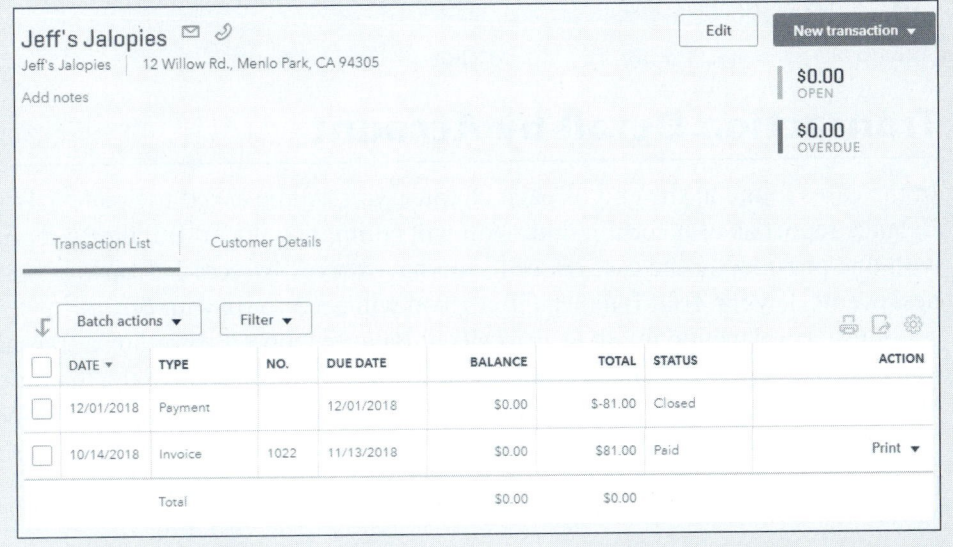

Figure 4.17

Jeff's Jalopies window (recent transactions)

12   Click the **+** icon, and select **Bank Deposit** from the Other column shown in Figure 4.18.

Figure 4.18

Create window (inputting a bank deposit)

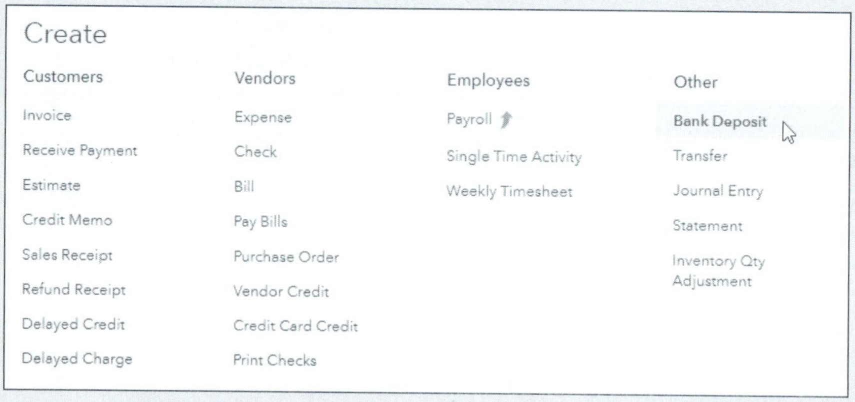

13 Select the payment received from Freeman Sporting Goods from the list of existing payments shown in Figure 4.19.

Figure 4.19

Deposit window

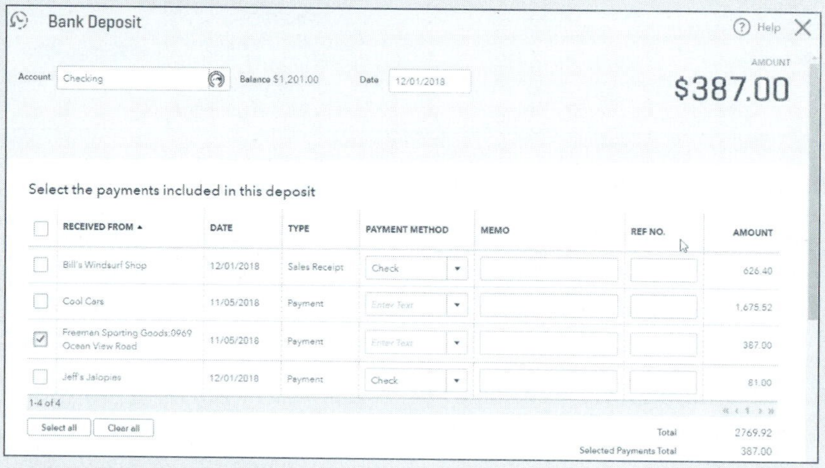

14 Click **Save and Close**.

Transaction Detail by Account

In the cases found at the end of each chapter, you will be asked to create a Trial Balance report as of a certain date. You will compare your Trial Balance report with one provided in the case to see if you have correctly recorded various business events. If your Trial Balance differs, you will need to fix your errors.

A usual explanation for an incorrect Trial Balance report is recording a transaction in an incorrect period, not recording it at all, or recording it incorrectly. To investigate, you will need to create a transaction detail by account report for a specific period. You can create such a report for all transactions to see if yours were recorded in the proper period and to see where you may have entered a wrong amount or account.

To create, print, and export a transaction detail by account report for all transactions, do the following:

1 Continue from your work earlier. (If you do not, none of your work in this chapter will be visible since it is not saved for the Sample Company.)

2 Click **Reports** from the navigation bar.

3 Type **Transaction** in the Find a report by name text box.

4 Select **Transaction Detail by Account**.

5 Select **All Dates** from the Report period drop-down text box. You may have to scroll to the top of this report to see the Report period text box.

6 Click **Run Report**. The top of the report is shown in Figure 4.20.

Craig's Design and Landscaping Services

TRANSACTION DETAIL BY ACCOUNT

All Dates

DATE	TRANSACTION TYPE	NUM	NAME	MEMO/DESCRIPTION	SPLIT	AMOUNT
▾ Checking						
06/22/2018	Deposit			Opening Balance	Opening Balance Equity	5,000.00
08/03/2018	Bill Payment (Check)	10	Robertson & Associates		Accounts Payable (A/P)	-300.00
08/11/2018	Payment	1053	Bill's Windsurf Shop		Accounts Receivable (A/R)	175.00
08/25/2018	Expense	12	Robertson & Associates		Legal & Professional Fees:Ac...	-250.00
09/16/2018	Check	4	Chin's Gas and Oil		Automobile:Fuel	-54.55

Figure 4.20

Transaction Detail by Account report (top section)

7 Scroll down the report until you locate the deposit you recorded from Freeman Sporting Goods shown in Figure 4.21.

DATE	TRANSACTION TYPE	NUM	NAME	MEMO/DESCRIPTION	SPLIT	AMOUNT
11/04/2018	Bill Payment (Check)	45	Tim Philip Masonry		Accounts Payable (A/P)	-666.00
11/04/2018	Deposit				-Split-	408.00
11/04/2018	Cash Expense		Chin's Gas and Oil		Automobile:Fuel	-63.15
11/04/2018	Bill Payment (Check)	6	PG&E		Accounts Payable (A/P)	-114.09
11/04/2018	Expense	108	Tania's Nursery		Job Expenses	-46.98
11/05/2018	Deposit				-Split-	868.15
11/05/2018	Check	75	Hicks Hardware		-Split-	-228.75
11/05/2018	Expense	76	Pam Seitz		Legal & Professional Fees	-75.00
11/08/2018	Cash Expense		Tania's Nursery		Job Expenses:Job Materials:...	-23.50
11/19/2018	Credit Card Credit				Mastercard	-900.00
12/01/2018	Deposit		Freeman Sporting Goods:09...		Undeposited Funds	387.00
Total for Checking						$1,588.00

Figure 4.21

Transaction Detail by Account report (partial view)

8 Click on **Deposit** for Freeman Sporting Goods to view the deposit recorded.

9 Close this window, scroll down the report, and investigate other transactions.

10 Scroll back to the top of this report, and click **Save customization**.

11 Click **Save**.

12 Click the **Print** icon to set this report up for printing; however, do not print this report since it is too long and unnecessary. Click **Close.**

13 Click the **Gear** icon, and click **Sign Out**.

This report can help identifying and correcting errors.

End Note

You have now added a customer, product, and service. You have recorded a sales receipt, invoice, payment received from a customer, and deposit to a bank account. These are operating activities. Additional operating activities related to purchases and cash payments follow in the next chapter.

Chapter 4 Questions

1   What steps need to be followed to add a new product or service?

2   What steps need to be followed to record a new sales receipt?

3   What steps need to be followed to record a new invoice?

4   What steps need to be followed to record a new payment from a customer?

5   What steps need to be followed to record a new deposit to the bank?

6   What are the differences between adding a new product and adding a new service?

7   What is the difference between a sales receipt and a sales invoice?

Chapter 4 Matching

a. Invoice

b. Sales receipt

c. Product

d. Service

e. + icon

f. Payment from a customer

g. Deposit

h. Pest control

i. Roses

j. Cool Cars

_____   A service in the Sample Company

_____   Providing the bank a payment from a customer

_____   Used when recording a sale on account

_____   Used to add invoices, sales receipts, or bank deposits

_____   A customer in the Sample Company

_____   Quantities of this are not tracked

_____   Used when cash is collected at the time of a sale

_____   Cash receipts received from a sale

_____   Quantities of this are tracked

_____   A product that is added in the Sample Company

Chapter 4 Cases

The following cases require you to open the company you updated in Chapter 3. Each of the following cases continues throughout the text in a sequential manner. For example, if you are assigned Case 01, you will use the file you modified in this chapter in all of the following chapters. Each of the following cases is similar in concepts assessed but differs in amounts and transactions. See the preface to this text for a matrix of each student case and its attributes.

To reopen your company, do the following:

1   Open your Internet browser.

2   Type **https://qbo.intuit.com** into your browser's address text box.

3   Type your User ID and Password into the text boxes as you have done before.

Case 1

Add some operating activities (sales and cash receipts) to your company. Based on what you learned in the text using the Sample Company, you are to make the following changes to the Case 1 company you modified in Chapter 3:

1 Add a new customer – Name: Sarah Hay, Company: Hey Hays Surf, Display name as: Sarah Hay, Address: 230 Beach Way, La Jolla, CA, 92039.

2 Add a new service – Tune-Up, Rate: $85.00, income account: Services.

3 Add a new product with quantity tracked – Fred Rubble, initial quantity on hand: 0, as of date 1/1/2018, price: $950.00, cost: $600.00, income account: Sales, expense account: Cost of Goods Sold.

4 Record a new sales receipt on 1/3/18 – Customer: Blondie's Boards, payment method: Check, reference no.: 893, deposit to: Undeposited Funds, product: Rook 15, quantity: 2.

5 Record a new invoice on 1/4/18 – Customer: Hey Hays Surf, terms: Net 30, service: Tune-Up, quantity: 2, product: The Water Hog, quantity: 1.

6 Record a new cash payment received on 1/5/18 – Customer: Blondie's Boards, payment method: Check, reference no.: 984, deposit to: Undeposited Funds, amount received: $5,000.00.

7 Record a deposit made on 1/8/18 to the checking account – Received from: Blondie's Boards, amount received: $1,300.00, related to: Sales Receipt.

8 Prepare a Trial Balance report with a From date of 1/1/18 and a To date of 1/31/18, save it as a customized report named Trial Balance 1/31/18, and share it with all users. Your report should look like Figure 4.22. If asked, indicate that your business is accrual based.

Figure 4.22

Trial Balance (as of 1/31/18)

Case 1
TRIAL BALANCE
As of January 31, 2018

	DEBIT	CREDIT
Checking	26,300.00	
Accounts Receivable	1,030.00	
Inventory Asset	6,700.00	
Prepaid Expenses	3,000.00	
Undeposited Funds	5,000.00	
Furniture & Fixtures:Depreciation		10,000.00
Furniture & Fixtures:Original cost	40,000.00	
Accounts Payable		4,500.00
Notes Payable		60,000.00
Common Stock		1,000.00
Opening Balance Equity		0.00
Retained Earnings		5,500.00
Sales		2,160.00
Services		170.00
Cost of Goods Sold	1,300.00	
TOTAL	$83,330.00	$83,330.00

9 If your trial balance differs from what is in Figure 4.22, do the following:

   a.   Make sure that all of your changes were dated in January 2018.

   b.   Click on the debit or credit balance to view a transactions report for each account, and investigate why your answer differs.

   c.   Ask your instructor for assistance.

   d.   Be sure your company matches the above since, in the following chapter, you will add additional business events.

10 Export your Trial Balance report to Excel, and save it with the file name: Student Name (replace with your name) Ch 04 Case 01 Trial Balance.xlsx.

11 Open and print the custom report you created in the previous chapter called Transaction Detail by Account.

12 Use your Transaction Detail by Account report to locate any differences in your Trial Balance report created above.

   a.   Make sure all of your changes were dated in January 2018.

   b.   Click on the line that does not match to view the transaction for that account, and investigate why your answer differs.

   c.   Ask your instructor for assistance.

   d.   Be sure your company matches the above since, in the following chapter, you will add additional business events.

13 Export your Transactions Detail by Account report to Excel and save it with the file name: Student Name (replace with your name) Ch 04 Case 01 Transaction Detail by Account.xlsx.

14 Sign out of your company.

Case 2

Add some operating activities (sales and cash receipts) to your company. Based on what you learned in the text using the Sample Company, you are to make the following changes to the Case 2 company you modified in Chapter 3:

1 Add a new customer – Hagen's Toys, 3983 Torrey Pines, La Jolla, CA, 92039.

2 Add a new service – Custom Painting, Rate: $45.00, income account: Services.

3 Add two new products with quantity tracked – GO Aircraft Radio, initial quantity on hand: 0, as of date 1/1/2019, price: $4,999.00, cost: $2,500.00, income account: Sales, expense account: Cost of Goods Sold and Taylor 22cc, initial quantity on hand: 0, as of date 1/1/2019, price: $2,999.00, cost: $1,500.00, income account: Sales, expense account: Cost of Goods Sold.

4 Record a new sales receipt on 1/3/19 – Customer: Benson's RC, payment method: Credit Card, reference no.: 16756, deposit to: Undeposited Funds, product: Broon F830 Ride, quantity: 3.

5 Record a new invoice on 1/4/19 – Customer: Hagen's Toys, terms: Net 30, service: Custom Painting, quantity: 5, product: Seawind Carbon Sailboat, quantity: 1.

6 Record a new cash payment received on 1/7/19 – Customer: Benson's RC, payment method: Check, reference no.: 9847, deposit to: Undeposited Funds, amount received: $925.00.

7 Record a deposit made on 1/7/19 to the checking account – Received from: Benson's RC, amount received: $4,500.00, related to: Sales Receipt.

8 Prepare a Trial Balance report with a From date of 1/1/19 and a To date of 1/31/19, save it as a customized report named Trial Balance 1/31/19, and share it with all users. Your report should look like Figure 4.23. If asked, indicate that your business is accrual based.

Figure 4.23

Trial Balance (as of 1/31/19)

Case 2
TRIAL BALANCE
As of January 31, 2019

	DEBIT	CREDIT
Checking	9,500.00	
Accounts Receivable	1,425.00	
Inventory Asset	2,040.00	
Prepaid Expenses	2,400.00	
Undeposited Funds	925.00	
Machinery & Equipment:Depreciation		1,000.00
Machinery & Equipment:Original cost	10,000.00	
Accounts Payable		1,900.00
Notes Payable		12,000.00
Common Stock		100.00
Opening Balance Equity		0.00
Retained Earnings		8,385.00
Sales		5,700.00
Services		225.00
Cost of Goods Sold	3,020.00	
TOTAL	$29,310.00	$29,310.00

9 If your trial balance differs from what is in Figure 4.23, do the following:

a. Make sure that all of your changes were dated in January 2019.

b. Click on the debit or credit balance to view a transactions report for each account, and investigate why your answer differs.

c. Ask your instructor for assistance.

d. Be sure your company matches the above since, in the following chapter, you will add additional business events.

10 Export your Trial Balance report to Excel and save it with the file name: Student Name (replace with your name) Ch 04 Case 02 Trial Balance.xlsx.

11 Open and print the custom report you created in the last chapter called Transaction Detail by Account.

12 Use your Transaction Detail by Account report to locate any differences in your Trial Balance report created above.

a. Make sure that all of your changes were dated in January 2019.

b. Click on the line that does not match to view the transaction for that account, and investigate why your answer differs.

c. Ask your instructor for assistance.

d. Be sure your company matches the above since, in the following chapter, you will add additional business events.

13 Export your Transactions Detail by Account report to Excel and save it with the file name: Student Name (replace with your name) Ch 04 Case 02 Transaction Detail by Account.xlsx.

14 Sign out of your company.

Case 3

Now it's time for you to add some operating activities (sales and cash receipts) to your company. Based on what you learned in the text using the Sample Company, you are to make the following changes to the Case 3 company you modified in Chapter 3:

1 Add a new customer – Surfer Sales, 3983 Torrey Pines, La Jolla, CA, 92039.

2 Add a new service – Phone Consulting, Rate: $35.00, income account: Services, not taxable.

3 Add two new products – Apple iPhone 6s, initial quantity on hand: 0, Inventory asset account: Inventory Asset, price: $549.00, cost: $349.00, income account: Sales of Product Income, expense account: Cost of Goods Sold, taxable and Apple iPhone 7 Plus, initial quantity on hand: 0, Inventory asset account: Inventory Asset, price: $800, cost: $600.00, income account: Sales of Product Income expense account: Cost of Goods Sold, taxable. (Use your current system date as the "as of date" for both products.)

4 Record a new sales receipt on 1/3/20 – customer: Surfer Sales, payment method: Credit Card, reference no.: 16756, deposit to: Undeposited Funds, (if no Undeposited Funds account exists, add it as a type Other Current Asset and detail type Undeposited Funds.) product: Apple iPhone 7, quantity: 6, and 3 hours of Phone Consulting. For this sale, and all sales following, be sure to override the sales tax rate to 10%. To do this click **Sales tax** at the bottom of the sales invoice then click **Override this amount**. Type **10** in the Rate text box and then select **Other** in the Reason drop-down list, then click **Confirm**. Click **Close**.

5 Record a new invoice on 1/6/20 – customer: GHO Marketing, terms: Net 30, 3 hours of Apple Repairs, product: iPhone 7, quantity: 3. For this sale, and all sales following, be sure to override the sales tax rate to 10%. To do this click **Sales tax** at the bottom of the sales invoice then click **Override this amount**. Type **10** in the Rate text box and then select **Other** in the Reason drop-down list, then click **Confirm**. Click **Close**.

6 Record a new cash payment received on 1/7/20 – customer: GHO Marketing, payment method: Check, reference no.: 9847, deposit to: Undeposited Funds, amount received: $4,125.00.

7 Record a deposit made on 1/9/20 to the checking account of $9,180.00 which was received from: Surfer Sales, amount $5,055.00, related to: Sales Receipt and GHO Marketing, amount $4,125.00, related to Payment.

8 Prepare a Trial Balance report with a From date of 1/1/20 and a To date of 1/31/20 and then save it as a customized report named Trial Balance 1/31/20 and share it with all users. Your report should look like Figure 4.24.

Figure 4.24

Trial Balance as of 1/31/20

TRIAL BALANCE		
As of January 31, 2020		
	DEBIT	CREDIT
Checking	21,180.00	
Accounts Receivable (A/R)	2,610.00	
Inventory Asset	1,700.00	
Prepaid Expenses	2,750.00	
Undeposited Funds	0.00	
Machinery & Equipment:Depreciation		2,000.00
Machinery & Equipment:Original cost	15,000.00	
Accounts Payable (A/P)		5,000.00
California State Board of Equalization Payable		675.00
Notes Payable		23,000.00
Opening Balance Equity		0.00
Owner's Equity		10,075.00
Sales of Product Income		6,750.00
Services		240.00
Cost of Goods Sold	4,500.00	
TOTAL	$47,740.00	$47,740.00

9   If your trial balance is different than Figure 4.24:

   a.   Make sure that all of your changes were dated in January 2020.

   b.   Click on the debit or credit balance to view a transactions report for each account and investigate why your answer is different.

   c.   Ask your instructor for assistance.

   d.   Be sure your company matches the above, as in the following chapter you'll be adding additional business events.

10   Export your Trial Balance report to Excel and save it with the file name: Student Name (replace with your name) Ch 04 Case 03 Trial Balance. xlsx.

11   Open and print the custom report you created in the previous chapter called Transaction Detail by Account.

12   Use your Transaction Detail by Account report to locate any differences in your Trial Balance report created above.

   a.   Make sure that all of your changes were dated January 2020.

   b.   Click on the line that doesn't match to view the transaction for that account and investigate why your answer is different.

   c.   Ask your instructor for assistance.

   d.   Be sure your company matches the above, as in the following chapter you'll be adding additional business events.

13 Export your Transactions Detail by Account report to Excel and save it with the file name: Student Name (replace with your name) Ch 04 Case 03 Transaction Detail by Account.xlsx.

14 Sign out of your company.

Case 4

Now it's time for you to add some operating activities (sales and cash receipts) to your company.

Based on what you learned in the text using the Sample Company, you are to make the following changes to the Case 4 company you modified in Chapter 3:

1 Add two new accounts –

   a. First account

      i)   Account Type – Other Current Assets

      ii) Detail Type/Name – Undeposited Funds

   b. Second account

      i)   Account Type – Expenses

      ii) Detail Type – Other Business Expenses

      iii) Name – Laundry Service

2 Add three new customers –

   a. Flyer Corporation, 32 Wilshire Blvd., Hollywood, CA 90028, terms: Net 30

   b. ABC Studios, 2300 W Riverside Dr., Burbank, CA 91506, terms: Net 30

   c. Sam Shepard, 10 Hollywood Blvd., Hollywood, CA 90028, terms: Due on receipt

3 Modify an existing customer (use help to learn how to do this)

   a. Company – Disney

   b. Address – 500 South Buena Vista Street, Burbank, CA 91505, terms: Net 30

4 Add three new vendors –

   a. Bowflex Inc., 3393 Main St., Vancouver, WA 98607, terms: Net 30

   b. NordicTrack Inc., 23 First St., Logan, UT 84321, terms: Net 30

   c. Laundry Service, 432 Sunset Blvd., Hollywood, CA, 90028, terms: Due on receipt

5   Modify an existing vendor (use help to learn how to do this)

a.   Company – Precor

b.   Address – 20031 142nd Avenue NE, Woodinville, WA 98072, terms: Net 30

6   Create a new service item as follows:

a.   Name/Sales information – Monthly Fee – Corporate Membership 50 Employees

b.   Sales information – Yes you do sell this service to customers

c.   Sales price/rate – $6,000

d.   Income account – Sales

e.   Is taxable – No

f.   Purchase information – No you don't purchase this service from a vendor

7   Modify two existing service items (use help to learn how to do this)

a.   Old name/Sales information – Monthly Fee – New name/Sales information – Monthly Fee – Individual

b.   Old name/Sales information – Training – New name/Sales information – Training – Individual

8   Add two new products –

a.   First product

i)   Name – Bowflex Dumbbells

ii)   Initial quantity on hand – 0

iii)   As of date – 12/31/2020

iv)   Inventory asset account – Inventory Asset

v)   Sales information – Bowflex Dumbbells

vi)   Sales price/rate – $249

vii)   Income account – Sales of Product Income

viii) Is taxable – Yes

ix)   Purchasing information – Bowflex Dumbbells

x)   Cost – $200

xi)   Expense account – Cost of Goods Sold

b.   Second product

i)   Name – Power Block Elite Dumbbells

ii)   Initial quantity on hand – 0

iii)   As of date – 12/31/2020

iv)   Inventory asset account – Inventory Asset

v)   Sales information – Power Block Elite Dumbbells

vi)   Sales price/rate – $299

vii)   Income account – Sales of Product Income

      viii)   Is taxable – Yes

      ix)   Purchasing information – Power Block Elite Dumbbells

      x)   Cost – $199

      xi)   Expense account – Cost of Goods Sold

9   Record a new sales receipt to Sam Shepard on 1/5/2021 for 6 months of Monthly Fee – Individual, 10 hours of Training – Individual, 1 T-shirt, and 1 pair of Yoga pants. Total $1,726.65 (including sales tax) received via check number 6571 and deposited to the Undeposited Funds account.

10   Record a new ABC Studios invoice 1002 on 1/6/2021 for 1 Monthly Fee – Corporate Membership 50 Employees and 50 T-shirts for a total amount of $7,368.75 (including sales tax).

11   Record a new Flyer Corporation invoice 1003 on 1/6/2021 for 1 Monthly Fee – Corporate Membership 50 Employees and 50 hours of Training – Individual and 50 pairs of Yoga pants for a total amount of $12,213.75 (including sales tax).

12   Record a partial cash payment of $6,000.00 received on 1/14/2021 from Disney using check 9744 recorded to the Undeposited Funds account.

13   Record a bank deposit of $7,726.65 made on 1/15/2021 from Disney and Sam Shepard.

14   Prepare and print a Trial Balance report with a custom reporting period of 1/1/2021 to 1/31/2021, then save it as a customized report named Trial Balance 1/31/2021. Your report should look like Figure 4.25.

Figure 4.25

Trial Balance as of 1/31/2021

Case 4 Student Name (Student ID)

TRIAL BALANCE
As of January 31, 2021

	DEBIT	CREDIT
Checking	34,726.65	
Accounts Receivable (A/R)	22,082.50	
Inventory Asset	3,868.00	
Prepaid Expenses	12,000.00	
Undeposited Funds	0.00	
Furniture:Depreciation		10,000.00
Furniture:Original cost	65,000.00	
Machinery & Equipment:Depreciation		6,500.00
Machinery & Equipment:Original cost	115,000.00	
Accounts Payable (A/P)		18,000.00
California State Board of Equalization Payable		339.15
Notes Payable		82,000.00
Common Stock		1,000.00
Opening Balance Equity		0.00
Retained Earnings		115,500.00
Sales		17,400.00
Sales of Product Income		3,570.00
Cost of Goods Sold	1,632.00	
TOTAL	$254,309.15	$254,309.15

15 Prepare and print a Transaction Detail by Account report for all transactions between 1/1/2021 and 12/31/2022, save it as a customized report named Transaction Detail by Account. If asked, indicate that your business is accrual based.

16 Use your Transaction Detail by Account report to locate any differences in your Trial Balance report created above.

    a. Make sure all your changes were dated in January 2021.

    b. Click on the line that does not match to view the transaction for that account and investigate why your answer differs.

    c. Ask your instructor for assistance.

    d. Be sure your company matches the above since, in the following chapter, you will be adding additional business events.

Operating Activities: Purchases and Cash Payments

Student Learning Outcomes

Upon completion of this chapter, the student will be able to do the following:

- Create a vendor
- Record a purchase order
- Record a bill for the receipt of products/services on account
- Record the payment of bills
- Record credit card charges
- Record checks
- Prepare a Trial Balance and drill down to a transaction report for an account

Overview

Intuit has provided a sample company online to provide new users a test drive of its QBO product. In this chapter, you will open this sample company and practice various features of QBO. You will be recording operating activities such as adding vendors, purchase orders, bills, bill payments, credit card charges, and checks to the Sample Company file. Remember, if you stop in the middle of this work, none of your work will be saved. So, when you return, the same Sample Company, without your work, will appear. In the end of chapter work, you will be asked to perform the same tasks completed on the Sample Company on your Student Company. That work, of course, will be saved. Your system date will differ from the date shown under the company name QBO. Transaction dates on your screen may also differ from the figures shown throughout this text.

Throughout this text, figures illustrating bills, expenses, checks, purchase orders, and credit card transactions will have the title Account details not Category details and the column title as Account and not Category as shown on your QBO software. Steps will also use the term Account when your QBO software will reflect the use of the term Category. Once again this change took place after this text was completed. See the Preface of this text for a complete discussion of the confusion this change created.

Vendors

In this section you will be adding new vendors. Recall that vendors are your company's suppliers of products and services. To add vendors you will use the Vendors menu item in the navigation bar.

To add new vendors to the Sample Company, do the following:

1 Open your Internet browser.

2 Type **https://qbo.intuit.com/redir/testdrive** into your browser's address text box, and then press [**Enter**] to view the Sample Company Dashboard.

3 Click **Expenses** and then click **Vendors** in the navigation bar, and then click the **New Vendor** button.

4 Type **Valley Rock** in the Company text box.

5 Type the address **290 Central Ave., Middletown, CA, 94482** in the appropriate text boxes.

6 Select **Net 30** from the Terms text box. A Vendor Information window is shown in Figure 5.1.

Figure 5.1

Vendor Information window

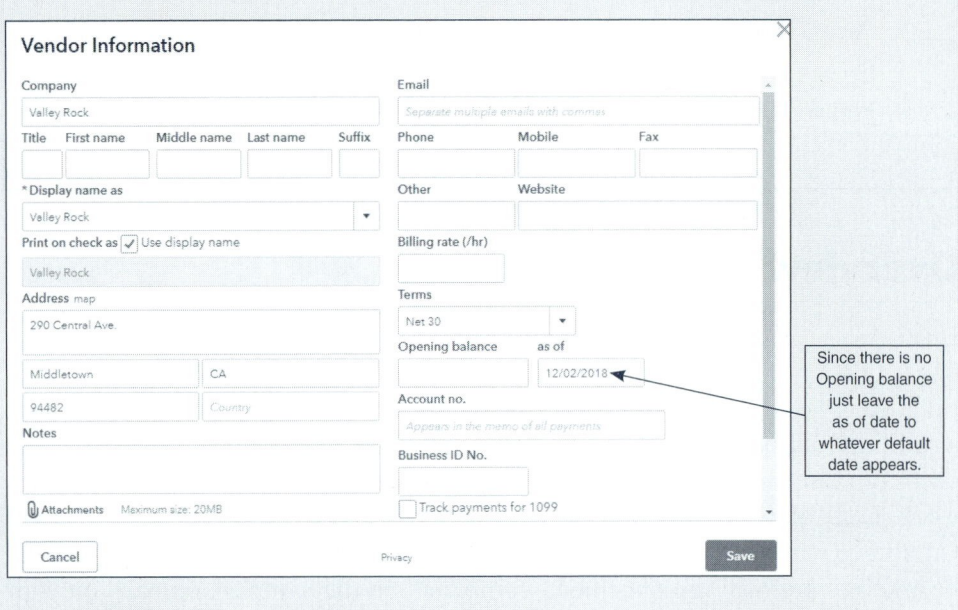

7 Click **Save**.

You have added a new vendor. Next up, adding purchase orders.

Purchase Orders

A business uses purchase orders to formally order products or services from its vendors. Purchase orders are also used as a reference and control for products received. During the creation of a purchase order, you can create a new product. Purchase orders can be for inventory or for products ordered for a specific customer.

To add two purchase orders and new product to the Sample Company, do the following:

1 Continue from where you left off above.

2 Click the + icon, and select **Purchase Order** as shown in Figure 5.2.

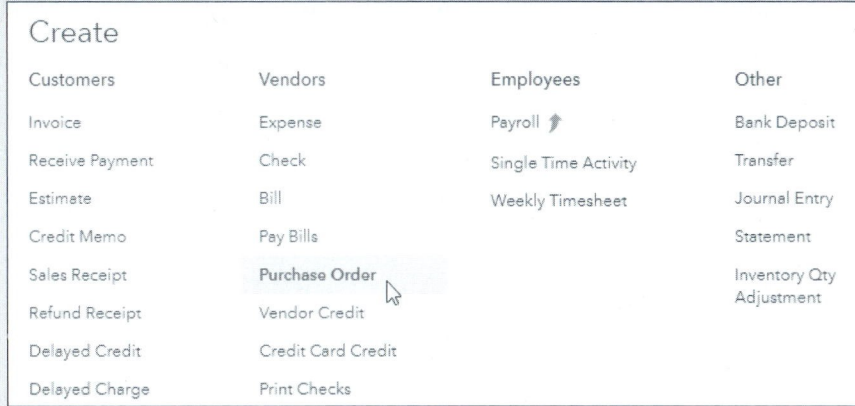

Figure 5.2

Create windows (adding a purchase order)

3 Select **Valley Rock** from the Choose a vendor drop-down list in the upper-left corner of the Purchase Order window.

4 Your computer's system date has been entered as the purchase order date.

5 Click in the **Product/Service** column on line 1 of the purchase order's Item details section, and select **Add New** shown in Figure 5.3.

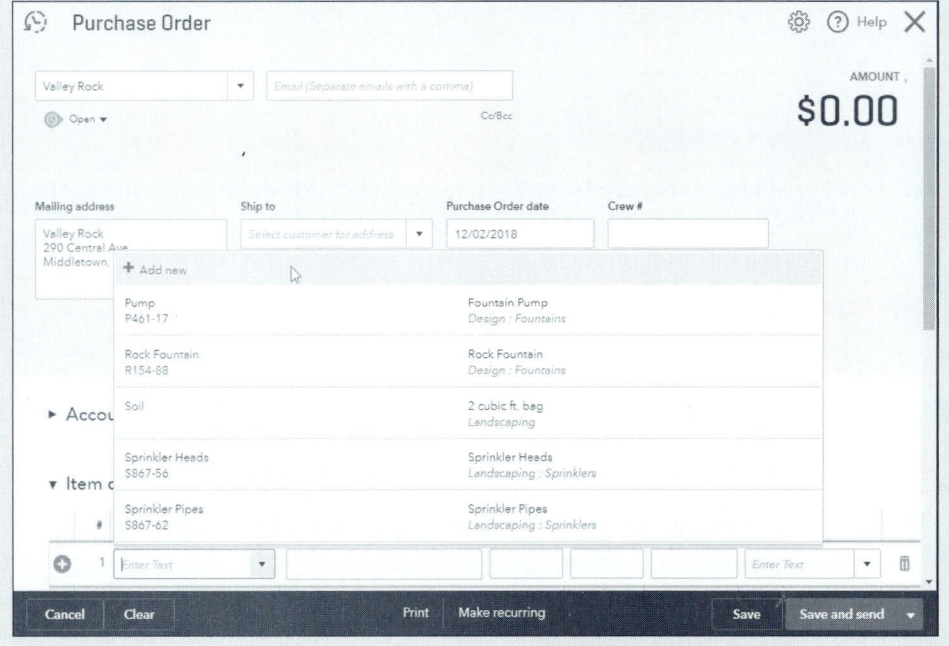

Figure 5.3

Purchase Order (adding a new product)

6 Create a new product, as you have done before – product type: **Inventory**, name and Sales/Purchase Information: **Landscape Rock**, initial quantity on hand: **0**, As of date: your system date, Category: **Landscaping**, inventory asset account: **Inventory Asset**, Sales price/rate: **75**, cost: **50**, income account: **Sales of Product Income**, expense account: **Cost of Goods Sold**, is taxable: **yes**. Click **Save and Close**.

7 Type **100** in the QTY column. Leave the Customer field blank as this order is for inventory. Your completed purchase order should look like Figure 5.4.

Figure 5.4

Purchase Order (for Valley Rock)

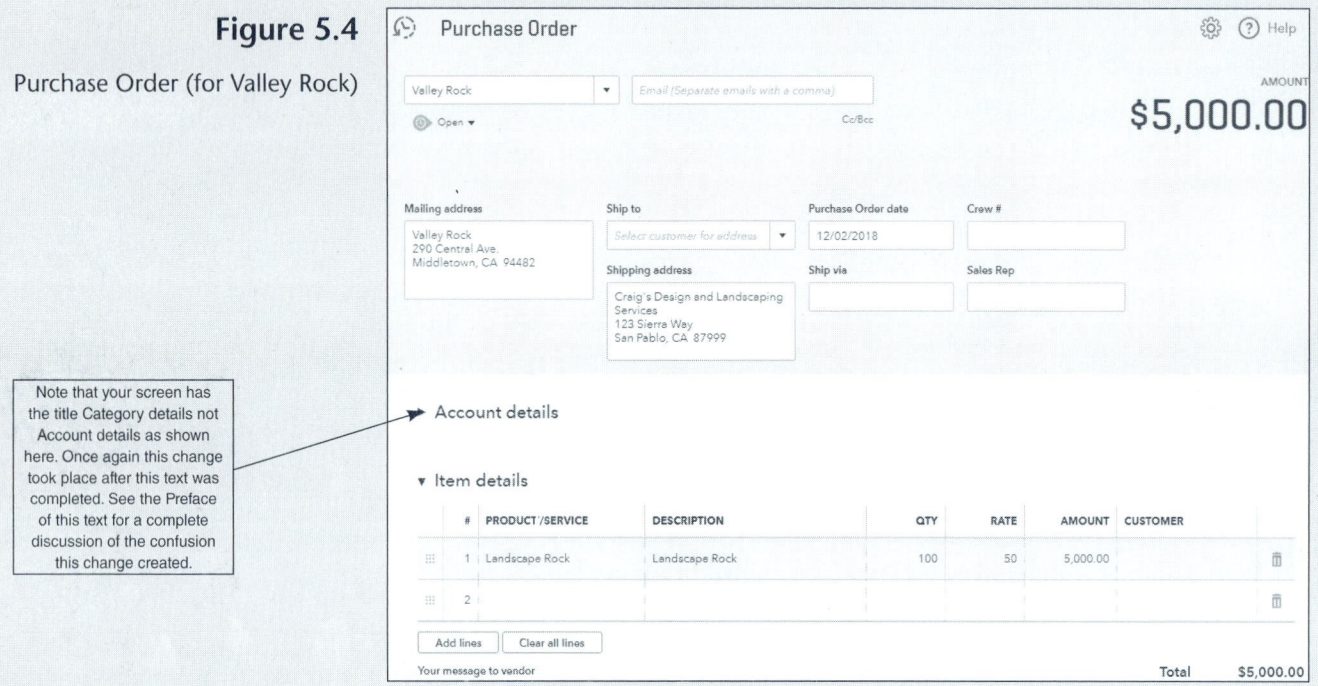

Note that your screen has the title Category details not Account details as shown here. Once again this change took place after this text was completed. See the Preface of this text for a complete discussion of the confusion this change created.

8 Click **Save and New**.

9 Select **Hicks Hardware** from the Choose a vendor drop-down list in the upper-left corner of the Purchase Order window. Accept your current system date as the purchase order date.

10 The Item details section of the purchase order is filled out with information from the last purchase order completed for this vendor. Leave all lines of the Product/Service column as it is.

11 Change the amounts in the QTY column as follows: Rock Fountain **3**, Sprinkler Heads **20**, Sprinkler Pipes **30**, and Pump **4**.

12 Select **Kookies by Kathy** in the Customer column for all four items so your purchase order looks like Figure 5.5.

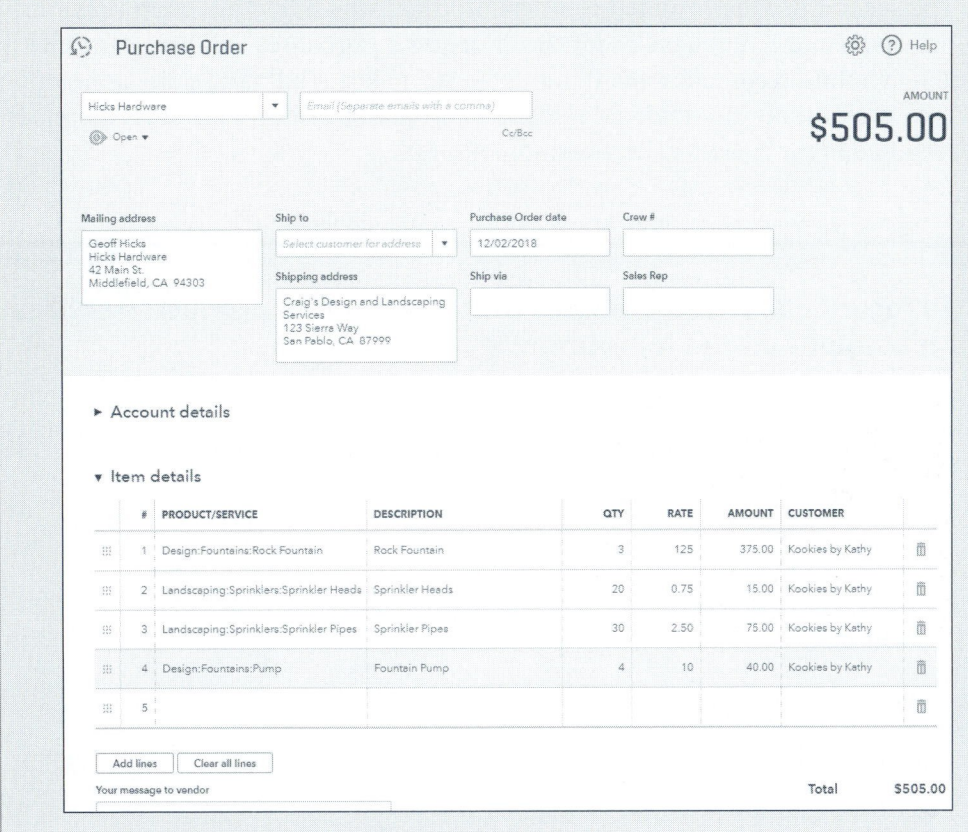

Figure 5.5

Purchase Order (to Hicks Hardware)

13   Click **Save and Close**.

Bills

In the previous chapter, you created invoices to customers for products or services rendered. That invoice served as a bill to that customer signifying a sales transaction for you and a bill to them. Likewise, when you enter into a business transaction, such as purchasing a product or service from a vendor, you expect them to send you an invoice. In QBO, the invoice you receive from a vendor is called a bill. Bills are recorded in QBO to signify the receipt of a product or service and a related liability, usually accounts payable. The inventory account is affected when the bill represents a product being delivered.

In QBO, the terms of those bills could be one of the following: due on receipt, net 10, net 15, net 30, or net 60. The net reference means the bill is due to be paid within a specified number of days, for example, 10, 15, 30, or 60 days. Other terms, for example, 2/10 net 30, provide for a 2% discount on the invoice if paid within 10 days; otherwise, a payment is required within 30 days. Even though you can set up such terms to appear on invoices to customers and bills from vendors, QBO does not calculate them automatically. To simplify your learning of QBO, discounts have not been implemented in this text.

In this section, you will focus on recording a bill for the receipt of services and products on account, meaning you will have been given terms (usually net 30), so you will not have to pay the bill for 30 days after the bill date. The first product purchased had been previously ordered using a purchase order.

The second product ordered is a new product, which had not been previously ordered using a purchase order. Both of these purchases will affect inventory and are, thus, recorded in the Items detail section of a bill. The third transaction is a service that was rendered and does not affect inventory and is, therefore, recorded in the Account detail section of a bill.

To record a bill from a vendor for the receipt of products/services on account, do the following:

1   Continue from where you left off.

2   Click the + icon, and click **Bill** in the Vendor column shown in Figure 5.6.

Figure 5.6

Create window (entering bills)

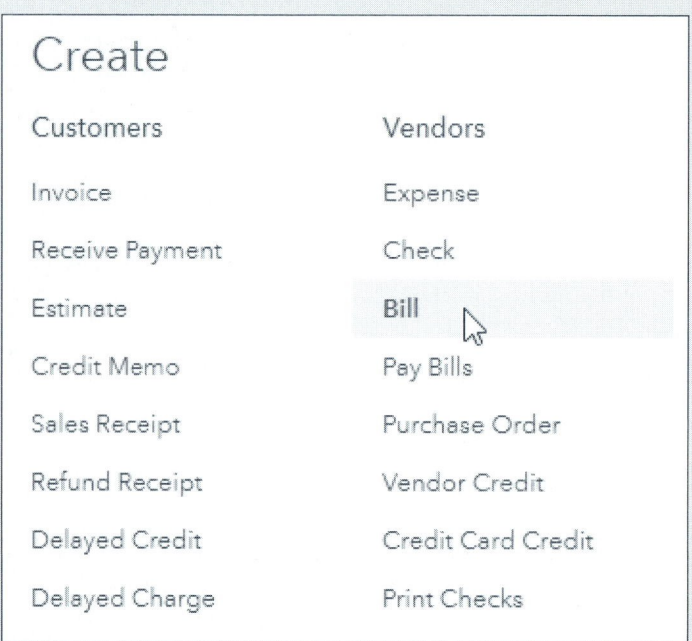

3   Select **Tim Phillip Masonry** from the Choose a vendor drop-down list.

4   Select **Net 30** from the drop-down list of terms. Accept your current system date as the Bill date.

5   Collapse the Account details section of the bill by clicking on the arrow next to **Account details.**

6   Expand the Item details section of the bill by clicking on the arrow next to **Item details.**

7   Click **Add All** in the Add to Bill section, which identifies an open purchase order #1002 from this vendor located on the right of the bill shown in Figure 5.7.

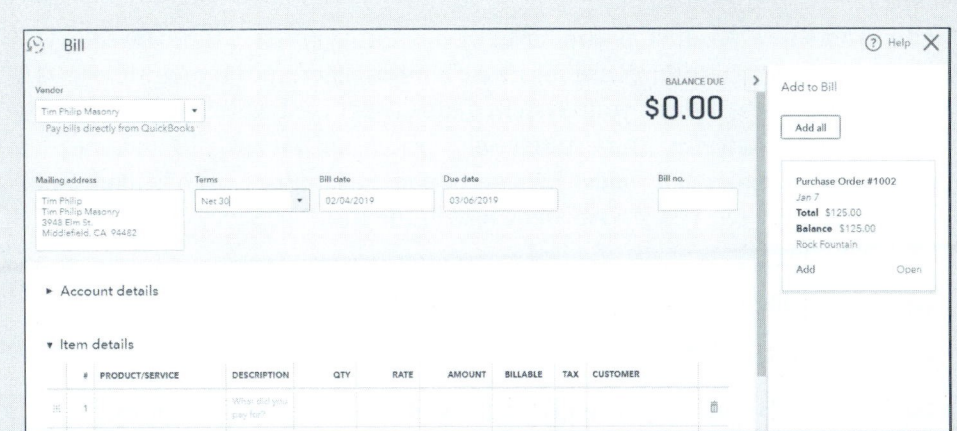

Figure 5.7

Bill (adding purchase order information)

8 The bill now contains information from purchase order #1002 as shown in Figure 5.8.

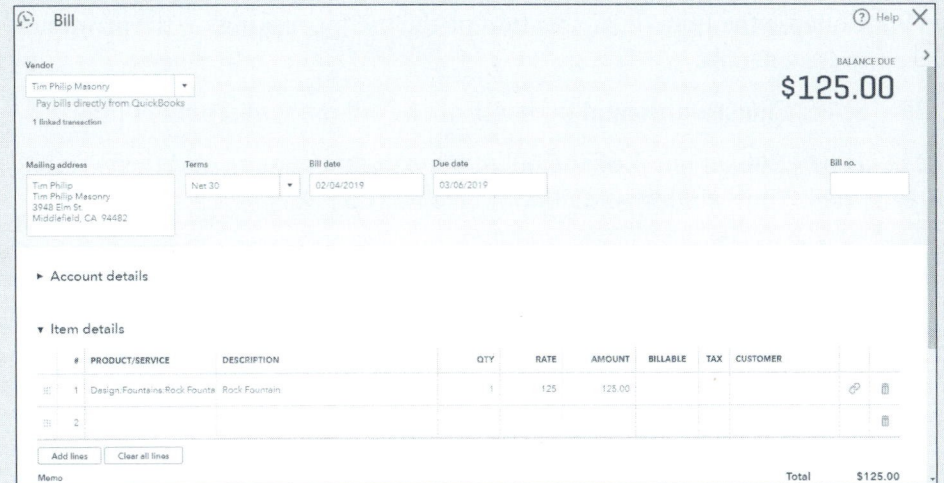

Figure 5.8

Bill (after purchase order information is added)

9 Click **Save and New**.

10 Select **Tania's Nursery** from the Choose a vendor drop-down list.

11 Select **Net 30** from the drop-down list of terms. Accept your current system date as the Bill date.

12 Collapse the Account details section and then expand the Item details section. Select **Add new** on line 1 of the bill in the Product/Service column of the Item details section. **Trouble?** If instead of seeing a Product/Service column you see an Account column you are in the Account details section instead of the Item details section. (a common mistake)? Note that this step has not been updated to reflect the change in terms from Account to Category. Steps from this point on will continue to use the Account term even though the QBO software will show the Category term.

13 Add a new product as you have done before – product type: **Inventory**, name and Sales/Purchase information: **Lavender**, initial quantity on hand: **0**, As of date: your system date, Category: **Landscaping**, inventory asset account: **Inventory Asset**, Sales price/rate: **15**, cost: **10**, income account: **Sales of Product Income**, expense account: **Cost of Goods Sold**, is taxable: **yes**. Click **Save and Close** in the Product/Service Information window.

14 Type **100** on line 1 of the bill in the QTY column.

15 Click **Save and New.**

16 Select **Computers by Jenni** from the Choose a vendor drop-down list.

17 Select **Net 30** from the drop-down list of terms. Accept your current system date as the Bill date.

18 Expand the Account details section of the bill by clicking on the **arrow next to Account details.**

19 Collapse the Item details section of the bill by clicking on the **arrow next to Item details.**

20 Select **Equipment Rental** on line 1 of the bill in the Account column.

21 Type **1,200** on line 1 of the bill in the Amount column and then press [**Tab**]. Your window should look like Figure 5.9.

Figure 5.9

Bill (for services)

Note that your screen has the title Category details not Account details and the column title is Category and not Account as shown here. Once again this change took place after this text was completed. See the Preface of this text for a complete discussion of the confusion this change created.

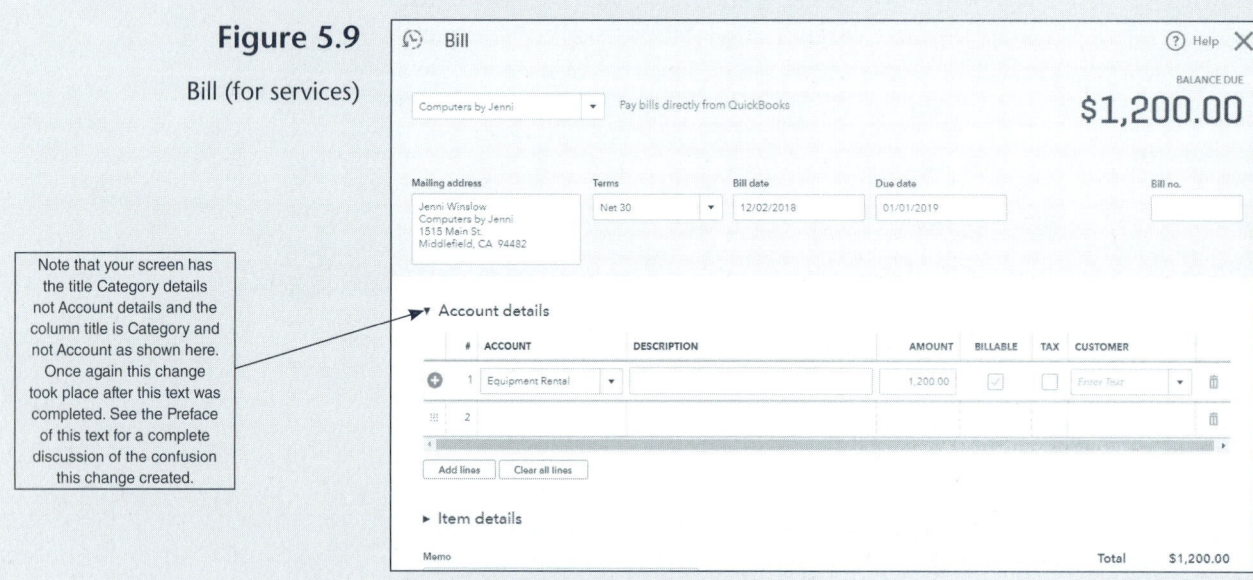

22 Click **Save and New.**

23 Select **Brosnahan Insurance Agency** from the Choose a vendor drop-down list.

24 Accept **Net 10** from the drop-down list of terms.

25 The bill information is filled in automatically based on the last bill entered for this vendor.

26   Select **Prepaid Expenses** on line 1 of the bill in the Account column replacing Insurance.

27   Type **1,800** on line 1 of the bill in the Amount column replacing the existing amount and then press [**Tab**]. Your window should look like Figure 5.10.

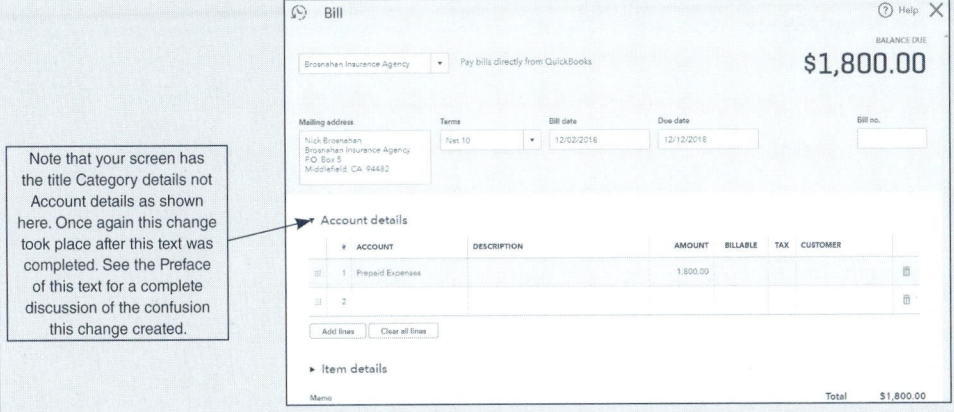

Note that your screen has the title Category details not Account details as shown here. Once again this change took place after this text was completed. See the Preface of this text for a complete discussion of the confusion this change created.

Figure 5.10

Bill for Prepaid Expenses (recording)

28   Click **Save and Close**.

All bills entered increased an asset or an expense account. Inventory purchases were all recorded in the Item details section and increased the quantity of those products (as long as they were originally set up as "tracked" products). Equipment rental was recorded as an expense and the prepaid insurance was recorded as an asset (Prepaid Expenses). All bills increased the accounts payable liability account.

Payment of Bills, Use of a Credit Card, Payments for Items Other than Bills

In this section, you will focus on recording the payment of a bill for the receipt of services and/or products on account, recording credit card charges, or recording the payment by check for other items.

To pay bills, do the following:

1   Continue from where you left off.

2   Click the **+** icon, and click **Pay Bills** in the Vendor column shown in Figure 5.11.

Figure 5.11

Create window (paying bills)

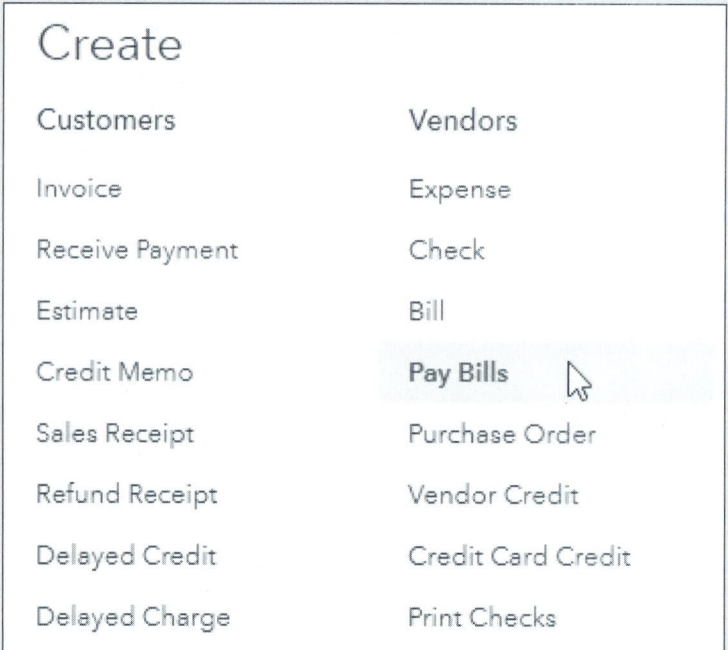

3 A listing of possible bills that can be paid appears. In the Pay Bills window, select **Checking** from the drop-down list in the Payment account box. Click the **PAYEE** column title to sort the listing by payee alphabetically. Your screen should look like Figure 5.12.

Figure 5.12

Bills to Pay

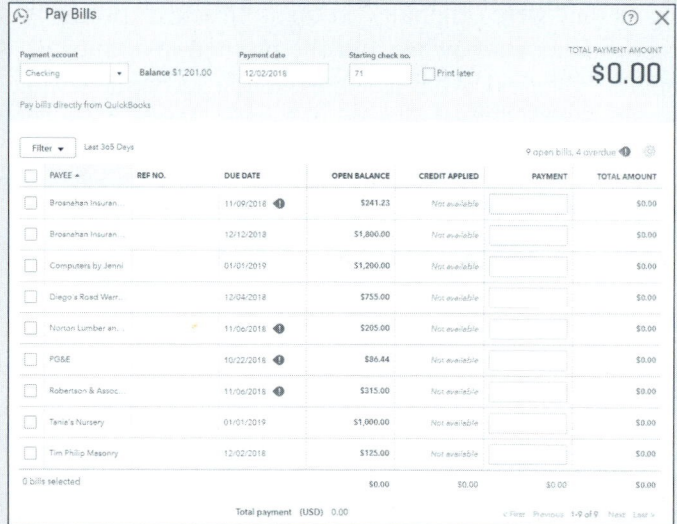

4 Click and hold your mouse between the PAYEE and REF NO. columns and drag to the right to increase the width of the PAYEE column.

5 Click and hold your mouse between the REF NO. and DUE DATE columns and drag to the left to decrease the width of the REF NO. column.

6 Click in the check box of payees PG&E, Norton Lumber and Building Materials, Robertson & Associates, and Brosnahan Insurance Agency shown in Figure 5.13. Remember your dates will be different than the figures shown.

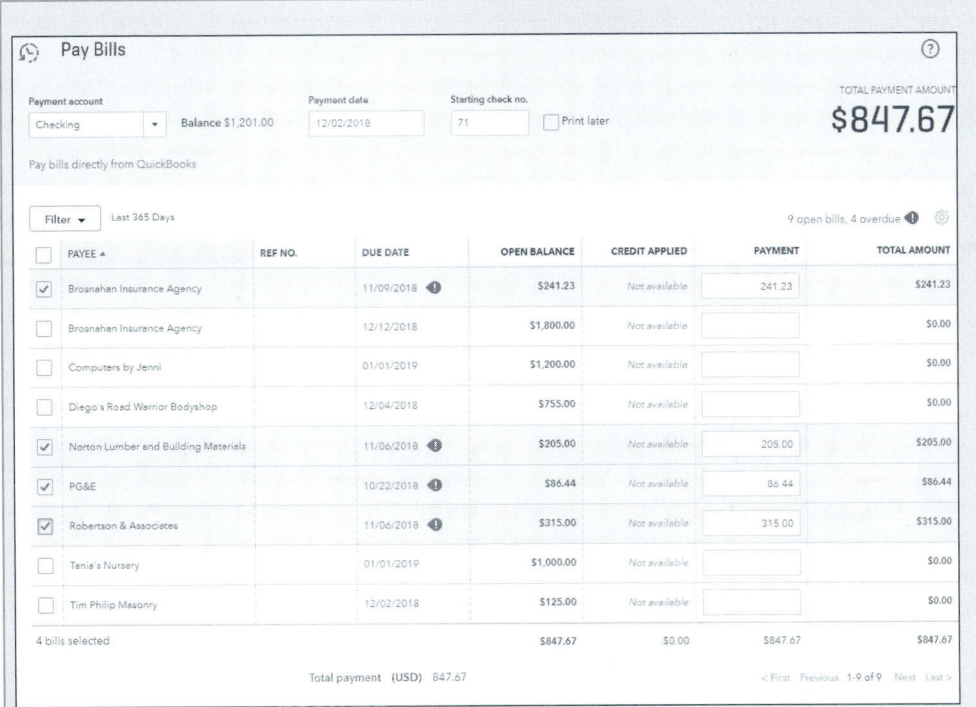

Figure 5.13

Bills to Pay (selecting)

7 Click **Save and Close**.

You have now paid bills for products/services received for which you received a bill. However, often you will pay for a product/service or another expense for which you have not received a bill. Often, these are vendors, who give you no terms, and require you to pay immediately. These terms are called *due on receipt*. For example, a credit card charge for fuel or a check for supplies. To record these transactions, you will use either the Expense task or the Check task after clicking the Create (+) icon. For ease of use, you will be directed to use the Expense task for all credit card transactions and the Check task for all checking account payments even though the Expense task can be used for either credit card charges or check payments.

To record a credit card or check payment, do the following:

1 Click the **+** icon.

2 Click **Expense** under the Vendor column.

3 Select **Chin's Gas and Oil** from the drop-down list in the Choose a payee text box.

4 Select **Mastercard** from the drop-down list in the Choose an account text box.

5 Accept **Automobile:Fuel** in the row 1 Account column and then type **85.00** as the amount replacing the existing 52.56 and then press [**Tab**]. Your window should look like Figure 5.14.

Figure 5.14

Credit Card Charge

Note that your screen has the title Category details not Account details and the column title is Category and not Account as shown here. Once again this change took place after this text was completed. See the Preface of this text for a complete discussion of the confusion this change created.

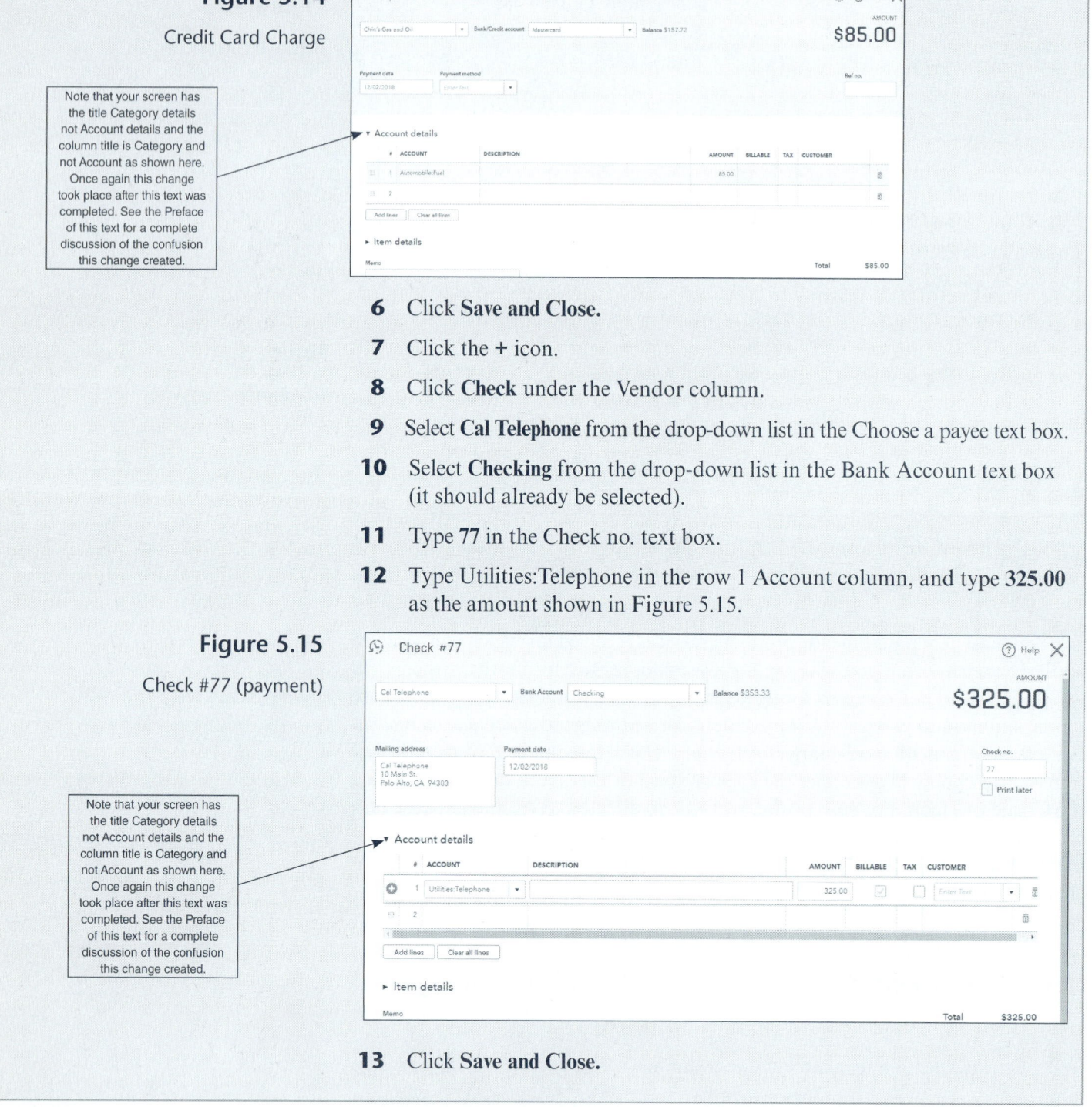

6   Click **Save and Close.**

7   Click the **+** icon.

8   Click **Check** under the Vendor column.

9   Select **Cal Telephone** from the drop-down list in the Choose a payee text box.

10   Select **Checking** from the drop-down list in the Bank Account text box (it should already be selected).

11   Type **77** in the Check no. text box.

12   Type Utilities:Telephone in the row 1 Account column, and type **325.00** as the amount shown in Figure 5.15.

Figure 5.15

Check #77 (payment)

Note that your screen has the title Category details not Account details and the column title is Category and not Account as shown here. Once again this change took place after this text was completed. See the Preface of this text for a complete discussion of the confusion this change created.

13   Click **Save and Close.**

Trial Balance

The work you completed in this chapter had an effect on the company's trial balance. You decided to create a Trial Balance report and investigate the checking, inventory asset, and accounts payable accounts. In the process, you realized that purchase orders do not affect a company's accounts until products are received or services are rendered.

Trouble? Recall the previous discussion of dates and amounts when using the Sample company. Dates in the text figures will be different than what you see in QBO when using the Sample company. Ending balances may also be different as they will all depend on what actual date you are entering transactions. Focus on the process rather than the resulting report dates or balances. This will not be the situation when you work on the end-of-chapter cases as those dates have been specifically identified.

To create a trial balance and investigate some account activity, do the following:

1   Click **Reports,** type **Trial Balance** into the Find report by name text box, and press [**Enter**]. The upper portion of that report is shown in Figure 5.16.

Craig's Design and Landscaping Services

TRIAL BALANCE
As of December 2, 2018

	DEBIT	CREDIT
Checking	28.33	
Savings	800.00	
Accounts Receivable (A/R)	5,281.52	
Inventory Asset	1,721.25	
Prepaid Expenses	1,800.00	
Undeposited Funds	2,062.52	
Truck:Original Cost	13,495.00	
Accounts Payable (A/P)		4,880.00
Mastercard		242.72
Arizona Dept. of Revenue Payable		0.00
Board of Equalization Payable		370.94
Loan Payable		4,000.00
Notes Payable		25,000.00
Opening Balance Equity	9,337.50	
Design income		2,250.00
Discounts given	89.50	
Landscaping Services		1,477.50
Landscaping Services:Job Materials:Fo…		2,246.50
Landscaping Services:Job Materials:Pl…		2,351.97
Landscaping Services:Job Materials:Sp…		138.00
Landscaping Services:Labor:Installation		250.00
Landscaping Services:Labor:Maintena…		50.00

Figure 5.16

Trial Balance (upper portion)

2   Click the Checking account balance of **28.33** to produce a Transaction Report for the Checking Account. The four bill payment checks you recorded earlier in this chapter and the check payment to Cal Telephone are shown in Figure 5.17.

Figure 5.17

Transaction Report (for the checking account)

Craig's Design and Landscaping Services
TRANSACTION REPORT
December 1-2, 2018

DATE	TRANSACTION TYPE	NUM	NAME	MEMO/DESCRIPTION	ACCOUNT	SPLIT	AMOUNT	BALANCE
▾ Checking								
Beginning Balance								1,201.00
12/02/2018	Check	77	Cal Telephone		Checking	Utilities:Telephone	-325.00	876.00
12/02/2018	Bill Payment (Check)	71	Brosnahan Insurance Agency	7653412	Checking	Accounts Payable (A/P)	-241.23	634.77
12/02/2018	Bill Payment (Check)	74	Robertson & Associates	000005641	Checking	Accounts Payable (A/P)	-315.00	319.77
12/02/2018	Bill Payment (Check)	73	PG&E	00649587213	Checking	Accounts Payable (A/P)	-86.44	233.33
12/02/2018	Bill Payment (Check)	72	Norton Lumber and Building	32980256	Checking	Accounts Payable (A/P)	-205.00	28.33
Total for Checking							$ -1,172.67	
TOTAL							$ -1,172.67	

3 Click the **Printer** icon to print this report.

4 Click **Back to report summary.**

5 Click the Inventory Asset account balance of **1,721.25** to produce a Transaction Report for the Inventory Asset account. The two bills for product purchases you recorded earlier in this chapter are shown in Figure 5.18.

Figure 5.18

Transaction Report (for the Inventory Asset Account)

Craig's Design and Landscaping Services
TRANSACTION REPORT
December 1-2, 2018

DATE	TRANSACTION TYPE	NUM	NAME	MEMO/DESCRIPTION	ACCOUNT	SPLIT	AMOUNT	BALANCE
▾ Inventory Asset								
Beginning Balance								596.25
12/02/2018	Bill		Tim Philip Masonry	Rock Fountain	Inventory Asset	Accounts Payable (A/P)	125.00	721.25
12/02/2018	Inventory Starting Value	START		Lavender - Opening Inventor...	Inventory Asset	Opening Balance Equity	0.00	721.25
12/02/2018	Inventory Starting Value	START		Landscape Rock - Opening in...	Inventory Asset	Opening Balance Equity	0.00	721.25
12/02/2018	Bill		Tania's Nursery	Lavender	Inventory Asset	Accounts Payable (A/P)	1,000.00	1,721.25
Total for Inventory Asset							$1,125.00	
TOTAL							$1,125.00	

6 Click the **Printer** icon to print this report.

7 Click **Back to report summary.**

8 Click the Accounts Payable (A/P) account balance of **4,880.00** to produce a Transaction Report for the Accounts Payable (A/P) account. The bills for product and service purchases and the bill payments you recorded earlier in this chapter are shown in Figure 5.19.

Figure 5.19

Transaction Report (for the Accounts Payable account)

Craig's Design and Landscaping Services
TRANSACTION REPORT
December 1-2, 2018

DATE	TRANSACTION TYPE	NUM	NAME	MEMO/DESCRIPTION	ACCOUNT	SPLIT	AMOUNT	BALANCE
▾ Accounts Payable (A/P)								
Beginning Balance								1,602.67
12/02/2018	Bill		Tim Philip Masonry		Accounts Payable (A/P)	Inventory Asset	125.00	1,727.67
12/02/2018	Bill		Tania's Nursery		Accounts Payable (A/P)	Inventory Asset	1,000.00	2,727.67
12/02/2018	Bill		Computers by Jenni		Accounts Payable (A/P)	Equipment Rental	1,200.00	3,927.67
12/02/2018	Bill Payment (Check)	74	Robertson & Associates		Accounts Payable (A/P)	Checking	-315.00	3,612.67
12/02/2018	Bill Payment (Check)	71	Brosnahan Insurance Agency		Accounts Payable (A/P)	Checking	-241.23	3,371.44
12/02/2018	Bill Payment (Check)	72	Norton Lumber and Building		Accounts Payable (A/P)	Checking	-205.00	3,166.44
12/02/2018	Bill Payment (Check)	73	PG&E		Accounts Payable (A/P)	Checking	-86.44	3,080.00
12/02/2018	Bill		Brosnahan Insurance Agency		Accounts Payable (A/P)	Prepaid Expenses	1,800.00	4,880.00
Total for Accounts Payable (A/P)							$3,277.33	
TOTAL							$3,277.33	

9 Click the **Printer** icon to print this report.

10 Click **Back to Summary Report.**

11 Click the **Gear** icon, and click **Sign Out.**

End Note

In this chapter, you added a vendor, a product, purchase orders, bills, payment of bills, a credit card purchase, and a check payment. You also produced a trial balance and drilled down through that trial balance to see the effect the bills and payment of bills affected accounts. In the next chapter, you will work with investing and financing activities.

Chapter 5 Questions

1 Why does a business use purchase orders?

2 Describe the steps to create a new product from within a purchase order.

3 What happens when you create a new purchase order to a vendor from whom you recently placed a different purchase order?

4 What accounts are affected when a bill from a vendor supplying you products is recorded?

5 What appears when you click Pay Bills after clicking the Create (+) icon?

6 Describe the process for increasing or decreasing the width of a column in the listing of bills to pay.

7 What are the steps to record a credit card charge?

8 What are the steps to record a check written to pay something other than bills?

9 What are the steps to view a transaction report for the checking account from a trial balance?

10 What are the steps to view a transaction report for the inventory account from a trial balance?

Chapter 5 Matching

a. Purchase order

b. Due on receipt

c. Bill

d. Net 30

e. Item detail section

f. Account detail section

g. Pay Bills

h. Check

i. Expense

j. Vendor

_____ Purchases that affect inventory are recorded here

_____ An invoice sent by a vendor to a customer

_____ Purchases that don't affect inventory are recorded here

_____ Task used to record checks in the checking account

_____ Suppliers of products and services

_____ A formal means to order products from vendors

_____ Pay a bill within 30 days after the bill date

_____ Task used to record credit card charges

_____ Terms that provide no credit

_____ Paying vendors who have billed you

Chapter 5 Cases

The following cases require you to open the company you updated in Chapter 4. Each of the following cases continues throughout the text in a sequential manner. For example, if you are assigned Case 01, you will use the file you modified in this chapter in all of the following chapters. Each of the following cases is similar in concepts assessed but differs in amounts and transactions. See the preface to this text for a matrix of each student case and its attributes.

To reopen your company, do the following:

1 Open your Internet browser.

2 Type **https://qbo.intuit.com** into your browser's address text box.

3 Type your User ID and Password into the text boxes as you have done before.

Case 1

Add some operating activities (purchases, credit card charges, and cash payments) to your company.

Based on what you learned in the text using the Sample Company, you are to make the following changes to the Case 1 company you modified in Chapter 4:

1 Add a new vendor – Stewart Surfboards, 2102 S El Camino Real, San Clemente, CA 92672, terms: net 30.

2 Add a new vendor – Village Travel, 100 S El Camino Real, San Clemente, CA 92672, terms: due on receipt.

3 Add a new vendor – Office Depot, 101 Main St., San Diego, CA 92600, terms: due on receipt.

4 Add a new account – category type: Credit Card, detail type: Credit Card, name: VISA.

5 Add a new account – category type: Other Current Assets, detail type: Other Current Assets, name: Supplies Asset.

6 Add a new tracked product – Name/description: California Nose Rider, initial quantity on hand: 0, inventory asset account: Inventory Asset, price: 3,200.00, cost: 1,700.00, income account: Sales, expense account: Cost of Goods Sold.

7 Add a new tracked product – Name/description: 808, initial quantity on hand: 0, inventory asset account: Inventory Asset, price: 2,700.00, cost: 1,500.00, income account: Sales, expense account: Cost of Goods Sold.

8 Record a new purchase order for products on 1/2/18 – Vendor: Channel Islands, product 1: Fred Rubble, QTY: 5, product 2: Rook 15, QTY: 4, product 3: The Water Hog, QTY: 1.

9 Record a new purchase order for products on 1/3/18 – Vendor: Stewart Surfboards, product 1: 808, QTY: 2, product 2: California Nose Rider, QTY: 1.

10 Record a new bill based on a purchase order #1001 on 1/5/18 – Vendor: Channel Islands, terms: Net 15. All items ordered were received.

11 Record a new bill without a purchase order on 1/8/18 – New vendor: San Diego Gas & Electric, terms: Net 15, account: Utilities, amount: 145.00.

12 Record a new bill without a purchase order on 1/9/18 – New vendor: Prime Properties, terms: Net 15, account 1: Rent or Lease, amount: 2,500.00, account 2: Prepaid Expenses, amount: 5,000.00.

13 Pay all bills due to Channel Islands on 1/19/18 using the checking account and starting with check no. 1001.

14 Record a credit card charge on 1/10/18, vendor: Village Travel, using credit card: VISA, account: Travel, amount: 1,800.00.

15 Record check on 1/11/18, no.: 1002, vendor: Office Depot, amount: 375.00, account: Supplies Asset.

16 Open your previously customized report named Trial Balance 1/31/18. If a cash or accrual message appears just close the message. Your report should look like Figure 5.20.

Figure 5.20

Trial Balance (as of 1/31/18)

Case 1
TRIAL BALANCE
As of January 31, 2018

	DEBIT	CREDIT
Checking	16,325.00	
Accounts Receivable	1,030.00	
Inventory Asset	11,800.00	
Prepaid Expenses	8,000.00	
Supplies Asset	375.00	
Undeposited Funds	5,000.00	
Furniture & Fixtures:Depreciation		10,000.00
Furniture & Fixtures:Original cost	40,000.00	
Accounts Payable		7,645.00
VISA		1,800.00
Notes Payable		60,000.00
Common Stock		1,000.00
Opening Balance Equity		0.00
Retained Earnings		5,500.00
Sales		2,160.00
Services		170.00
Cost of Goods Sold	1,300.00	
Rent or Lease	2,500.00	
Travel	1,800.00	
Utilities	145.00	
TOTAL	$88,275.00	$88,275.00

17 Create and print a Transaction Report for the Checking account as you did earlier in the chapter.

18 Create and print a Transaction Report for the Inventory Asset account as you did earlier in the chapter.

19 Create and print a Transaction Report for the Accounts Payable (A/P) account as you did earlier in the chapter.

20 If your trial balance differs from what is in Figure 5.20, do the following:

    a. Make sure all of your changes were dated in January 2018.

    b. View the Transaction Reports you just created to locate any errors.

    c. Ask your instructor for assistance.

    d. Be sure your company matches the above, as in the following chapter you'll be adding additional business events.

21 Export your Trial Balance report to Excel and save it with the file name: Student Name (replace with your name) Ch 05 Case 01 Trial Balance.xlsx.

22 Open and print the custom report you created in the last chapter called Transaction Detail by Account.

23 Export your Transactions Detail by Account report to Excel and save it with the file name: Student Name (replace with your name) Ch 05 Case 01 Transaction Detail by Account.xlsx.

24 Sign out of your company.

Case 2

Add some operating activities (purchases, credit card charges, and cash payments) to your company.

Based on what you learned in the text using the Sample Company, you are to make the following changes to the Case 2 company you modified in Chapter 4:

1 Add a new vendor – E-flite, 700 Annapolis Ln N Suite #175, Plymouth, MN, 55447, terms: net 15.

2 Add a new vendor – Village Steak House, 100 S El Camino Real, San Clemente, CA 92672, terms: due on receipt.

3 Add a new vendor – Staples, 101 Main St., San Diego, CA 92600, terms: due on receipt.

4 Add a new account – category type: Credit Card, detail type: Credit Card, name: AMEX.

5 Add a new account – category type: Other Current Assets, detail type: Other Current Assets, name: Supplies Asset.

6 Add a new tracked product – name/description: Sport Cub S, initial quantity on hand: 0, inventory asset account: Inventory Asset, price: 600.00, cost: 479.00, income account: Sales, expense account: Cost of Goods Sold.

7 Add a new tracked product – name/description: Mystique RES, initial quantity on hand: 0, inventory asset account: Inventory Asset, price: 450.00, cost: 325.00, income account: Sales, expense account: Cost of Goods Sold.

8 Record a new purchase order for products on 1/2/19 – vendor: E-flite, product 1: Sport Cub S, QTY: 5, product 2: Mystique RES, QTY: 3.

9 Record a new purchase order for products on 1/3/19 – vendor: Kyosho, product 1: Broon F830 Ride, QTY: 4, product 2: GO Aircraft Radio, QTY: 2, product 3: Seawind Carbon Sailboat, QTY: 1.

10 Record a new bill based on a purchase order #1001 on 1/7/19 – vendor: E-flite, terms: Net 15. All items ordered were received.

11 Record a new bill without a purchase order on 1/8/19 – new vendor: San Diego News-Press, terms: Net 15, account: Advertising, amount: 500.00.

12 Record a new bill without a purchase order on 1/10/19 – new vendor: Gomez Insurance, terms: Net 15, account 1: Insurance, amount: 400.00, account 2: Prepaid Expenses, amount: 4,400.00.

13 Pay bill due to Kyosho on 1/18/19 using the checking account and starting with check no. 1001.

14 Record a credit card charge on 1/11/19, vendor: Village Steak House, using credit card: AMEX, account: Meals and Entertainment, amount: 240.00.

15 Record check on 1/14/19, no.: 1002, vendor: Staples, amount: 450.00, account: Supplies Asset.

16 Open your previously customized report named Trial Balance 1/31/19. Your report should look like Figure 5.21.

Figure 5.21

Trial Balance (as of 1/31/19)

Case 2
TRIAL BALANCE
As of January 31, 2019

	DEBIT	CREDIT
Checking	7,150.00	
Accounts Receivable	1,425.00	
Inventory Asset	5,410.00	
Prepaid Expenses	6,800.00	
Supplies Asset	450.00	
Undeposited Funds	925.00	
Machinery & Equipment:Depreciation		1,000.00
Machinery & Equipment:Original cost	10,000.00	
Accounts Payable		8,670.00
AMEX		240.00
Notes Payable		12,000.00
Common Stock		100.00
Opening Balance Equity		0.00
Retained Earnings		8,385.00
Sales		5,700.00
Services		225.00
Cost of Goods Sold	3,020.00	
Advertising	500.00	
Insurance	400.00	
Meals and Entertainment	240.00	
TOTAL	**$36,320.00**	**$36,320.00**

17 Create and print a Transaction Report for the Checking account as you did earlier in the chapter.

18 Create and print a Transaction Report for the Inventory Asset account as you did earlier in the chapter.

19 Create and print a Transaction Report for the Accounts Payable (A/P) account as you did earlier in the chapter.

20 If your trial balance differs from what is in Figure 5.21, do the following:

    a. Make sure that all of your changes were dated in January 2019.

    b. View the Transaction Reports you created to locate any errors.

    c. Ask your instructor for assistance.

    d. Be sure your company matches the above since, in the following chapter, you will add additional business events.

21 Export your Trial Balance report to Excel and save it with the file name: Student Name (replace with your name) Ch 05 Case 02 Trial Balance.xlsx.

22 Open and print the custom report you created in the last chapter called Transaction Detail by Account.

23 Export your Transactions Detail by Account report to Excel and save it with the file name: Student Name (replace with your name) Ch 05 Case 02 Transaction Detail by Account.xlsx.

24 Sign out of your company.

Case 3

Now it's time for you to add some operating activities (purchases, credit card charges, and cash payments) to your company.

Based on what you learned in the text using the Sample Company, you are to make the following changes to the Case 3 company you modified in Chapter 4:

1 Add a new vendor – Google, Inc., 1600 Amphitheatre Parkway, Mountain View, CA 94043, terms: Net 15.

2 Add a new vendor – Samsung, Inc., 105 Challenger Rd., Ridgefield Park, NJ 07660, terms: Net 15.

3 Add a new vendor – Staples, Inc., 101 Main St., San Diego, CA 92600, terms: Net 30.

4 Modify Apple, Inc. (existing Vendor) – Name should be Apple Computer, Inc., address: 1 Infinite Loop Cupertino, CA 95014, terms: Net 15.

5 Add a new account – category type: Credit Card, detail type: Credit Card, name: AMEX.

6 Add a new account – category type: Other Current Assets, detail type: Other Current Assets, name: Supplies Asset.

7 Add a new taxable product – Name/Sales & Purchase information: Samsung Galaxy 8, initial quantity on hand: 0, inventory asset account: Inventory Asset, Sales price: 450.00, cost: 350.00, income account: Sales of Product Income, expense account: Cost of Goods Sold. (Use your current system date as the "as of date".)

8 Add a new taxable product – Name/Sales & Purchase information: Samsung Note, initial quantity on hand: 0, inventory asset account: Inventory Asset, Sales price: 850.00, cost: 650.00, income account: Sales of Product Income, expense account: Cost of Goods Sold. (Use your current system date as the "as of date".)

9 Record a new purchase order (1001) for products on 1/6/20 – vendor: Google, Inc., Pixel, QTY: 10

10 Record a new purchase order (1002) for products on 1/7/20 – vendor: Samsung, Inc., product 1: Samsung Galaxy 8, QTY: 5, product 2: Samsung Note, QTY: 8.

11 Record a new bill based on a purchase order #1001 dated 1/6/20 – vendor: Google, Inc., terms: Net 15. All items ordered were received on 1/10/20 (the bill date).

12 Record a new bill without a purchase order on 1/8/20 – new vendor: News-Press, terms: Net 15, account: Advertising, amount: 1,300.00.

13 Record a new bill without a purchase order on 1/10/20 – new vendor: Hathaway Insurance, terms: Net 15, account 1: Insurance, amount: 300.00, account 2: Prepaid Expenses, amount: 3,300.00.

14 Pay bill due to Apple Computer, Inc. on 1/18/20 using the checking account and starting with check no. 321.

15 Record a credit card charge on 1/11/20, new vendor: Village Steak House, using credit card: AMEX, account: Meals and Entertainment, amount: 123.00.

16 Record check on 1/14/20, no.: 322, vendor: Staples, amount: 327.00, account: Supplies Asset.

17 Open and print your previously customized report named Trial Balance 1/31/20. Your report should look like Figure 5.22.

Figure 5.22

Trial Balance as of 1/31/20

Case 3 - Student Name (ID number)

TRIAL BALANCE

As of January 31, 2020

	DEBIT	CREDIT
Checking	15,853.00	
Accounts Receivable (A/R)	2,610.00	
Inventory Asset	5,700.00	
Prepaid Expenses	6,050.00	
Supplies Asset	327.00	
Undeposited Funds	0.00	
Machinery & Equipment:Depreciation		2,000.00
Machinery & Equipment:Original cost	15,000.00	
Accounts Payable (A/P)		8,900.00
AMEX		123.00
State Board of Equalization Payable		675.00
Notes Payable		23,000.00
Opening Balance Equity		0.00
Owner's Equity		10,075.00
Sales of Product Income		6,750.00
Services		240.00
Cost of Goods Sold	4,500.00	
Advertising	1,300.00	
Insurance	300.00	
Meals and Entertainment	123.00	
TOTAL	$51,763.00	$51,763.00

18 Create and print a Transaction Report for the Checking account like you did in the chapter.

19 Create and print a Transaction Report for the Accounts Receivable (A/R) account.

20 Create and print a Transaction Report for the Inventory Asset account like you did in the chapter.

21 Create and print a Transaction Report for the Accounts Payable (A/P) account like you did in the chapter.

22 If your trial balance is different than Figure 5.22:

    a. Make sure that all of your changes were dated in January 2020.

    b. View the Transaction Reports you just created to locate any errors.

    c. Ask your instructor for assistance.

    d. Be sure your company matches the above, as in the following chapter you'll be adding additional business events.

23 Export your Trial Balance report to Excel and save it with the file name: Student Name (replace with your name) Ch 05 Case 03 Trial Balance.xlsx.

24   Open and print the custom report you created in the last chapter called Transaction Detail by Account.

25   Export your Transactions Detail by Account report to Excel and save it with the file name: Student Name (replace with your name) Ch 05 Case 03 Transaction Detail by Account.xlsx.

26   Sign out of your company.

Case 4

Now it's time for you to add some operating activities (purchases and cash payments) to your company.

Based on what you learned in the text using the Sample Company, you are to make the following changes to the Case 4 company you modified in Chapter 4:

1   Add a new vendor – GEICO Insurance, 335 Park Ave., Los Angeles, CA 90034, terms: Net 15.

2   Add a new account – Account Type: Other Current Assets, Detail Type: Other Current Assets, name: Supplies.

3   Add a new account – Account Type: Credit Card, Detail Type: Credit Card, name: VISA.

4   Add a new service – Name and Sales information: Towel Service, Sales price/rate: 20.00, income account: Sales, Is taxable: No.

5   Record sales receipt 1004 to a new customer: Enterprise Inc., on 1/4/2021 for 5 Monthly Fee – Corporate Membership 50 Employees and 50 Towel Service. Check no. 9847 was received and immediately deposited to the company's checking account in the amount of $31,000.

6   Record a new purchase order (1001) for products on 1/7/21 – vendor: Bowflex, product: Bowflex Dumbbells, QTY: 25.

7   Record a new purchase order (1002) for products on 1/8/21 – vendor: Precor, product: Power Block Elite Dumbbells, QTY: 15.

8   Record a new bill based on a purchase order #1001 dated 1/15/21 – vendor: Bowflex, terms: Net 15. All items ordered were received on 1/15/21 (the bill date).

9   Record a new bill without a purchase order on 1/16/21 – new vendor: Supreme Marketing, terms: Net 15, account: Advertising & Marketing, amount: $1,800.00.

10   Record a new bill without a purchase order on 1/18/21 – vendor: Laundry Service, terms: Net 15, account: Supplies, amount: $1,400.00.

11   Pay bills due to Precor and Laundry Service on 1/18/21 using the checking account and starting with check no. 25498.

12   Record credit card charge on 1/20/2021 vendor: GEICO Insurance, using credit card: VISA, account: Insurance, amount: $2,400.00.

13   Record check on 1/21/2021, check no.: 25500, vendor: NordicTrack, amount: $750.00, account: Repairs & Maintenance.

14   Prepare and print the Trial Balance 1/31/2021 report you saved previously. Your report should look like Figure 5.23.

Figure 5.23

Trial Balance as of 1/31/21

Case 4 Student Name (Student ID)

TRIAL BALANCE
As of January 31, 2021

	DEBIT	CREDIT
Checking	45,576.65	
Accounts Receivable (A/R)	22,082.50	
Inventory Asset	8,868.00	
Prepaid Expenses	12,000.00	
Supplies	1,400.00	
Undeposited Funds	0.00	
Furniture:Depreciation		10,000.00
Furniture:Original cost	65,000.00	
Machinery & Equipment:Depreciation		6,500.00
Machinery & Equipment:Original cost	115,000.00	
Accounts Payable (A/P)		6,800.00
VISA		2,400.00
California State Board of Equalization Payable		339.15
Notes Payable		82,000.00
Common Stock		1,000.00
Opening Balance Equity		0.00
Retained Earnings		115,500.00
Sales		48,400.00
Sales of Product Income		3,570.00
Cost of Goods Sold	1,632.00	
Advertising & Marketing	1,800.00	
Insurance	2,400.00	
Repairs & Maintenance	750.00	
TOTAL	$276,509.15	$276,509.15

15 Create and print a Transaction Report for the Checking account.

16 Create and print a Transaction Report for the Accounts Receivable (A/R) account.

17 Create and print a Transaction Report for the Inventory Asset account.

18 Create and print a Transaction Report for the Accounts Payable (A/P) account.

19 Investigate differences between your trial balance and the trial balance shown above.

20 If necessary, prepare and print the Transaction Detail by Account report you saved previously to investigate identified differences.

   a. Make sure all your changes were dated in January 2021.

   b. Click on the line that does not match to view the transaction for that account and investigate why your answer differs.

   c. Ask your instructor for assistance.

   d. Be sure your company matches the above since, in the following chapter, you will be adding additional business events.

Investing and Financing Activities

Upon completion of this chapter, the student will be able to do the following:

- Record the acquisition of a fixed asset
- Record the acquisition of a long-term investment
- Record the sale of common stock
- Record the payment of a dividend
- Record a long-term borrowing (long-term debt)
- Record payment on long-term borrowing (long-term debt)
- Record the acquisition of a fixed asset by taking on new debt

Overview

Intuit has provided a Sample Company online to provide new users a test drive of its QBO product. In this chapter, you will open this Sample Company and practice various features of QBO. You will be recording investing activities such as acquiring a long-term investment and a fixed asset to the Sample Company file. In addition, you will be recording financing activities, such as selling common stock, paying a dividend, borrowing on a long-term basis, and making payments on long-term debt to the Sample Company file. Lastly, you will record an investing activity, acquiring a new fixed asset, and a financing activity by borrowing funds to purchase the fixed asset. Remember, if you stop in the middle of this work, none of your work will be saved. So when you return, the same sample company, without your work, will appear. In some parts of the chapter, you'll be asked to sign out of the Sample Company and sign back in so the Sample Company is reset to its original state. In the end of chapter work, you will be asked to perform the same tasks completed on the Sample Company on your Student Company. That work, of course, will be saved.

Throughout this text, figures illustrating bills, expenses, checks, purchase orders, and credit card transactions will have the title Account details not Category details and the column title as Account and not Category as shown on your QBO software. Steps will also use the term Account when your QBO software will reflect the use of the term Category. Once again this change took place after this text was completed. See the Preface of this text for a complete discussion of the confusion this change created.

Fixed Assets

In this section, you will be recording the acquisition of fixed assets. Fixed assets are long-term tangible property that a firm owns and uses in the production of its income and is not expected to be consumed or converted into cash any sooner than at least one year's time. Normally, a fixed asset's cost is depreciated over time as a means of allocating its cost over its useful life. The depreciation is recorded to a depreciation expense account and added to an accumulated depreciation (contra-asset) account. That process will be explained in the chapter on adjusting entries.

To add an asset, you will use the Check task accessed by clicking the + icon. Alternatively, you could purchase new fixed assets with using a credit card or take on new debt. The Sample Company had a fixed asset account for trucks, which you'll use to record the purchase of a truck. If you were to purchase some other type of fixed asset, equipment for example, you would need to create a new fixed asset account named Equipment and two additional subaccounts to the Equipment account: Original Cost and Accumulated Depreciation.

To record the purchase of a new truck and new equipment in the Sample Company, do the following:

1 Open your Internet browser.

2 Type **https://qbo.intuit.com/redir/testdrive** into your browser's address text box and then press [**Enter**] to view the Sample Company Dashboard.

3 Click the + icon and then click **Check**.

4 Select + **Add new** from the drop-down list in the Choose a payee text box.

5 Type **Sunset Auto** in the Name text box, select **Vendor** as the Type, and click **Save**.

6 Accept the given Payment date and Check no. provided by QBO.

7 Type **Truck:Original Cost** in the Account column of line 1.

8 Type **2,500.00** in the Amount column of line 1 and the press [**Tab**]. Your screen should look like Figure 6.1.

Check #71					⑦ Help
					AMOUNT
Sunset Auto ▼	Bank Account	Checking ▼	Balance $1,201.00		**$2,500.00**

Mailing address	Payment date			Check no.
Sunset Auto	12/03/2018			71
				☐ Print later

▼ Account details

#	ACCOUNT	DESCRIPTION	AMOUNT	BILLABLE	TAX	CUSTOMER	
1	Truck:Original Cost		2,500.00				🗑
2							🗑

Figure 6.1

Purchase of Truck

9   Click **Save and new**.

10 Select **Tania's Nursery** from the drop-down list in the Choose a payee text box.

11 Select **+ Add new** from the drop-down list in Account column of line 1.

12 Select **Fixed Assets** from the drop-down list in the Account Type text box.

13 Select **Machinery & Equipment** from the drop-down list in the Detail type text box.

14 Leave Machinery & Equipment in the Name text box, then place a check in the Track depreciation of this asset check box, and then click **Save and Close**.

15 Type **Machinery & Equipment:Original Cost** in the Account column of line 1.

16 Type **1,000.00** in the Amount column of line 1 and then press **[Tab]** to see Figure 6.2.

17 Click **Save and close**.

Figure 6.2

Purchase of Equipment

You have recorded the purchase of two new fixed assets.

Long-Term Investments

The acquisition of a long-term investment is another type of investing activity. In general, a long-term investment is the purchase of a financial instrument (bond, common stock, and preferred stock) that matures in more than one year.

To record the purchase of a long-term investment in the Sample Company, do the following:

1 Continue from where you left off. If you closed the Sample Company, follow the steps to reopen it found at the beginning of this chapter.

2 Click the + icon, and select **Check**.

3 Select + **Add new** from the drop-down list in the Choose a payee text box.

4 Type **Scottrade** in the Name text box, select **Vendor** as the Type, and click **Save.**

5 Accept the given Payment date and Check no. provided by QBO.

6 Select + **Add new** from the drop-down list in Account column of line 1.

7 Select **Other Assets** from the drop-down list in the Category Type text box.

8 Select **Other Long-term Assets** from the drop-down list in the Detail type text box.

9 Type **Investments** in the Name text box, and click **Save and Close**.

10 Type **3,000.00** in the Amount column of line 1 and then press [**Tab**] to see Figure 6.3.

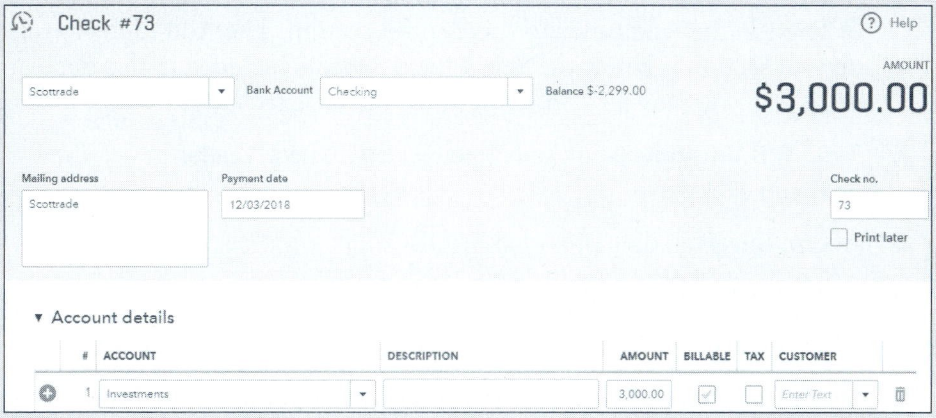

Figure 6.3

Purchase of a Long-Term Investment

11 Click **Save and close**.

12 Click the **Gear** icon, and click **Sign out** to reset the Sample Company.

You have recorded the purchase of a long-term investment.

Common Stock and Dividends

The sale of common stock and the payment of cash dividends to shareholders are two common financing activities. Common stock is a stockholders' equity account. Dividends are a distribution of earnings to shareholders and are accounted for as a reduction in retained earnings. Both of these are cash activities in that the sale of stock results in a cash receipt (you will account for it as a bank deposit), whereas the payment of a cash dividend results in a cash payment. Two previous payments from customers appear when you attempt to record a bank deposit from the issuance of stock. These payments have been received but not recorded. Ignore those for now. To simplify this transaction, we will assume that the common stock is no-par common stock, and thus, no additional paid-in capital exists. Also, we'll assume that the declaration, record, and payment dates are all the same.

To record the sale of stock and payment of cash dividends in the Sample Company, do the following:

1   Continue from where you left off. If you closed the Sample Company, follow the steps to reopen it found at the beginning of this chapter.

2   Click the + icon and then select **Bank Deposit**.

3   Select + **Add new** from the drop-down list in the Received From column of line 1 in the Add funds to this deposit section. The Add funds to this deposit section is below the Select the payments included in this deposit section so you may have to scroll down the page to find it.

4   Type **WB Investments** in the Name text box, select **Vendor** in the Type box, and click **Save**.

5   Accept the given date provided by QBO.

6   Select + **Add new** from the drop-down list in the Account column of line 1.

7   Select **Equity** from the drop-down list in the Account Type text box.

8   Select **Common Stock** from the drop-down list in the Detail Type text box.

9   Accept **Common Stock** in the Name text box, and click **Save and Close**.

10   Select **Check** as the Payment Method.

11   Type **10,000.00** in the Amount column of line 1, and press [**Tab**]. Your screen should look like Figure 6.4.

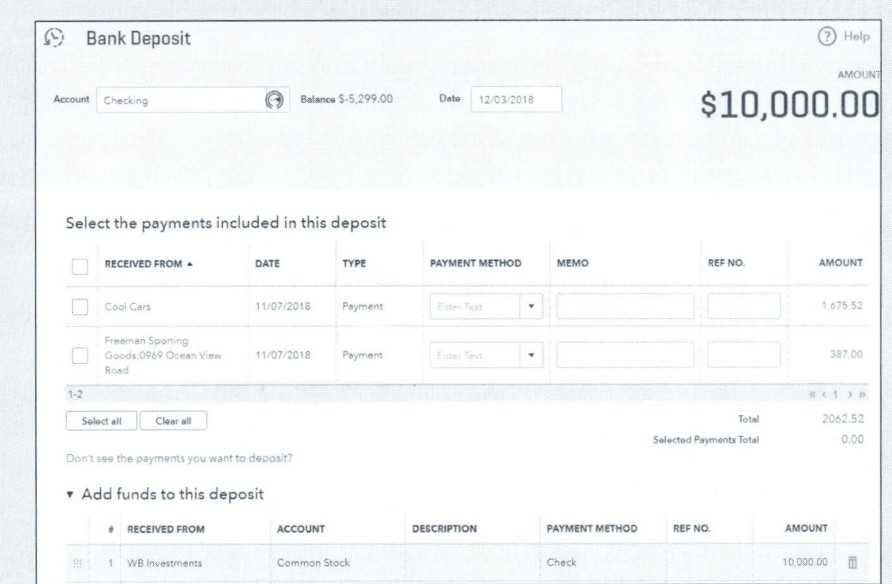

Figure 6.4

Recording the Deposit of Funds from the Sale of Common Stock

12 Click **Save and close**.

13 Click the + icon, and select **Check**.

14 Select + **Add new** from the drop-down list in the Choose a payee text box.

15 Type **Shareholders** in the Name text box, select **Vendor** in the Type box, and click **Save**.

16 Accept the given Payment date and Check no. provided by QBO.

17 Select **Retained Earnings** from the drop-down list in the Account column of line 1.

18 Type **1,250.00** in the Amount column of line 1, and press [**Tab**]. Your screen should look like Figure 6.5.

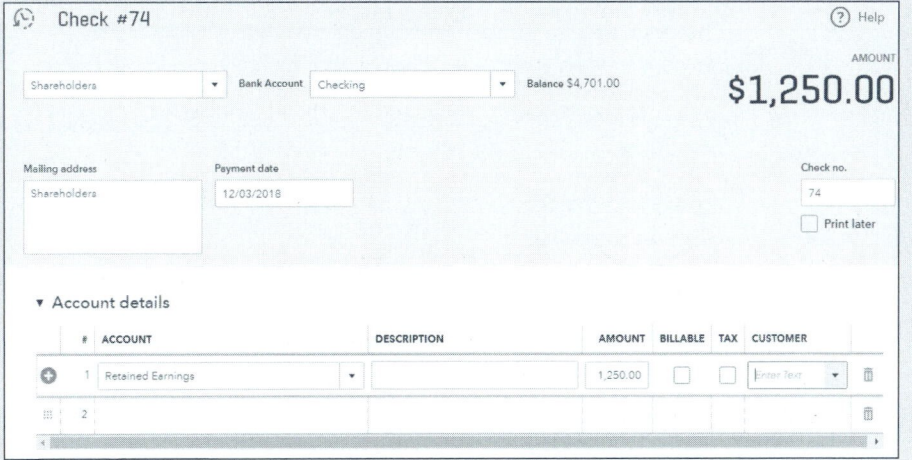

Figure 6.5

Payment of Dividends

19 Click **Save and close**.

20 Do not sign out of the Sample Company.

Long-Term Debt

The borrowing of funds on a long-term basis and the repayment of debt are two additional financing activities. Both of these are cash activities in that the borrowing of funds results in a cash receipt (you will account for it as a bank deposit), whereas the payment of the debt results in a cash payment. There are two previous payments from customers that appear when you attempt to record a bank deposit from the borrowing of funds. These payments have been received but not recorded. You'll ignore those for now. This company decided to take the funds from the stock sale recorded above and the new borrowings below to pay off the old long-term debt with interest.

To record the receipt of funds from borrowing and the payment of long-term debt in the Sample Company, do the following:

1   Continue from where you left off. If you closed the Sample Company, follow the steps to reopen it found at the beginning of this chapter.

2   Click the + icon and then select **Bank Deposit**.

3   Select + **Add new** from the drop-down list in the Received From column of line 1 in the Add funds to this deposit section.

4   Type **Bank of La Jolla** in the Name text box, select **Vendor** in the Type box, and click **Save**.

5   Accept the given date provided by QBO.

6   Select **Notes Payable** from the drop-down list in Account column of line 1.

7   Select **Check** from the drop-down list in the Payment Method column of line 1.

8   Type **15,000.00** in the Amount column of line 1, and press [**Tab**]. Your screen should look like Figure 6.6.

Figure 6.6

Recording the Deposit of Funds from Borrowing

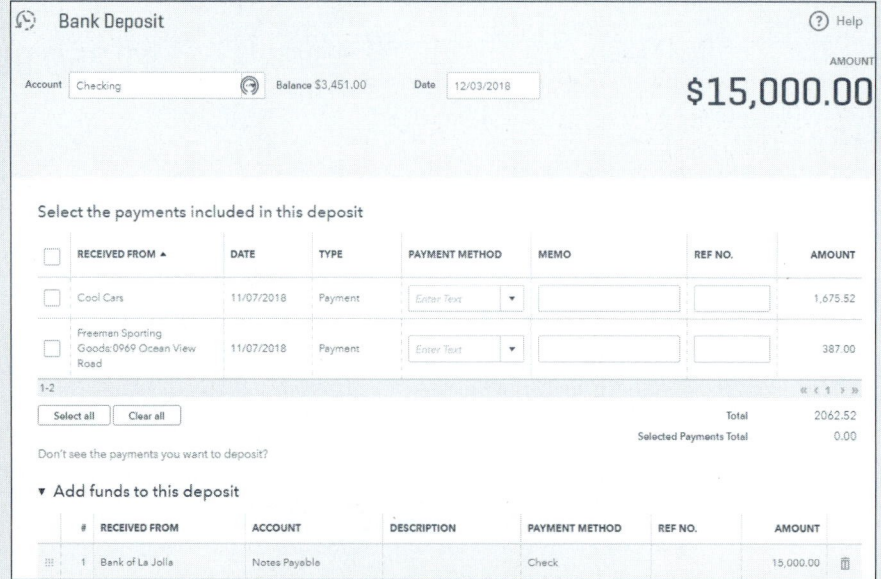

9 Click **Save and close**.

10 Click the + icon, and select **Check**.

11 Select + **Add new** from the drop-down list in the Choose a payee text box.

12 Type **Bank of San Diego** in the Name text box, select **Vendor** in the Type box, and click **Save**.

13 Accept the given Payment date and Check no. provided by QBO.

14 Select **Notes Payable** from the drop-down list in the Account column of line 1.

15 Type **25,000.00** in the Amount column of line 1 and then press [**Tab**].

16 Select + **Add new** from the drop-down list in the Account column of line 2.

17 Select **Expenses** from the drop-down list in the Account Type text box.

18 Select **Interest Paid** from the drop-down list in the Detail Type text box.

19 Type **Interest Expense** in the Name text box and click **Save and Close**.

20 Type **1,000.00** in the Amount column of line 2, and press [**Tab**]. Your screen should look like Figure 6.7.

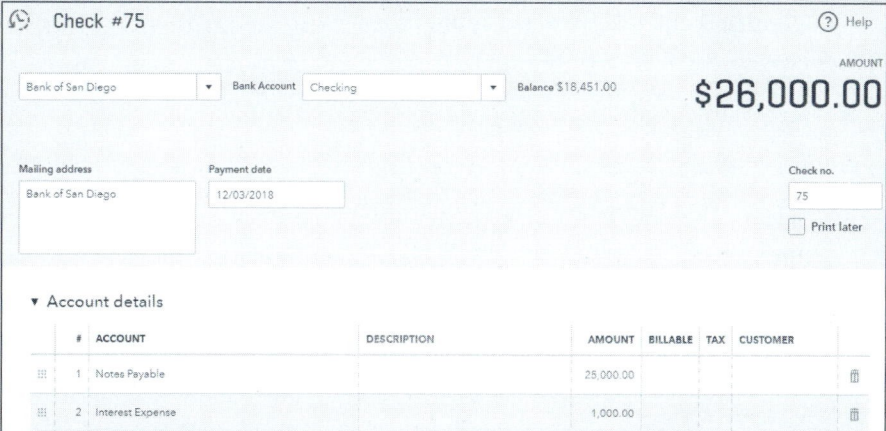

Figure 6.7

Repayment of Long-Term Debt with Interest

21 Click **Save and close**. If a warning message appears indicating a duplicate check number, just click **Yes**.

22 Do not sign out of the Sample Company.

Acquisition of a Fixed Asset in Exchange for Long-Term Debt

You completed the process for recording an investing activity (purchase of a fixed asset) and a financing activity (borrowing on a long-term basis). Both of these transactions were recorded by affecting the checking account (cash).

Occasionally, a company acquires a fixed asset by issuing long-term debt, for example, purchasing another truck in exchange for a note payable. This cannot be recorded using the checking account since no funds were exchanged. Instead, you will use the journal entry process to record the fixed asset acquisition and the long-term debt borrowing.

To record the purchase of a fixed asset by issuing debt, do the following:

1 Continue from where you left off. If you closed the Sample Company, follow the steps to reopen it found at the beginning of this chapter.

2 Click the + icon, and select **Journal Entry.**

3 Accept the Journal date and Journal no. provided by QBO.

4 Select **Truck:Original Cost** from the drop-down list in the Account column of line 1.

5 Type **3,400.00** in the Debits column of line 1.

6 Select **Notes Payable** from the drop-down list in the Account column of line 2.

7 Accept **3,400.00** in the Credits column of line 2, and press [**Tab**] to view the journal entry shown in Figure 6.8.

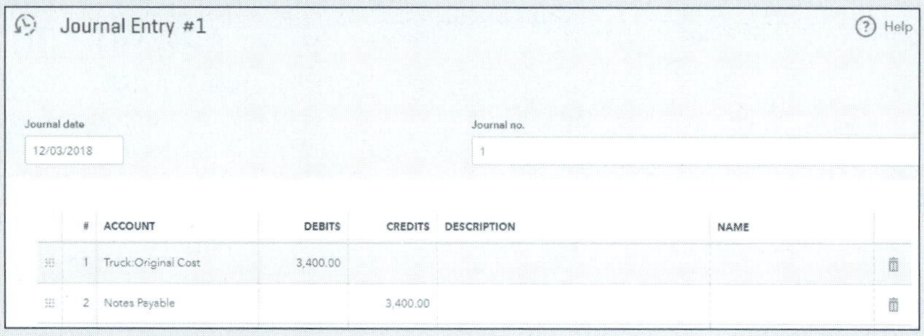

Figure 6.8

Journal Entry to Record Purchase of Fixed Asset in Exchange for Long-Term Debt

8 Click **Save and close**.

9 Sign out of the Sample Company.

End Note

In this chapter, you recorded investing activities: the acquisition of fixed assets and of long-term investments, the sale of common stocks, the payment of a dividend, the borrowing and payment of long-term debt, and the acquisition of fixed assets by taking on new debt. In the next chapter, you will work with payroll.

Chapter 6 Questions

1 What are the steps to record the acquisition of a fixed asset using a check?

2 What are the steps to record the acquisition of a fixed asset for a note payable?

3 What are the steps to record the sale of common stock?

4 What are the steps to record the payment of dividends?

5 What are the steps to record borrowing on a note payable?

Chapter 6 Matching

a. Operating activity	_____	Long-term tangible property that a firm owns
b. Investing activity	_____	Distribution of earnings to shareholders
c. Financing activity	_____	A stockholders' equity account
d. Fixed assets	_____	Used to record purchase of a fixed asset for a note
e. Long-term investment	_____	A 5-year note payable
f. Common stock	_____	Sales receipt
g. Dividends	_____	A financial instrument that matures in more than 1 year
h. Long-term debt	_____	Used to record amounts received from a note payable
i. Bank deposit	_____	Sale of common stock
j. Journal entry	_____	Purchase of common stock

Chapter 6 Cases

The following cases require you to open the company you updated in Chapter 5. Each of the following cases is continued throughout the text in a sequential manner. For example, if you are assigned Case 01, you will use the file you modified in this chapter in all following chapters. Each of the following cases is similar in concepts assessed but differs in amounts and transactions.

To reopen your company, do the following:

1 Open your Internet browser.

2 Type **https://qbo.intuit.com** into your browser's address text box.

3 Type your User ID and Password into the text boxes as you have done before.

Case 1

Now add some investing and financing activities to your company.

Based on what you learned in the text using the Sample Company, you are to make the following changes to the Case 1 company you modified in Chapter 5:

1. Create three new fixed asset accounts: category type: Fixed Asset, detail type: Machinery & Equipment and Accumulated Depreciation (where appropriate), account names: Equipment, Original Cost (a sub-account of Equipment), and Accumulated Depreciation (a sub-account of Equipment).

2. Create a new asset account with a category type: Other Assets, detail type: Other Long-Term Assets, name: Investments.

3. Record the purchase of a new computer on 1/10/18 from Office Depot, check: 1003, amount: $1,375.00, account: Equipment:Original Cost.

4. Record a long-term investment on 1/11/18 to Etrade (a new vendor), check: 1004, amount: $4,000, account: Investments.

5. Record the sale of common stock on 1/12/18 to Shareholders (a new vendor), deposit amount: $20,000, account: Common Stock.

6. Record the payment of dividends to Shareholders on 1/15/18, check 1005, in the amount of $500.

7. Record the deposit of funds from a new note payable signed on 1/16/18 with Bank of CA (a new vendor) in the amount of $65,000.

8. Record the payment to Rabo Bank (a new vendor) to retire an existing note payable on 1/16/18 of $60,000 with interest of $600 using check 1006.

9. Record the purchase of an additional computer on 1/17/18 from Office Depot in exchange for a note payable of $1,800.

10. Open your previously customized report named Trial Balance 1/31/18. Your report should look like Figure 6.9.

11. Create and print a Transaction Report for the Checking account.

12. Create and print a Transaction Report for the Equipment:Original Cost account.

13. Create and print a Transaction Report for the Notes Payable account.

14. Create and print a Transaction Report for the Common Stock account.

15. If your trial balance differs from Figure 6.9, do the following:

    a. Make sure that all of your changes were dated in January 2018.

    b. View the Transaction Reports you just created to locate any errors.

    c. Ask your instructor for assistance.

    d. Be sure your company matches the above, as in the following chapter you'll be adding additional business events.

Figure 6.9

Trial Balance as of 1/31/18

Case 1
TRIAL BALANCE
As of January 31, 2018

	DEBIT	CREDIT
Checking	34,850.00	
Accounts Receivable	1,030.00	
Inventory Asset	11,800.00	
Prepaid Expenses	8,000.00	
Supplies Asset	375.00	
Undeposited Funds	5,000.00	
Equipment:Original Cost	3,175.00	
Furniture & Fixtures:Depreciation		10,000.00
Furniture & Fixtures:Original cost	40,000.00	
Investments	4,000.00	
Accounts Payable		7,645.00
VISA		1,800.00
Notes Payable		66,800.00
Common Stock		21,000.00
Opening Balance Equity		0.00
Retained Earnings		5,000.00
Sales		2,160.00
Services		170.00
Cost of Goods Sold	1,300.00	
Interest Expense	600.00	
Rent or Lease	2,500.00	
Travel	1,800.00	
Utilities	145.00	
TOTAL	**$114,575.00**	**$114,575.00**

16 Export your Trial Balance report to Excel, and save it with the file name: Student Name (replace with your name) Ch 06 Case 01 Trial Balance.xlsx.

17 Open and print the custom report you created in the last chapter called Transaction Detail by Account.

18 Export your Transactions Detail by Account report to Excel, and save it with the file name: Student Name (replace with your name) Ch 06 Case 01 Transaction Detail by Account.xlsx.

19 Sign out of your company.

Case 2

Now add some investing and financing activities to your company.

Based on what you learned in the text using the Sample Company, you are to make the following changes to the Case 2 company you modified in Chapter 5:

1 Create three new fixed asset accounts: category type: Fixed Asset, detail type: Furniture & Fixtures and Accumulated Depreciation (where appropriate), account names: Furniture, Original Cost (a sub-account of Furniture), and Accumulated Depreciation (a sub-account of Furniture).

2   Create a new asset account with a category type: Other Assets, detail type: Other Long-Term Assets, name: Investments.

3   Record the purchase of new furniture on 1/11/19 from Staples, check: 1003, amount: $2,250.00, account: Furniture:Original Cost.

4   Record a long-term investment on 1/11/19 to Raymond James (a new vendor), check: 1004, amount: $3,200, account: Investments.

5   Record the sale of common stock on 1/14/19 to Shareholders (a new vendor), deposit amount: $25,000, account: Common Stock.

6   Record the payment of dividends to Shareholders on 1/15/19, check: 1005, in the amount of $800.

7   Record the deposit of funds from a new note payable signed on 1/16/19 with Bank of TJ (a new vendor) in the amount of $25,000.

8   Record the payment to Community Bank (a new vendor) to retire an existing note payable on 1/16/19 of $12,000 with interest of $300 using check 1006.

9   Record the purchase of additional furniture from Staples on 1/17/19 in exchange for a note payable of $2,625.

10   Open your previously customized report named Trial Balance 1/31/19. Your report should look like Figure 6.10.

Figure 6.10

Trial Balance as of 1/31/19

Case 2
TRIAL BALANCE
As of January 31, 2019

	DEBIT	CREDIT
Checking	38,600.00	
Accounts Receivable	1,425.00	
Inventory Asset	5,410.00	
Prepaid Expenses	6,800.00	
Supplies Asset	450.00	
Undeposited Funds	925.00	
Furniture:Original Cost	4,875.00	
Machinery & Equipment:Depreciation		1,000.00
Machinery & Equipment:Original cost	10,000.00	
Investments	3,200.00	
Accounts Payable		8,670.00
AMEX		240.00
Notes Payable		27,625.00
Common Stock		25,100.00
Opening Balance Equity		0.00
Retained Earnings		7,585.00
Sales		5,700.00
Services		225.00
Cost of Goods Sold	3,020.00	
Advertising	500.00	
Insurance	400.00	
Interest Expense	300.00	
Meals and Entertainment	240.00	
TOTAL	$76,145.00	$76,145.00

11 Create and print a Transaction Report for the Checking account.

12 Create and print a Transaction Report for the Furniture:Original Cost account.

13 Create and print a Transaction Report for the Notes Payable account.

14 Create and print a Transaction Report for the Common Stock account.

15 If your trial balance differs from Figure 6.10, do the following:

   a. Make sure that all of your changes were dated in January 2019.

   b. View the Transaction Reports you created to locate any errors.

   c. Ask your instructor for assistance.

   d. Be sure your company matches the above, because in the following chapter, you will be adding additional business events.

16 Export your Trial Balance report to Excel, and save it with the file name: Student Name (replace with your name) Ch 06 Case 02 Trial Balance.xlsx.

17 Open and print the custom report you created in the last chapter called Transaction Detail by Account.

18 Export your Transactions Detail by Account report to Excel, and save it with the file name: Student Name (replace with your name) Ch 06 Case 02 Transaction Detail by Account.xlsx.

19 Sign out of your company.

Case 3

Now it's time for you to add some investing and financing activities to your company.

Based on what you learned in the text using the Sample Company, you are to make the following changes to the Case 3 company you modified in Chapter 5:

1 Create three new fixed asset accounts. Each are category type: Fixed Asset, detail type: Buildings and Accumulated Depreciation (where appropriate), account names: Buildings, Original Cost (a sub-account of Buildings), and Accumulated Depreciation (a sub-account of Buildings).

2 Create a new asset account with a category type: Other Assets, detail type: Other Long-Term Assets, name: Investments. In addition, change the name of the Interest Paid expense account to Interest Expense.

3 Create a new equity account with a category type: Equity, detail type: Common Stock, and name: Common Stock.

4 Record the purchase of a new equipment on 1/12/20 from Staples, Inc., check: 323, amount: $3,000.00, account: Machinery & Equipment: Original Cost.

5 Record a long-term investment on 1/13/20 to E-Trade (a new vendor), check: 324, amount: $5,700.00, account: Investments.

6 Record the sale of common stock on 1/14/20 to Shareholders (a new vendor) after receiving a check that was immediately deposited in the amount: $40,000.00 to account: Common Stock.

7 Record the deposit of funds from a new note payable signed on 1/16/20 with Chase Bank (a new vendor) in the amount of $32,000.00.

8 Record the payment to Rabobank (a new vendor) to retire an existing note payable on 1/17/20 of $23,000 with interest of $300 using check 325 for a total of $23,300.

9 Record the purchase of a building from Leeds, Inc. (a new vendor) on 1/17/20 in exchange for a note payable of $31,800.00.

10 Open and print your previously customized report named Trial Balance 1/31/20. Your report should look like Figure 6.11.

Figure 6.11

Trial Balance as of 1/31/20

TRIAL BALANCE
As of January 31, 2020

	DEBIT	CREDIT
Checking	55,853.00	
Accounts Receivable (A/R)	2,610.00	
Inventory Asset	5,700.00	
Prepaid Expenses	6,050.00	
Supplies Asset	327.00	
Undeposited Funds	0.00	
Buildings:Original cost	31,800.00	
Machinery & Equipment:Depreciation		2,000.00
Machinery & Equipment:Original cost	18,000.00	
Investments	5,700.00	
Accounts Payable (A/P)		8,900.00
AMEX		123.00
California State Board of Equalization Payable		675.00
Notes Payable		63,800.00
Common Stock		40,000.00
Opening Balance Equity		0.00
Owner's Equity		10,075.00
Sales of Product Income		6,750.00
Services		240.00
Cost of Goods Sold	4,500.00	
Advertising & Marketing	1,300.00	
Insurance	300.00	
Interest Paid	300.00	
Meals & Entertainment	123.00	
TOTAL	$132,563.00	$132,563.00

11 Create and print a Transaction Report for the Checking account.

12 Create and print a Transaction Report for the Buildings:Original Cost account.

13 Create and print a Transaction Report for the Notes Payable account.

14 Create and print a Transaction Report for the Common Stock account.

15 If your trial balance is different than Figure 6.11:

    a. Make sure that all of your changes were dated in January 2020.

    b. View the Transaction Reports you just created to locate any errors.

    c. Ask your instructor for assistance.

    d. Be sure your company matches the above, as in the following chapter you'll be adding additional business events.

16 Export your Trial Balance report to Excel and save it with the file name: Student Name (replace with your name) Ch 06 Case 03 Trial Balance.xlsx.

17 Open and print the custom report you created in the last chapter called Transaction Detail by Account.

18 Export your Transactions Detail by Account report to Excel and save it with the file name: Student Name (replace with your name) Ch 06 Case 03 Transaction Detail by Account.xlsx.

19 Sign out of your company.

Case 4

Now it's time for you to add some investing and financing activities to your company.

Based on what you learned in the text using the Sample Company, you are to make the following changes to the Case 4 company you modified in Chapter 5:

1 Create a new fixed asset account with an account type: Fixed Asset, detail type: Buildings, name: Buildings. Track depreciation of this asset.

2 Create a new asset account with an account type: Other Assets, detail type: Other Long-Term Assets, name: Investments.

3 Change the name of the Interest Paid expense account to Interest Expense.

4 Record the signing of a new 8% 24-month note payable on 1/01/21 with Coast Bank (a new vendor) in the amount of $18,000.00. A check was received from Coast Bank and immediately deposited.

5 Record the purchase of a new building on 1/23/21 from ABC Holdings (a new vendor), check: 25501, amount: $35,000.00.

6 Record the purchase of a long-term investment on 1/25/21 from Barber Investments, Inc. (a new vendor), check: 25502, amount: $8,000.00.

7   Record the sale of common stock on 1/26/21 to Shareholders (a new vendor) receiving a $10,000.00 check that was immediately deposited.

8   Record the purchase of furniture from Pacific Furniture (a new vendor) on 1/27/21 in exchange for a note payable of $6,000.00.

9   Record the payment of principle ($694.00) and interest ($120.00) to Coast Bank on the $18,000.00 note payable on 1/31/21 with check 25503.

10 Record the payment of $1,000.00 in dividends to Shareholders on 1/31/21, check: 25504.

11 Prepare and print the Trial Balance 1/31/2021 report you saved previously. Your report should look like Figure 6.12.

Figure 6.12

Trial Balance as of 1/31/21

Case 4 Student Name (Student ID)

TRIAL BALANCE
As of January 31, 2021

	DEBIT	CREDIT
Checking	28,762.65	
Accounts Receivable (A/R)	22,082.50	
Inventory Asset	8,868.00	
Prepaid Expenses	12,000.00	
Supplies	1,400.00	
Undeposited Funds	0.00	
Buildings:Original cost	35,000.00	
Furniture:Depreciation		10,000.00
Furniture:Original cost	71,000.00	
Machinery & Equipment:Depreciation		6,500.00
Machinery & Equipment:Original cost	115,000.00	
Investments	8,000.00	
Accounts Payable (A/P)		6,800.00
VISA		2,400.00
California State Board of Equalization Payable		339.15
Notes Payable		105,306.00
Common Stock		11,000.00
Opening Balance Equity		0.00
Retained Earnings		114,500.00
Sales		48,400.00
Sales of Product Income		3,570.00
Cost of Goods Sold	1,632.00	
Advertising & Marketing	1,800.00	
Insurance	2,400.00	
Interest Expense	120.00	
Repairs & Maintenance	750.00	
TOTAL	$308,815.15	$308,815.15

12 Investigate differences between your trial balance and the trial balance shown above.

13 If necessary, prepare and print the Transaction Detail by Account report you saved previously to investigate identified differences.

    a. Make sure all your changes were dated in January 2021.

    b. Click on the line that does not match to view the transaction for that account and investigate why your answer differs.

    c. Ask your instructor for assistance.

    d. Be sure your company matches the above since, in the following chapter, you will be adding additional business events.

7

Payroll

Upon completion of this chapter, the student will be able to do the following:

- Add a new employee
- Add payroll-related general ledger accounts
- Pay employees and record payroll expenses and liabilities

Overview

Intuit has provided a Sample Company online to let new users test drive its QBO product. In this chapter, you will open this Sample Company and practice payroll activities in QBO. QBO Payroll is an add-on feature to QBO. You can use a trial version of QBO Payroll, but it only lasts for 30 days. Even though the payroll features available through QBO Payroll are extensive and helpful, they focus on real companies and real-time frames. Thus, this chapter will focus on the creation of new employees, general ledger accounts, and payment to employees without the use of QBO Payroll.

Remember, if you stop in the middle of this work, none of your work will be saved. So, when you return, the same sample company, without your work, will appear. In some parts of the chapter, you will be asked to sign out of the Sample Company and sign back in so the Sample Company is reset to its original state. In the end of chapter work, you will be asked to perform the same tasks completed on the Sample Company on your Student Company. That work, of course, will be saved.

Throughout this text, figures illustrating bills, expenses, checks, purchase orders, and credit card transactions will have the title Account details not Category details and the column title as Account and not Category as shown on your QBO software. Steps will also use the term Account when your QBO software will reflect the use of the term Category. Once again this change took place after this text was completed. See the Preface of this text for a complete discussion of the confusion this change created.

Employees

In this section, you will be adding a new employee to QBO.

To add a new employee to the Sample Company, do the following:

1 Open your Internet browser.

2 Type **https://qbo.intuit.com/redir/testdrive** into your browser's address text box, and press [**Enter**] to view the Sample Company Dashboard.

3 Click **Workers** and then click **Employees** from the navigation bar.

4 Click the **Add an employee** button.

5 Click the **Not right now** button when asked to Turn payroll on.

6 Type **May West** as the employee's name and provide the following address information: **2393 Ridge Place #3, Rancho Mar, CA, 93154**. Type **178** as the Employee ID No. Your screen should look like Figure 7.1.

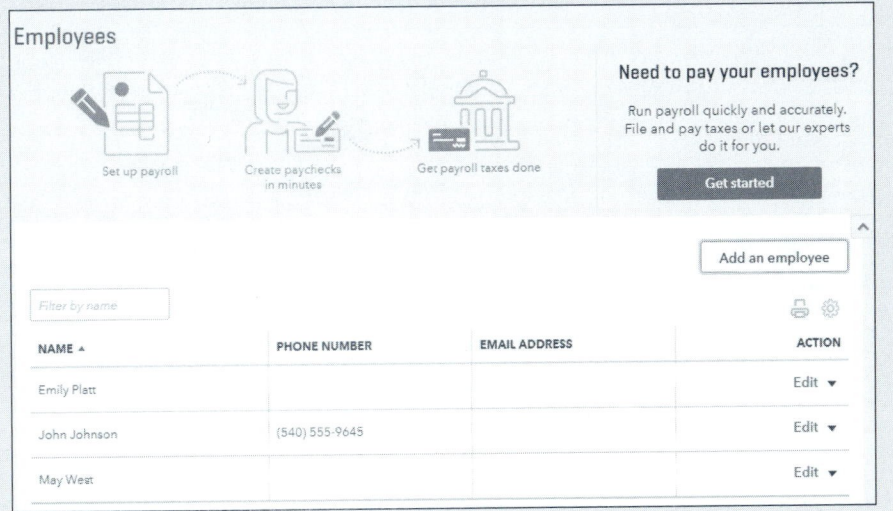

Figure 7.1

Employee Information (adding a new employee)

7 Click **Save**.

8 Your Employee window should now reflect three employees shown in Figure 7.2.

Figure 7.2

Employees

Payroll Accounts

Once again, if you were using QuickBooks Payroll Online, general ledger accounts to capture payroll information would be created for you in the setup process. However, since you are not using QuickBooks Payroll Online, you will have to create them on your own. To keep things simple, you can create the minimum two new accounts for payroll: Payroll (expense) and Payroll Tax Payable (liability).

An employer agrees to pay its employees a salary per month or an hourly rate. In either case, for the agreed upon salary or hourly rate times hours worked, amounts are recorded to the Payroll (expense) account. Depending on the state, employees are often required to have an estimated amount of federal and state income taxes withheld from their paychecks by their employers. In addition, employers must withhold social security (6.2%) and Medicare (1.45%) taxes. Amounts withheld from employees will be recorded in the Payroll Tax Payable (liability) account until remitted to the U.S. Treasury and state government entities. Employers must match those amounts for social security (6.2%) and Medicare (1.45%) taxes. These matching costs will be recorded as additional Payroll expense.

To add payroll-related accounts to the Sample Company, do the following:

1 Continue from where you left off. If you closed the Sample Company, follow the steps to reopen it found at the beginning of this chapter.

2 Click the **Gear** icon and then click **Chart of Accounts**.

3 Click **See your Chart of Accounts** and then click **New**.

4 Select **Expenses** from the drop-down list in the **Account Type** text box.

5 Select **Payroll Expenses** from the drop-down list in the **Detail Type** text box.

6 Type **Payroll** in the Name text box replacing Payroll Expenses as shown in Figure 7.3.

Figure 7.3

Account (adding a new payroll account)

Account

Account Type	*Name
Expenses ▼	Payroll
*Detail Type	Description
Payroll Expenses ▼	

7 Click **Save and New**.

8 Select **Other Current Liabilities** from the drop-down list in the **Account Type** text box.

9 Select **Payroll Tax Payable** from the drop-down list in the **Detail Type** text box.

10 Accept **Payroll Tax Payable** in the **Name** text box.

11 Click **Save and Close**.

You have added two payroll-related general ledger accounts.

Pay Employees

The payment of employees requires gathering information from each employee that helps determine withholding amounts and payroll expenses. The federal and state governments provide formulas and/or tables to help employers calculate these amounts. In this text, you will be provided these amounts. Additional taxes such as training, unemployment, etc., are ignored for this illustration. Since payroll is a recurring event, it will help to make these checks recur, which can be edited for each payroll for changes in hours worked where applicable. In this example payroll is paid semi-monthly.

See Figure 7.4 for a payroll for your Sample Company:

Pay/Tax/Withholding	Emily	John	May	Total
Hours if applicable	n/a	80	60	
Annual salary or hourly rate	$ 60,000	$ 18.00	$ 18.00	
Gross pay	2,500.00	1,440.00	1,080.00	5,020.00
Federal withholding	342.50	197.28	147.96	687.74
Social security employee (6.2%)	155.00	89.28	66.96	311.24
Medicare employee (1.45%)	36.25	20.88	15.66	72.79
Employee withholding	533.75	307.44	230.58	1,071.77
Social security employer (6.2%)	155.00	89.28	66.96	311.24
Medicare company employer (1.45%)	36.25	20.88	15.66	72.79
Employer payroll tax expense	191.25	110.16	82.62	384.03
Net Check amount	1,966.25	1,132.56	849.42	3,948.23

Figure 7.4

Semi-Monthly Payroll Information

To record the payment of employees in the Sample Company, do the following:

1 Continue from where you left off.

2 Click the + icon, and select **Check**.

3   Select **Emily Platt** from the drop-down list (Note: Employees are located at the bottom of the list.) in the **Choose a payee** text box.

4   Accept the given date and check number QBO provides.

5   Select **Payroll** from the drop-down list in Account column of line 1.

6   Type **2,500** in the Amount column of line 1 and press [**Tab**] once.

7   Select **Payroll Tax Payable** from the drop-down list in Account column of line 2.

8   Type **−533.75** in the Amount column of line 1 and press [**Tab**] once. (Be sure to enter this amount as a negative number.)

9   Select **Payroll** from the drop-down list in Account column of line 3.

10 Type **191.25** in the Amount column of line 3 and press [**Tab**] once.

11 Select **Payroll Tax Payable** from the drop-down list in Account column of line 4.

12 Type **−191.25** in the Amount column of line 4 and press [**Tab**] once. (Be sure to enter this amount as a negative number.) Your screen should look like Figure 7.5.

Figure 7.5

Check #71 (paycheck for Emily Platt)

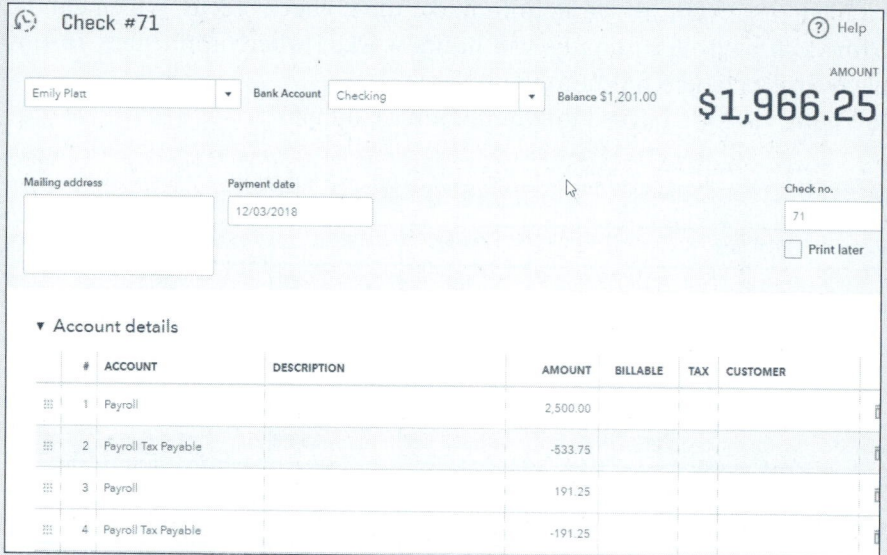

13 Click **Make Recurring** located at the bottom of the screen.

14 Select **Unscheduled** from the drop-down list in the **Type** text box.

15 Click **Save template**.

16 Click the **Gear** icon.

17 Select **Recurring Transactions** located in the List column.

18 Click **Use** located in the Action column of the Emily Platt row. The check window will appear again completed like that shown in Figure 7.5.

19 Make sure the date is correct and then click **Save and New**.

20 Enter payroll information found in Figure 7.4 for John and May in the same way as you entered payroll information for Emily above. Be sure to make each of these unscheduled recurring events.

21 After entering the last check to record payroll above, click **Save and Close**.

22 Click **Reports** from the navigation bar.

23 Type **Trial Balance** in the Find report by name search box and then press [**Enter**] to view a current trial balance, the top of which is shown in Figure 7.6.

Figure 7.6

Trial Balance (partial view)

Craig's Design and Landscaping Services

TRIAL BALANCE
As of December 3, 2018

	DEBIT	CREDIT
Checking		2,747.23
Savings	800.00	
Accounts Receivable (A/R)	5,281.52	
Inventory Asset	596.25	
Undeposited Funds	2,062.52	
Truck:Original Cost	13,495.00	
Accounts Payable (A/P)		1,602.67
Mastercard		157.72
Arizona Dept. of Revenue Pay…		0.00
Board of Equalization Payable		370.94
Loan Payable		4,000.00
Payroll Tax Payable		1,455.80
Notes Payable		25,000.00
Opening Balance Equity	9,337.50	

24 Click the **2,747.23** amount on the Checking line to view a transaction report for the checking account shown in Figure 7.7. Note that this amount represents a credit balance in the account. Remember that this is a sample company created by Intuit and thus the balances may or many not make sense.

Figure 7.7

Transaction Report (checking account)

Craig's Design and Landscaping Services

TRANSACTION REPORT
December 1-3, 2018

DATE	TRANSACTION TYPE	NUM	NAME	MEMO/DESCRIPTION	ACCOUNT	SPLIT	AMOUNT	BALANCE
▾ Checking								
Beginning Balance								1,201.00
12/03/2018	Check	71	Emily Platt		Checking	-Split-	-1,966.25	-765.25
12/03/2018	Check	73	May West		Checking	-Split-	-849.42	-1,614.67
12/03/2018	Check	72	John Johnson		Checking	-Split-	-1,132.56	-2,747.23
Total for Checking							$ -3,948.23	
TOTAL							$ -3,948.23	

25 Match your screen with Figure 7.7, which may be in a different order than yours. (It shows different dates.)

26 Click **John Johnson** to view the payroll check shown in Figure 7.8.

Figure 7.8

Check #72 (John Johnson payroll check)

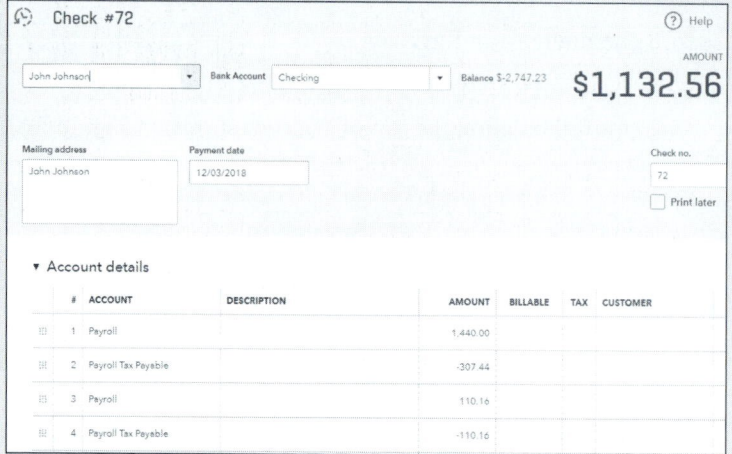

27 Match your screen to Figure 7.8, and close the check window.

28 Click **Back to report summary** to return to the Trial Balance report.

You have recorded payroll for one semi-monthly period. You can practice with another payroll using the recurring transactions you have set up.

29 Click the **Gear** icon, and click **Recurring transactions** located in the Lists column to view a list of recurring transactions shown in Figure 7.9. (If your list does not contain the three employees you recorded, you will need to return to these transactions, and click the Make recurring button.)

Figure 7.9

Recurring Transactions

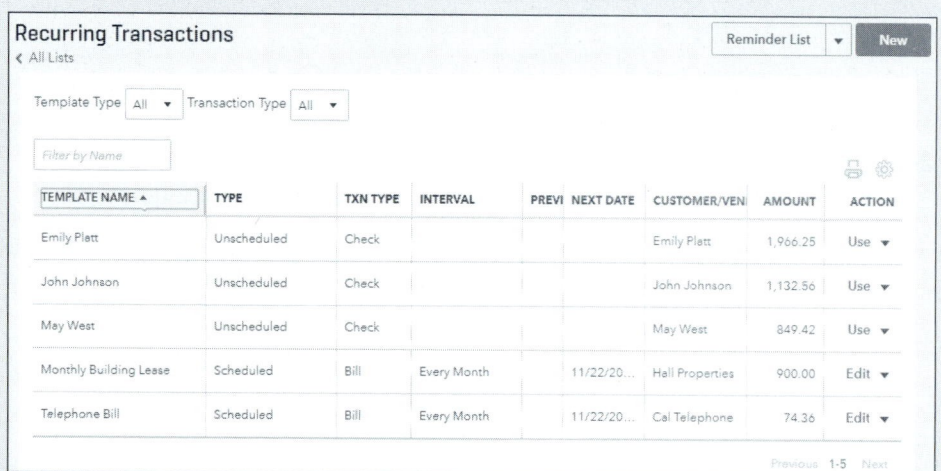

30 Click **Use** on the May West template to view a new payroll check for May.

31 Add 14 days to the **Payment date** text box representing the next semi-monthly period. In this example, the new date is 12/17/18; of course, yours will differ.

32 Payroll information for this next semi-monthly period is shown in Figure 7.10. Note the hours worked are different and John received an increase in his hourly rate.

Pay/Tax/Withholding	Emily	John	May	Total
Hours if applicable	n/a	75	63	
Annual salary or hourly rate	$ 60,000	$ 20.00	$ 18.00	
Gross pay	2,500.00	1,500.00	1,134.00	5,134.00
Federal withholding	342.50	205.50	155.36	703.36
Social security employee (6.2%)	155.00	93.00	70.31	318.31
Medicare employee (1.45%)	36.25	21.75	16.44	74.44
Employee withholding	533.75	320.25	242.11	1,096.11
Social security employer (6.2%)	155.00	93.00	70.31	318.31
Medicare company employer (1.45%)	36.25	21.75	16.44	74.44
Employer payroll tax expense	191.25	114.75	86.75	392.75
Net Check amount	1,966.25	1,179.75	891.89	4,037.89

Figure 7.10

Semi-Monthly Payroll Information

33 Type **1,134** in the Amount column on line 1.

34 Type **−242.11** in the Amount column on line 2.

35 Type **86.75** in the Amount column on line 3.

36 Type **−86.75** in the Amount column on line 4. Your screen should now look like Figure 7.11.

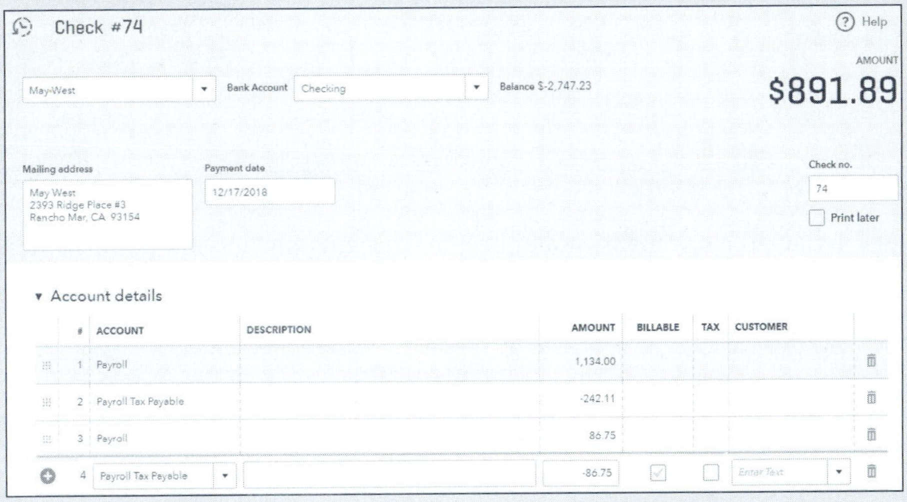

Figure 7.11

Check #74 (May West payroll check)

37 Click **Save and close**.

38 Use the same process (clicking **Use** from the Recurring Transactions list) for John and Emily to record their paychecks based on the new information shown in Figure 7.10. (Since Emily is salaried, her information remains the same each pay period, so nothing needs to be changed from the recurring transaction information provided.) Click **Yes** to accept a duplicate check number if QBO identifies that the check number you are proposing has been used.

39 Click **Reports** from the navigation bar.

40 Type **Trial Balance** in the Find report by name search box, and press [**Enter**].

41 Scroll to the top of the Trial Balance report. Change the To: date in the report to include whatever date you used to enter the most recent semi-monthly payroll. In our example, that date was 12/31/18. Your date will differ. When changed, click **Run report** to see a partial view of the trial balance shown in Figure 7.12.

Figure 7.12

Trial Balance (partial view)

Craig's Design and Landscaping Services
TRIAL BALANCE
As of December 31, 2018

	DEBIT	CREDIT
Checking		6,785.12
Savings	800.00	
Accounts Receivable (A/R)	5,281.52	
Inventory Asset	596.25	
Undeposited Funds	2,062.52	
Truck:Original Cost	13,495.00	
Accounts Payable (A/P)		1,602.67
Mastercard		157.72
Arizona Dept. of Revenue Payable		0.00
Board of Equalization Payable		370.94
Loan Payable		4,000.00
Payroll Tax Payable		2,944.66
Notes Payable		25,000.00
Opening Balance Equity	9,337.50	

42 Click the **6,785.12** amount on the Checking line to view a transaction report for the checking account shown in Figure 7.13.

Figure 7.13

Transaction Report (checking account)

Craig's Design and Landscaping Services
TRANSACTION REPORT
December 2018

DATE	TRANSACTION TYPE	NUM	NAME	MEMO/DESCRIPTION	ACCOUNT	SPLIT	AMOUNT	BALANCE
▾ Checking								
Beginning Balance								1,201.00
12/03/2018	Check	71	Emily Platt		Checking	-Split-	-1,966.25	-765.25
12/03/2018	Check	72	John Johnson		Checking	-Split-	-1,132.56	-1,897.81
12/03/2018	Check	73	May West		Checking	-Split-	-849.42	-2,747.23
12/17/2018	Check	74	May West		Checking	-Split-	-891.89	-3,639.12
12/17/2018	Check	75	John Johnson		Checking	-Split-	-1,179.75	-4,818.87
12/17/2018	Check	76	Emily Platt		Checking	-Split-	-1,966.25	-6,785.12
Total for Checking							$ -7,986.12	
TOTAL							$ -7,986.12	

43 Match your screen with Figure 7.13, which may be in a different order than yours. It will show different dates. Take note of any differences.

44 Click any payroll-related transaction if you want to drill down to the payroll check you recorded to see if you can fix any differences noted.

45 Fix any errors you discover.

46 Sign out of this Sample Company.

You have recorded two semi-monthly payroll checks for the Sample Company. Keep in mind that since you are not using QuickBooks Payroll Online, there are no employee records of earnings or taxes.

End Note

In this chapter, you added a new employee, a new payroll (expense) account, and a new payroll tax payable (liability) account and paid employees. In the next chapter, you will work with budgets and bank reconciliations.

chapter

7

Chapter 7 Questions

1   What are the steps to create a new employee?

2   What are the steps to create a new account?

3   What are the two minimum accounts needed to account for payroll?

4   What types of costs are included in the Payroll (expense) account?

5   What types of costs are included in the Payroll Tax Payable (liability) account?

Chapter 7 Matching

a. 6.2%

b. 1.45%

c. Payroll

d. Payroll tax payable

e. QBO Payroll

f. Gross pay

g. Recurring transactions

h. Transaction report

i. Unscheduled

j. Record as negative amounts

_____   Account used to record the liability for Federal income tax withheld

_____   An add-on feature to QBO

_____   Rate used to calculate an employee's Medicare tax

_____   Hours worked times hourly rate

_____   Use to more efficiently record periodic payroll

_____   Payroll tax payable

_____   Accessed by clicking an amount on the trial balance

_____   One type of recurring event

_____   Account used to record all payroll expenses

_____   Rate used to calculate an employee's social security tax

Chapter 7 Cases

The following cases require you to open the company you updated in Chapter 6. Each of the following cases continues throughout the text in a sequential manner. For example, if you are assigned Case 01, you will use the file you modified in this chapter in all following chapters. Each of the following cases is similar in concepts assessed but differs in amounts and transactions.

To reopen your company, do the following:

1   Open your Internet browser.

2   Type **https://qbo.intuit.com** into your browser's address text box.

3   Type your User ID and Password into the text boxes as you have done before.

Case 1

Now add some payroll activities to your company. Do not install QBO Payroll. Based on what you learned in the text using the Sample Company, you are to make the following changes to the Case 1 company you modified in Chapter 6:

1   Add two new accounts like you did in the chapter: Payroll (expense) and Payroll Tax Payable (liability).

2   Add a new employee: Ben Franklin, 32 Ocean View Lane, La Jolla, CA, 92037, social security number: 556-12-3467.

3   Add a second employee: Betsy Ross, 2323 1st Street, La Jolla, CA, 92037, social security number: 458-87-1974.

4   Payroll is paid twice a month on the 17th and the last day of each month.

5   Record payroll (as you did in the chapter) for 1/17/18 based on the information shown in Figure 7.14. After recording each employee's check, be sure to designate it as a recurring transaction.

Pay/Tax/Withholding	Ben	Betsy	Total
Hours if applicable	n/a	73	
Annual salary or hourly rate	$ 95,000	$ 21.50	
Gross pay	3,958.33	1,569.50	5,527.83
Federal withholding	542.29	215.02	757.31
Social security employee (6.2%)	245.42	97.31	342.73
Medicare employee (1.45%)	57.40	22.76	80.16
Employee withholding	845.11	335.09	1,180.20
Social security employer (6.2%)	245.42	97.31	342.73
Medicare company employer (1.45%)	57.40	22.76	80.16
Employer payroll tax expense	302.82	120.07	422.89
Net Check amount	3,113.22	1,234.41	4,347.63

Figure 7.14

Payroll Information (for 1/17/18)

6   Use the recurring transactions template you created above to help you record payroll (as you did in the chapter) for 1/31/18 based on the information shown in Figure 7.15.

Figure 7.15

Payroll Information (for 1/31/18)

Pay/Tax/Withholding	Ben	Betsy	Total
Hours if applicable	n/a	68	
Annual salary or hourly rate	$ 95,000	$ 21.50	
Gross pay	**3,958.33**	**1,462.00**	**5,420.33**
Federal withholding	542.29	200.29	**742.58**
Social security employee (6.2%)	245.42	90.64	**336.06**
Medicare employee (1.45%)	57.40	21.20	**78.60**
Employee withholding	**845.11**	**312.13**	**1,157.24**
Social security employer (6.2%)	245.42	90.64	**336.06**
Medicare company employer (1.45%)	57.40	21.20	**78.60**
Employer payroll tax expense	**302.82**	**111.84**	**414.66**
Net Check amount	3,113.22	1,149.87	**4,263.09**

7 Open your previously customized report named Trial Balance 1/31/18. Your report should look like Figure 7.16.

Figure 7.16

Trial Balance (as of 1/31/18)

	DEBIT	CREDIT
Checking	26,239.28	
Accounts Receivable	1,030.00	
Inventory Asset	11,800.00	
Prepaid Expenses	8,000.00	
Supplies Asset	375.00	
Undeposited Funds	5,000.00	
Equipment:Original Cost	3,175.00	
Furniture & Fixtures:Depreciation		10,000.00
Furniture & Fixtures:Original cost	40,000.00	
Investments	4,000.00	
Accounts Payable		7,645.00
Visa		1,800.00
Payroll Tax Payable		3,174.99
Notes Payable		66,800.00
Common Stock		21,000.00
Opening Balance Equity		0.00
Retained Earnings		5,000.00
Sales		2,160.00
Services		170.00
Cost of Goods Sold	1,300.00	
Interest Expense	600.00	
Payroll	11,785.71	
Rent or Lease	2,500.00	
Travel	1,800.00	
Utilities	145.00	
TOTAL	$117,749.99	$117,749.99

Handwritten annotations: 1149.87 over (next to Checking); short 3,174.99, 423.97 (next to Payroll Tax Payable / Notes Payable); short 1573.84 (next to Payroll)

8 Create and print a Transaction Report for the Checking account.

9 Create and print a Transaction Report for the Payroll Tax Payable account.

10 If your trial balance differs from the one in Figure 7.16, do the following:

    a. Make sure all of your changes were dated in January 2018.

    b. View the Transaction Reports you created to locate any errors.

    c. Ask your instructor for assistance.

    d. Be sure your company matches the above since, in the following chapter, you will add additional business events.

11 Export your Trial Balance report to Excel, and save it with the file name: Student Name (replace with your name) Ch 07 Case 01 Trial Balance.xlsx.

12 Open and print the custom report you created in the last chapter called Transaction Detail by Account.

13 Export your Transactions Detail by Account report to Excel, and save it with the file name: Student Name (replace with your name) Ch 07 Case 01 Transaction Detail by Account.xlsx.

14 Sign out of your company.

Case 2

Now add some payroll activities to your company. Do not install QBO Payroll. Based on what you learned in the text using the Sample Company, you are to make the following changes to the Case 2 company you modified in Chapter 6:

1 Add two new accounts like you did in the chapter: Payroll (expense) and Payroll Tax Payable (liability).

2 Add a new employee: Frank Benjamin, 32 Ocean View Lane, La Jolla, CA, 92037, social security number: 556-12-3467.

3 Add a second employee: Sara Juarez, 2323 1st Street, La Jolla, CA, 92037, social security number: 458-87-1974.

4 Payroll is paid twice a month on the 16th and the last day of each month.

5 Record payroll (like you did in the chapter) for 1/16/19 based on the information shown in Figure 7.17. After recording each employee's check, be sure to designate it as a recurring transaction.

Figure 7.17

Payroll Information (for 1/16/19)

Pay/Tax/Withholding	Frank	Sara	Total
Hours if applicable	n/a	71	
Annual salary or hourly rate	$ 72,000	$ 18.75	
Gross pay	**3,000.00**	**1,331.25**	**4,331.25**
Federal withholding	411.00	182.38	**593.38**
Social security employee (6.2%)	186.00	82.54	**268.54**
Medicare employee (1.45%)	43.50	19.30	**62.80**
Employee withholding	**640.50**	**284.22**	**924.72**
Social security employer (6.2%)	186.00	82.54	**268.54**
Medicare company employer (1.45%)	43.50	19.30	**62.80**
Employer payroll tax expense	**229.50**	**101.84**	**331.34**
Net Check amount	2,359.50	1,047.03	**3,406.53**

6   Use the recurring transactions template you created above to help you record payroll (as you did in the chapter) for 1/31/19 based on the information shown in Figure 7.18.

Figure 7.18

Payroll Information (for 1/31/19)

Pay/Tax/Withholding	Frank	Sara	Total
Hours if applicable	n/a	66	
Annual salary or hourly rate	$ 72,000	$ 18.75	
Gross pay	**3,000.00**	**1,237.50**	**4,237.50**
Federal withholding	411.00	169.54	**580.54**
Social security employee (6.2%)	186.00	76.73	**262.73**
Medicare employee (1.45%)	43.50	17.94	**61.44**
Employee withholding	**640.50**	**264.21**	**904.71**
Social security employer (6.2%)	186.00	76.73	**262.73**
Medicare company employer (1.45%)	43.50	17.94	**61.44**
Employer payroll tax expense	**229.50**	**94.67**	**324.17**
Net Check amount	2,359.50	973.29	**3,332.79**

7 Open your previously customized report named Trial Balance 1/31/19. Your report should look like Figure 7.19.

Case 2
TRIAL BALANCE
As of January 31, 2019

	DEBIT	CREDIT
Checking	31,860.68	
Accounts Receivable	1,425.00	
Inventory Asset	5,410.00	
Prepaid Expenses	6,800.00	
Supplies Asset	450.00	
Undeposited Funds	925.00	
Furniture:Original Cost	4,875.00	
Machinery & Equipment:Depreciation		1,000.00
Machinery & Equipment:Original cost	10,000.00	
Investments	3,200.00	
Accounts Payable		8,670.00
AMEX		240.00
Payroll Tax Payable		2,484.94
Notes Payable		27,625.00
Common Stock		25,100.00
Opening Balance Equity		0.00
Retained Earnings		7,585.00
Sales		5,700.00
Services		225.00
Cost of Goods Sold	3,020.00	
Advertising	500.00	
Insurance	400.00	
Interest Expense	300.00	
Meals and Entertainment	240.00	
Payroll	9,224.26	
TOTAL	$78,629.94	$78,629.94

Figure 7.19

Trial Balance (as of 1/31/19)

8 Create and print a Transaction Report for the Checking account.

9 Create and print a Transaction Report for the Payroll Tax Payable account.

10 If your trial balance differs from the one in Figure 7.19, do the following:

a. Make sure all of your changes were dated in January 2019.

b. View the Transaction Reports you created to locate any errors.

c. Ask your instructor for assistance.

d. Be sure your company matches the above since, in the following chapter, you will add additional business events.

11 Export your Trial Balance report to Excel, and save it with the file name: Student Name (replace with your name) Ch 07 Case 02 Trial Balance.xlsx.

12 Open and print the custom report you created in the last chapter called Transaction Detail by Account.

13 Export your Transactions Detail by Account report to Excel, and save it with the file name: Student Name (replace with your name) Ch 07 Case 02 Transaction Detail by Account.xlsx.

14 Sign out of your company.

Case 3

Now add some payroll activities to your company. Do not install QBO Payroll. Based on what you learned in the text using the Sample Company, you are to make the following changes to the Case 3 company you modified in Chapter 6:

1 Add two new accounts like you did in the chapter: Payroll (expense) and Payroll Tax Payable (liability).

2 Add a new employee: Kira Jennings, 32 Ocean View Lane, La Jolla, CA, 92037, employee ID number: 556-33-3467.

3 Add a second employee: Jedi Vu, 2323 1st Street, La Jolla, CA, 92037, employee ID number: 458-22-1974.

4 Payroll is paid twice a month on the 16th and the last day of each month.

5 Record payroll (like you did in the chapter) for 1/16/20 based on the information shown in Figure 7.20 using checks 326 and 327. After recording each employee's check, be sure to designate it as a recurring transaction.

Figure 7.20

Payroll Information for 1/16/20

Pay/Tax/Withholding	Kira	Jedi	Total
Hours if applicable	n/a	70	
Annual salary or hourly rate	$ 48,000	$ 17.00	
Gross pay	**2,000.00**	**1,190.00**	**3,190.00**
Federal withholding	274.00	163.03	**437.03**
Social security employee (6.2%)	124.00	73.78	**197.78**
Medicare employee (1.45%)	29.00	17.26	**46.26**
Employee withholding	**427.00**	**254.07**	**681.07**
Social security employer (6.2%)	124.00	73.78	**197.78**
Medicare company employer (1.45%)	29.00	17.26	**46.26**
Employer payroll tax expense	**153.00**	**91.04**	**244.04**
Net Check amount	1,573.00	935.93	**2,508.93**

6 Use the recurring transactions template you created above to help you record payroll (like you did in the chapter) for 1/31/20 based on the information shown in Figure 7.21 using checks 328 and 329.

Pay/Tax/Withholding	Kira	Jedi	Total
Hours if applicable	n/a	75	
Annual salary or hourly rate	$ 48,000	$ 17.00	
Gross pay	**2,000.00**	**1,275.00**	**3,275.00**
Federal withholding	274.00	174.68	**448.68**
Social security employee (6.2%)	124.00	79.05	**203.05**
Medicare employee (1.45%)	29.00	18.49	**47.49**
Employee withholding	**427.00**	**272.22**	**699.22**
Social security employer (6.2%)	124.00	79.05	**203.05**
Medicare company employer (1.45%)	29.00	18.49	**47.49**
Employer payroll tax expense	**153.00**	**97.54**	**250.54**
Net Check amount	1,573.00	1,002.78	**2,575.78**

Figure 7.21

Payroll Information for 1/31/20

7 Open your previously customized report named Trial Balance 1/31/20. Your report should look like Figure 7.22.

Figure 7.22

Trial Balance as of 1/31/20

TRIAL BALANCE
As of January 31, 2020

	DEBIT	CREDIT
Checking	50,768.29	
Accounts Receivable (A/R)	2,610.00	
Inventory Asset	5,700.00	
Prepaid Expenses	6,050.00	
Supplies Asset	327.00	
Undeposited Funds	0.00	
Buildings:Original cost	31,800.00	
Machinery & Equipment:Depreciation		2,000.00
Machinery & Equipment:Original cost	18,000.00	
Investments	5,700.00	
Accounts Payable (A/P)		8,900.00
AMEX		123.00
California State Board of Equalization Payable		675.00
Payroll Tax Payable		1,874.87
Notes Payable		63,800.00
Common Stock		40,000.00
Opening Balance Equity		0.00
Owner's Equity		10,075.00
Sales of Product Income		6,750.00
Services		240.00
Cost of Goods Sold	4,500.00	
Advertising & Marketing	1,300.00	
Insurance	300.00	
Interest Paid	300.00	
Meals & Entertainment	123.00	
Payroll	6,959.58	
TOTAL	$134,437.87	$134,437.87

8 Create and print a Transaction Report for the Checking account.

9 Create and print a Transaction Report for the Payroll Tax Payable account.

10 If your trial balance is different than Figure 7.22:

    a. Make sure that all of your changes were dated in January 2020.

    b. View the Transaction Reports you just created to locate any errors.

    c. Ask your instructor for assistance.

    d. Be sure your company matches the above as in the following chapter you'll be adding additional business events.

11 Export your Trial Balance report to Excel and save it with the file name: Student Name (replace with your name) Ch 07 Case 03 Trial Balance.xlsx.

12 Open and print the customized report you created in the last chapter called Transaction Detail by Account.

13 Export your Transactions Detail by Account report to Excel and save it with the file name: Student Name (replace with your name) Ch 07 Case 03 Transaction Detail by Account.xlsx.

14 Sign out of your company.

Case 4

Now add some payroll activities to your company. Do not install QBO Payroll. Based on what you learned in the text using the Sample Company, you are to make the following changes to the Case 4 company you modified in Chapter 6:

1   Add two new accounts like you did in the chapter: Payroll (expense) and Payroll Tax Payable (liability).

2   Add a new employee: Graham O'Leary.

3   Add additional employees: Allegra Munoz and Beckett Yamamomo.

4   Payroll is paid twice a month on the 15th and the last day of each month.

5   Record payroll (like you did in the chapter) for 1/15/21 based on the information shown in Figure 7.23. After recording each employee's check, be sure to designate it as a recurring transaction.

Pay/Tax/Withholding	Graham	Allegra	Beckett	Total
Hours if applicable	n/a	75	83	
Annual salary or hourly rate	$ 75,000	$ 25.00	$ 22.00	
Gross pay	**3,125.00**	**1,875.00**	**1,826.00**	**6,826.00**
Federal withholding	428.13	256.88	250.16	**935.16**
Social security employee (6.2%)	193.75	116.25	113.21	**423.21**
Medicare employee (1.45%)	45.31	27.19	26.48	**98.98**
Employee withholding	**667.19**	**400.31**	**389.85**	**1,457.35**
Social security employer (6.2%)	193.75	116.25	113.21	**423.21**
Medicare company employer (1.45%)	45.34	27.19	26.48	**99.01**
Employer payroll tax expense	**239.09**	**143.44**	**139.69**	**522.22**
Net Check amount	2,457.81	1,474.68	1,436.15	**5,368.64**

Figure 7.23

Payroll Information for 1/15/21

6   Use the recurring transactions template you created above to help you record payroll (as you did in the chapter) for 1/31/21 based on the information shown in Figure 7.24.

Figure 7.24

Payroll Information for 1/31/21

Pay/Tax/Withholding	Graham	Allegra	Beckett	Total
Hours if applicable	n/a	70	88	
Annual salary or hourly rate	$ 75,000	$ 25.00	$ 22.00	
Gross pay	**3,125.00**	**1,750.00**	**1,936.00**	**6,811.00**
Federal withholding	428.13	239.75	265.23	**933.11**
Social security employee (6.2%)	193.75	108.50	120.03	**422.28**
Medicare employee (1.45%)	45.31	25.38	28.07	**98.76**
Employee withholding	**667.19**	**373.63**	**413.34**	**1,454.15**
Social security employer (6.2%)	193.75	108.50	120.03	**422.28**
Medicare company employer (1.45%)	45.34	25.38	28.07	**98.79**
Employer payroll tax expense	**239.09**	**133.88**	**148.10**	**521.07**
Net Check amount	2,457.81	1,376.37	1,522.67	**5,356.85**

7   Prepare and print the Trial Balance 1/31/21 report you saved previously. Your report should look like Figure 7.25.

Case 4 Student Name (Student ID)

TRIAL BALANCE
As of January 31, 2021

	DEBIT	CREDIT
Checking	18,037.16	
Accounts Receivable (A/R)	22,082.50	
Inventory Asset	8,868.00	
Prepaid Expenses	12,000.00	
Supplies	1,400.00	
Undeposited Funds	0.00	
Buildings:Original cost	35,000.00	
Furniture:Depreciation		10,000.00
Furniture:Original cost	71,000.00	
Machinery & Equipment:Depreciation		6,500.00
Machinery & Equipment:Original cost	115,000.00	
Investments	8,000.00	
Accounts Payable (A/P)		6,800.00
VISA		2,400.00
California State Board of Equalization ...		339.15
Payroll Tax Payable		3,954.80
Notes Payable		105,306.00
Common Stock		11,000.00
Opening Balance Equity		0.00
Retained Earnings		114,500.00
Sales		48,400.00
Sales of Product Income		3,570.00
Cost of Goods Sold	1,632.00	
Advertising & Marketing	1,800.00	
Insurance	2,400.00	
Interest Expense	120.00	
Payroll	14,680.29	
Repairs & Maintenance	750.00	
TOTAL	$312,769.95	$312,769.95

Figure 7.25

Trial Balance as of 1/31/21

8   Investigate differences between your trial balance and the trial balance shown above.

9   If necessary, prepare and print the Transaction Detail by Account report you saved previously to investigate identified differences.

   a.   Make sure all your changes were dated in January 2021.

   b.   Click on the line that does not match to view the transaction for that account and investigate why your answer differs.

   c.   Ask your instructor for assistance.

   d.   Be sure your company matches the above since, in the following chapter, you will be adding additional business events.

Budgets and Bank Reconciliations

Student Learning Outcomes

Upon completion of this chapter, the student will be able to do the following:

- Add budget amounts to create a budget
- Create Profit and Loss budget reports
- Reconcile a checking account and print a reconciliation report

Overview

Intuit has provided a sample company online to provide new users a test drive of its QBO product. In this chapter, you will open this sample company and practice budget activities in QBO and reconcile a bank account. Budgets and bank reconciliations provide internal control over business activities. Significant deviations between actual and budget amounts could identify and help resolve problems. Unexplained differences identified in bank reconciliations can point to possible fraud or incompetency issues.

Remember, if you stop in the middle of this work none of your work will be saved. So, when you return, the same sample company, without your work, will appear. In some parts of the chapter, you will be asked to sign out of the Sample Company and then sign back in so the Sample Company is reset to its original state. In the end of chapter work, you will be asked to perform the same tasks completed on the Sample Company on your Student Company. That work, of course, will be saved.

Throughout this text, figures illustrating bills, expenses, checks, purchase orders, and credit card transactions will have the title Account details not Category details and the column title as Account and not Category as shown on your QBO software. Steps will also use the term Account when your QBO software will reflect the use of the term Category. Once again this change took place after this text was completed. See the Preface of this text for a complete discussion of the confusion this change created.

Budget Creation

In this section, you will be establishing a Profit and Loss budget in QBO, which tracks amounts in income and expense accounts. QBO will interview you to determine budget amounts. You will be creating your budget from scratch since you have no historical amounts in QBO.

To create a Profit and Loss budget for the Sample Company, do the following:

1 Open your Internet browser.

2 Type **https://qbo.intuit.com/redir/testdrive** into your browser's address text box, and press [**Enter**] to view the Sample Company Dashboard.

3 Click the **Gear** icon, and select **Budgeting** shown in Figure 8.1.

Figure 8.1

Budgeting window (accessing the budgeting process)

Craig's Design and Landscaping Services

Your Company	Lists	Tools
Account and Settings	All Lists	Import Data
Manage Users	Products and Services	Export Data
Custom Form Styles	Recurring Transactions	Reconcile
Chart of Accounts	Attachments	**Budgeting**
QuickBooks Labs		Audit Log
		Order Checks ↗
		SmartLook

4 Click **Add budget**. Read page 1 of the Creating a budget instructions, if it is presented and then click **Next**.

5 Leave the default fiscal year provided, and type **Budget 1** as the Budget name. (The default fiscal year will change based on the date you use for the Sample Company. Thus, the dates in QBO will not match the dates shown in the text figures for the Sample Company.)

6 Click **Next**.

7 Click in the **Design income** account, which will activate the Edit – Design income section of the worksheet.

8 Type **3,000** in the Jan: text box, then place your cursor over the **Copy Across** button as shown in Figure 8.2.

Figure 8.2

Profit and Loss (budget worksheet)

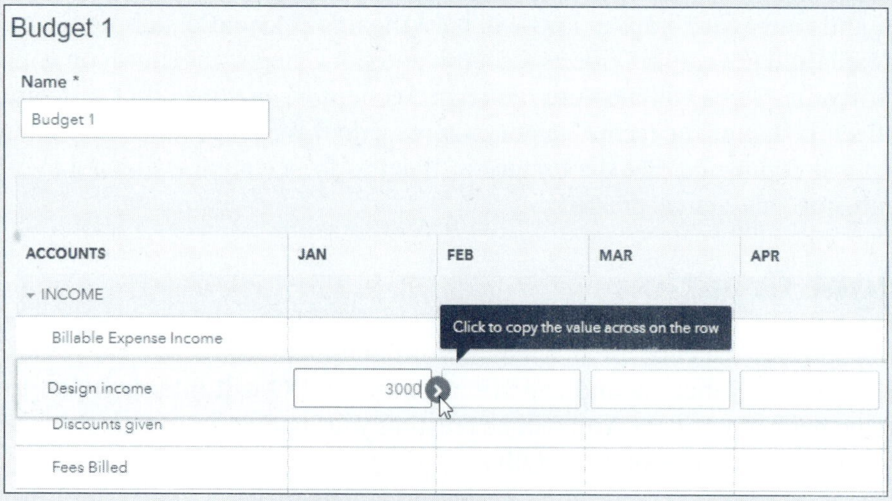

Budget 1

Name *

Budget 1

ACCOUNTS	JAN	FEB	MAR	APR
▾ INCOME				
Billable Expense Income				
Design income	3000 ⟩			
Discounts given				
Fees Billed				

Click to copy the value across on the row

9 Click the **Copy Across** button to view Figure 8.3.

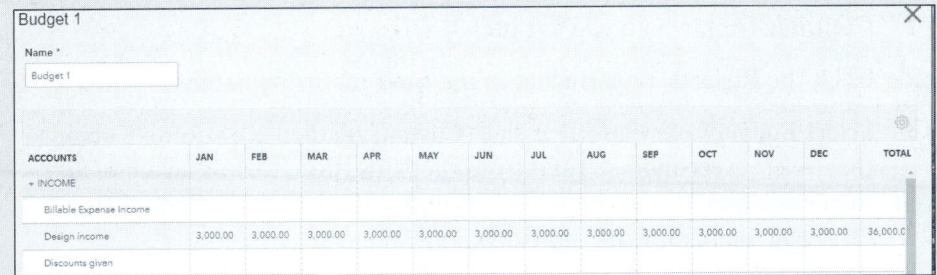

Figure 8.3

Profit and Loss (design income budget amounts)

10 Scroll down the budget worksheet as needed to enter the amounts shown in Figure 8.4.

ACCOUNTS	JAN	FEB	MAR	APR	MAY	JUN	JUL	AUG	SEP	OCT	NOV	DEC	TOTAL
▾ Landscaping Services													
▾ Job Materials													
Decks and Patios													
Fountains and Garden Ligh..	2,000.00	2,000.00	2,000.00	2,000.00	2,000.00	2,000.00	2,000.00	2,000.00	2,000.00	2,000.00	2,000.00	2,000.00	24,000.0
Plants and Soil	2,000.00	2,000.00	2,000.00	2,000.00	2,000.00	2,000.00	2,000.00	2,000.00	2,000.00	2,000.00	2,000.00	2,000.00	24,000.0
Sprinklers and Drip Systems	500.00	500.00	500.00	500.00	500.00	500.00	500.00	500.00	500.00	500.00	500.00	500.00	6,000.0
Total Job Materials	4,500.00	4,500.00	4,500.00	4,500.00	4,500.00	4,500.00	4,500.00	4,500.00	4,500.00	4,500.00	4,500.00	4,500.00	54,000.0
▾ Labor													
Installation	300.00	300.00	300.00	300.00	300.00	300.00	300.00	300.00	300.00	300.00	300.00	300.00	3,600.0
Maintenance and Repair	50.00	50.00	50.00	50.00	50.00	50.00	50.00	50.00	50.00	50.00	50.00	50.00	600.0
Total Labor	350.00	350.00	350.00	350.00	350.00	350.00	350.00	350.00	350.00	350.00	350.00	350.00	4,200.0
Total Landscaping Services	4,850.00	4,850.00	4,850.00	4,850.00	4,850.00	4,850.00	4,850.00	4,850.00	4,850.00	4,850.00	4,850.00	4,850.00	58,200.0
Other Income													
Pest Control Services	100.00	100.00	100.00	100.00	100.00	100.00	100.00	100.00	100.00	100.00	100.00	100.00	1,200.0
Refunds-Allowances													
Sales of Product Income	1,000.00	1,000.00	1,000.00	1,000.00	1,000.00	1,000.00	1,000.00	1,000.00	1,000.00	1,000.00	1,000.00	1,000.00	12,000.0
Services	400.00	400.00	400.00	400.00	400.00	400.00	400.00	400.00	400.00	400.00	400.00	400.00	4,800.0

Figure 8.4

Profit and Loss (budget worksheet)

11 After entering the above amounts, click **Save**. (This needs to be done even though you are not finished so QBO doesn't time out and make you start again.)

12 Scroll down the budget worksheet, and add additional <u>monthly</u> amounts for cost of goods sold: **400**, advertising: **100**, automobile: **500**, equipment rental: **100**, insurance: **250**, job expenses: **1,000**, legal and professional: **950**, maintenance and repair: **900**, rent or lease: **800**, utilities: **500**, Miscellaneous: **3,000**.

13 Click **Save and close**.

You have entered budgeted amounts and stored them in QBO. Now, view budget reports.

Budget Reports

QBO has two basic budget-related reports: Budget Overview and Budget vs. Actual. The overview report only lists budget data. The Budget vs. Actual lists budget data compared to actual transactions inputted into QBO.

To view budget reports in the Sample Company, do the following:

1 Continue from where you left off.

2 Click the **Reports**, type **Budget** in the Find report by name text box.

3 Select **Budget Overview**, then click **Customize**, then click **Rows/Columns**, then select **Accounts vs. Total** from the Show Grid drop-down list, and then click **Run Report**. Now click **Collapse** to view the collapsed Budget Overview report for the year shown in Figure 8.5.

Figure 8.5

Budget Overview (collapsed report)

Craig's Design and Landscaping Services	
BUDGET OVERVIEW: BUDGET 1 - FY18 P&L	
January - December 2018	
	TOTAL
▾ Income	
Design income	36,000.00
Landscaping Services	58,200.00
Pest Control Services	1,200.00
Sales of Product Income	12,000.00
Services	4,800.00
Total Income	**$112,200.00**
▾ Cost of Goods Sold	
Cost of Goods Sold	4,800.00
Total Cost of Goods Sold	**$4,800.00**
GROSS PROFIT	**$107,400.00**
▾ Expenses	
Advertising	1,200.00
Automobile	6,000.00
Equipment Rental	1,200.00
Insurance	3,000.00
Job Expenses	12,000.00
Legal & Professional Fees	11,400.00
Maintenance and Repair	10,800.00
Rent or Lease	9,600.00
Utilities	6,000.00
Total Expenses	**$61,200.00**
NET OPERATING INCOME	**$46,200.00**
▾ Other Expenses	
Miscellaneous	36,000.00
Total Other Expenses	**$36,000.00**
NET OTHER INCOME	**$ -36,000.00**
NET INCOME	**$10,200.00**

4 Click **Customize** to modify the Budget Overview report.

5 Change the From: and To: dates to the current month and year (In this case, the new From: is 12/01/2018 and the new To: is 12/31/2018. If your current system date, today's date, is, for example, 10/8/2019, you would change the From: to 10/1/2019 and the To: to 10/31/2019.)

6 Check the **Without Cents** check box as shown in Figure 8.6.

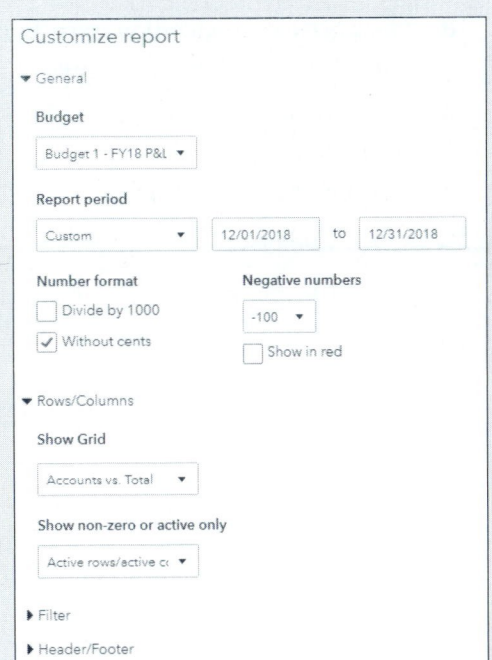

Figure 8.6

Customizing Budget Overview

7 Click **Run Report** to view the customized **Budget Overview** report shown in Figure 8.7.

Figure 8.7

Budget Overview (customized report)

Craig's Design and Landscaping Services	
BUDGET OVERVIEW: BUDGET 1 - FY18 P&L	
December 2018	

	TOTAL
▾ Income	
Design income	3,000
Landscaping Services	4,850
Pest Control Services	100
Sales of Product Income	1,000
Services	400
Total Income	**$9,350**
▾ Cost of Goods Sold	
Cost of Goods Sold	400
Total Cost of Goods Sold	**$400**
GROSS PROFIT	**$8,950**
▾ Expenses	
Advertising	100
Automobile	500
Equipment Rental	100
Insurance	250
Job Expenses	1,000
Legal & Professional Fees	950
Maintenance and Repair	900
Rent or Lease	800
Utilities	500
Total Expenses	**$5,100**
NET OPERATING INCOME	**$3,850**
▾ Other Expenses	
Miscellaneous	3,000
Total Other Expenses	**$3,000**
NET OTHER INCOME	**$ -3,000**
NET INCOME	**$850**

8 Click **Save customization**, type **Budget Overview** in the Custom report name text box then click **Save**.

9 Click **Reports**, then once again type **Budget** into the Find report by name text box, and then select **Budget vs. Actuals** from the list of recommended reports.

10 Click **Collapse**.

11 Click **Customize** to modify the Budget vs. Actuals report.

12 Change the From: and To: dates to the current month and year. (In this case, the new From: is 12/01/2018 and the new To: is 12/31/2018. If your current system date, today's date, is, for example, 10/8/2019, you would change the From: to 10/01/2019 and the To: to 10/31/2019.)

13 Click **Rows/Columns** and then select **Accounts vs. Total** in the drop-down list in the Show Grid text box and then check the **Without Cents** check box as shown in Figure 8.8.

Figure 8.8

Customizing Budget vs. Actuals

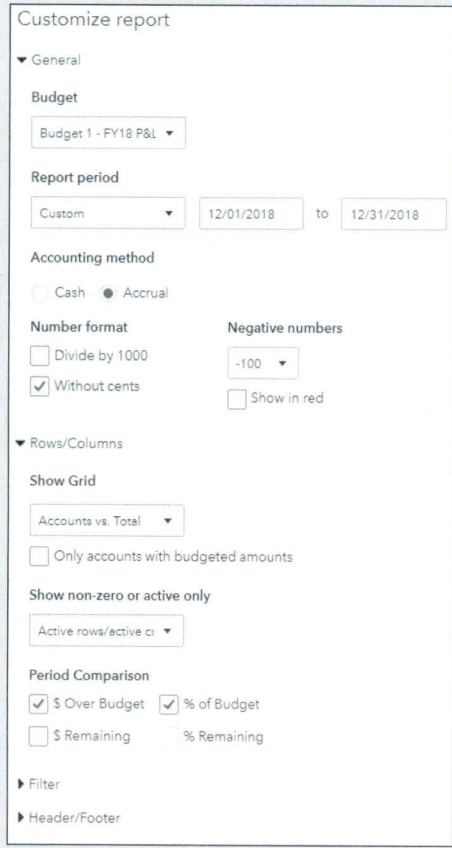

14 Click **Run Report**. A partial view of the customized Budget vs. Actuals report is shown in Figure 8.9. Note: Your budget amounts should match this figure but your actual amounts will be different since the actual data changes based on when you are using the Sample Company.

Figure 8.9

Budget vs. Actual report

Craig's Design and Landscaping Services

BUDGET VS. ACTUALS: BUDGET 1 - FY18 P&L

December 2018

	ACTUAL	BUDGET	OVER BUDGET	% OF BUDGET
▾ Income				
Design income		3,000	-3,000	
Landscaping Services		4,850	-4,850	
Pest Control Services		100	-100	
Sales of Product Income		1,000	-1,000	
Services		400	-400	
Total Income	$0	$9,350	$ -9,350	0%
▾ Cost of Goods Sold				
Cost of Goods Sold		400	-400	
Total Cost of Goods Sold	$0	$400	$ -400	0%
GROSS PROFIT	$0	$8,950	$ -8,950	0%
▾ Expenses				
Advertising		100	-100	
Automobile	34	500	-466	7.00 %
Equipment Rental		100	-100	
Insurance		250	-250	
Job Expenses		1,000	-1,000	
Legal & Professional Fees		950	-950	
Maintenance and Repair		900	-900	
Rent or Lease		800	-800	
Utilities		500	-500	
Total Expenses	$34	$5,100	$ -5,066	1.00 %
NET OPERATING INCOME	$ -34	$3,850	$ -3,884	-1.00 %
▾ Other Expenses				
Miscellaneous		3,000	-3,000	
Total Other Expenses	$0	$3,000	$ -3,000	0%
NET OTHER INCOME	$0	$ -3,000	$3,000	0.00 %
NET INCOME	$ -34	$850	$ -884	-4.00 %

15 Click **Save customization**, type **Budget vs. Actuals** in the Custom report name text box, and then click **Save**.

16 Sign out of the Sample Company.

Bank Reconciliation

Good internal control requires frequent reconciliations between bank records and a company's records of cash receipts and payments completed by someone other than the accountant or bookkeeper who is responsible for maintaining accounting records. The process involves comparing items that appear in the checking account with those items appearing on the bank statement. Deposits that appear in the checking account but do not appear on the bank statement are referred to as deposits in transit. Checks that appear in the checking account but do not appear on the bank statement are referred to as outstanding checks. They usually appear as checks on the next bank statement.

In QBO, if you discover a deposit recorded by the bank but not recorded in the checking account (determined to be an error in the checking account), you should correct the checking account by recording the deposit. Likewise, if you discover a check recorded by the bank but not recorded in the checking account (determined to be an error in the checking account), you should correct the checking account by recording the check. In the following example, neither was identified.

To create reconciliation for the Sample Company, do the following:

1   Open your Internet browser.

2   Type **https://qbo.intuit.com/redir/testdrive** into your browser's address text box, and press [**Enter**] to view the Sample Company Dashboard.

3   Click the **Gear** icon, and select **Reconcile** as shown in Figure 8.10.

Figure 8.10

Reconciliation process (access)

4   Click **Reconcile an account**, then click **Maybe later**, and then make sure the **Checking** account is selected in the Reconcile window shown in Figure 8.11.

Figure 8.11

Reconcile window

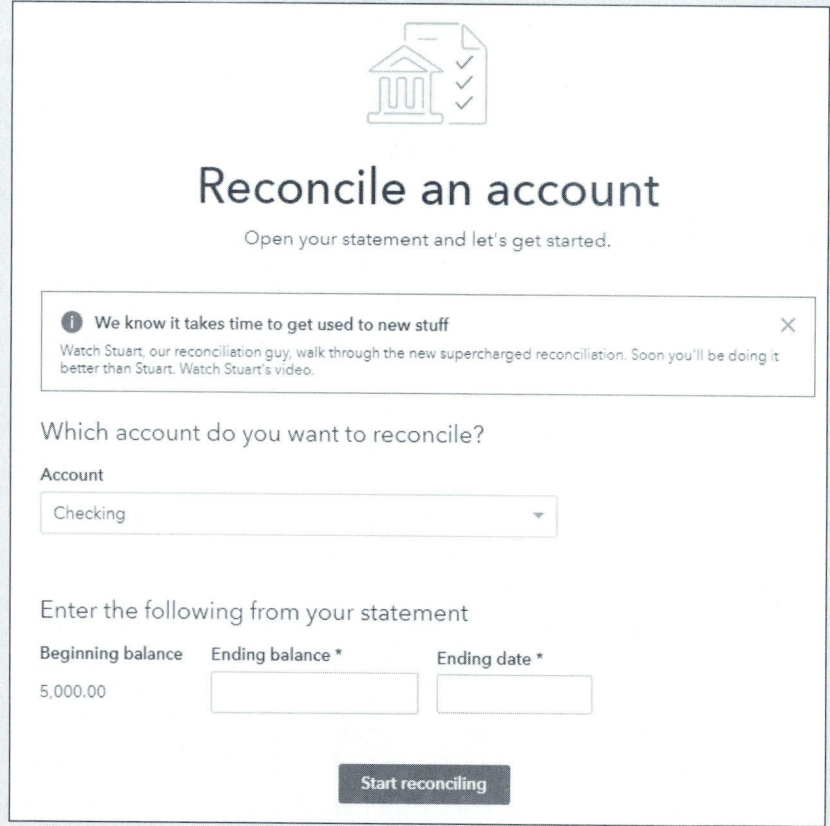

5 Type the last day of the month prior to your current system date as the Statement Ending date, and type **1,026.41** as the Ending Balance. Your date will differ than the figure shown below depending on your current system date.

6 Click **Start reconciling**.

7 The Reconcile – Checking form shown in Figure 8.12 should appear. Note: The column widths in this figure have been adjusted.

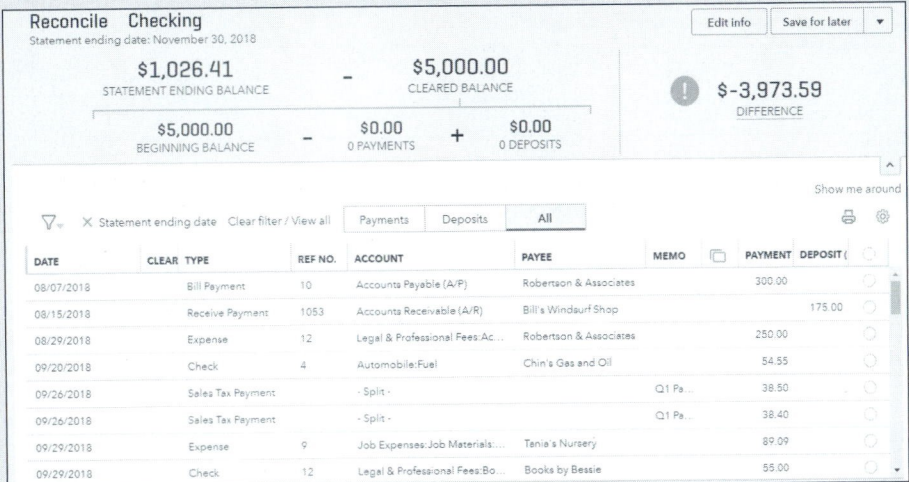

Figure 8.12

Partial View of the Reconcile – Checking form

8 After a review of the company's most recent bank statement and a comparison with the company's checking account, you discover some checks and payments recorded in the checking account that did not appear on the bank statement. Click the **Payments** tab. Place a check next to all checks and payments <u>except</u> for check **13** to Hicks Hardware for 215.66, check **75** to Hicks Hardware for 228.75, and check **76** to Pam Seitz for 75.00, none of which had cleared the bank.

9 After a review of the company's most recent bank statement and a comparison with the company's checking account, you discover some deposits and other credits recorded in the checking account that did not appear on the bank statement. Click the **Deposits** tab. Place a check next to all deposits and other credits <u>except</u> for payment **1886** from Cool Cars for 694.00 which had not cleared the bank.

10 Click the **All** tab. Your account is reconciled as shown by the 0.00 difference between the Statement Ending Balance and the Cleared Balance. Scroll down the listing of payments and deposits until a Bill Payment ref no 11 is located and the top of the payments and deposits listing as shown in Figure 8.13. Be sure all the items referenced in the above steps (checks and payments as well as deposits and other credits) are properly checked or unchecked. Note the two items shown on your screen (a deposit of $694.00 and a payment of $215.66) and shown in the figure below are unchecked.

Figure 8.13

Reconcile – Checking form
(reconciled account)

11 Once you have reconciled the checking account and the $0.00 difference is displayed, click **Finish Now** and then click **Done**.

12 Click the text **History by account**. A summary of all reconciliation reports completed should appear shown in Figure 8.14.

Figure 8.14

Reconcile (reconciliation summary)

History by account   Summary | Reconcile | Sh

Account		Report period				
Checking ▼		Since 365 Days Ago ▼				
STATEMENT ENDING ...	RECONCILED ON	ENDING BALANCE		CHANGES	AUTO ADJUSTMENT	ACTION
2018						
11/30/2018	12/05/2018	1,026.41		0.00		View report ▼

13 Click **View report** to view the reconciliation report. The upper summary portion of that report is shown in Figure 8.15.

Figure 8.15

Summary Reconciliation Report

Craig's Design and Landscaping Services
Checking, Period Ending 11/30/2018

RECONCILIATION REPORT

Reconciled on: 12/05/2018

Reconciled by: Craig Carlson

Any changes made to transactions after this date aren't included in this report.

Summary	USD
Statement beginning balance	5,000.00
Checks and payments cleared (29)	-6,550.94
Deposits and other credits cleared (10)	2,577.35
Statement ending balance	1,026.41
Uncleared transactions as of 11/30/2018	174.59
Register balance as of 11/30/2018	1,201.00

14 Click the **Printer** icon, click **Print**, and click **Close** to print the report and close its window.

15 Sign out of the Sample Company.

End Note

In this chapter, you created a Profit and Loss budget for 12 months, prepared a Budget Overview report and Budget vs. Actual report, and reconciled your checking account. In the next chapter, you will work with adjusting journal entries.

Chapter 8 Questions

1 What are the steps to create a Profit and Loss budget?

2 What value do budgets provide a business?

3 Why should a business reconcile a checking account?

4 Who should prepare a bank reconciliation?

5 Explain the difference between the Budget Overview report and the Budget vs. Actual report.

6 What button is used to replicate amounts across several months in the budget worksheet?

7 How do you know if you have correctly reconciled an account?

8 What are the steps to change a Budget Overview report from covering a year to covering just one month?

9 What should you do if you discover a deposit was recorded by the bank but not recorded in the checking account (determined to be an error in the checking account)?

10 What are the initial steps to begin a bank reconciliation?

Chapter 8 Matching

a. Budget Overview report   _____   Condenses a report

b. Budget vs. Actual report   _____   Do not appear on the bank statement

c. Deposits in transit   _____   Used to change report dates

d. Outstanding checks   _____   Includes only budget amounts

e. Collapse   _____   Usually appear as checks on the next bank statement

f. Customize   _____   Includes both budget and actual amounts

Chapter 8 Cases

The following cases require you to open the company you updated in Chapter 7. Each of the following cases continues throughout the text in a sequential manner. For example, if you are assigned Case 01, you will use the file you modified in this chapter in all following chapters. Each of the following cases is similar in concepts assessed but differs in amounts and transactions.

To reopen your company, do the following:

1 Open your Internet browser.

2 Type **https://qbo.intuit.com** into your browser's address text box.

3 Type your User ID and Password into the text boxes as you have done before.

Case 1

Now it is time to create a budget and reconcile a bank account. Based on what you learned in the text using the Sample Company, you are to make the following changes to the Case 1 company you modified in Chapter 7:

✓ 1   Add an invoice on 1/30/18 to customer: Blondie's Boards, terms: Net 30, for 4 Fred Rubbles, 7 Water Hogs, and 8 Rook 15 surfboards.

✓ 2   Add an invoice on 1/31/18 to a new customer: Surf Rider Foundation, terms: Net 30, for 100 hours of consulting.

3   Create a new budget titled "Budget 1." Be sure to select FY 2018 (Jan 2018–Dec 2018) from the Fiscal Year drop-down list in the new budget window. Enter the following budgeted amounts: sales: 40,000, services: 3,000, cost of goods sold: 23,500, interest expense: 600, payroll: 12,000, rent or lease: 2500, travel: 500, utilities: 200. Amounts provided should be input for each month of 2018.

4   Create and customize, save customization as Budget Overview Budget 1, print, and export to Excel a Budget Overview report for the month of January 2018. Your report should look like Figure 8.16.

Figure 8.16

Budget Overview (January 2018)

Case 1 BUDGET OVERVIEW: BUDGET 1 - FY18 P&L January 2018	
	TOTAL
Income	
Sales	40,000.00
Services	3,000.00
Total Income	**$43,000.00**
Cost of Goods Sold	
Cost of Goods Sold	23,500.00
Total Cost of Goods Sold	**$23,500.00**
Gross Profit	**$19,500.00**
Expenses	
Interest Expense	600.00
Payroll	12,000.00
Rent or Lease	2,500.00
Travel	500.00
Utilities	200.00
Total Expenses	**$15,800.00**
Net Operating Income	**$3,700.00**
Net Income	**$3,700.00**

5   Create and customize, save customization as Budget vs. Actual Budget 1, print, and export to Excel a Budget vs. Actuals report for the month of January 2018. Your report should look like Figure 8.17.

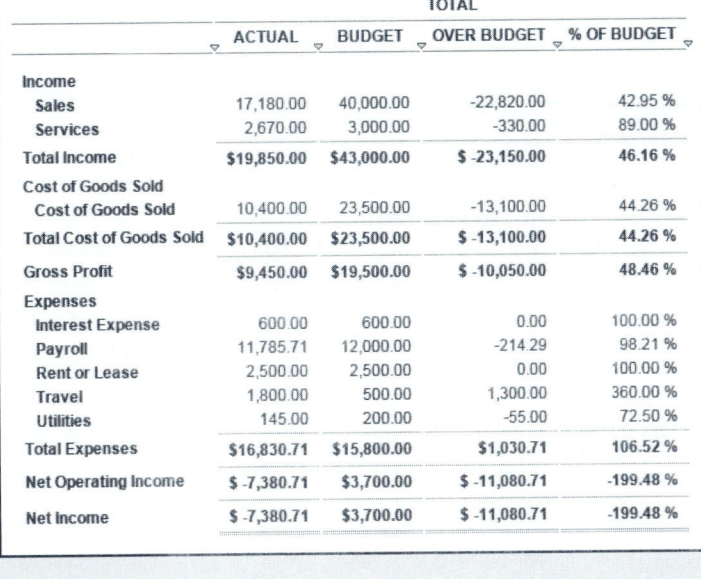

Figure 8.17

Budget vs. Actuals (January 2018)

Case 1
BUDGET VS. ACTUALS: BUDGET 1 - FY18 P&L
January 2018

	TOTAL			
	ACTUAL	BUDGET	OVER BUDGET	% OF BUDGET
Income				
Sales	17,180.00	40,000.00	-22,820.00	42.95 %
Services	2,670.00	3,000.00	-330.00	89.00 %
Total Income	**$19,850.00**	**$43,000.00**	**$ -23,150.00**	**46.16 %**
Cost of Goods Sold				
Cost of Goods Sold	10,400.00	23,500.00	-13,100.00	44.26 %
Total Cost of Goods Sold	**$10,400.00**	**$23,500.00**	**$ -13,100.00**	**44.26 %**
Gross Profit	**$9,450.00**	**$19,500.00**	**$ -10,050.00**	**48.46 %**
Expenses				
Interest Expense	600.00	600.00	0.00	100.00 %
Payroll	11,785.71	12,000.00	-214.29	98.21 %
Rent or Lease	2,500.00	2,500.00	0.00	100.00 %
Travel	1,800.00	500.00	1,300.00	360.00 %
Utilities	145.00	200.00	-55.00	72.50 %
Total Expenses	**$16,830.71**	**$15,800.00**	**$1,030.71**	**106.52 %**
Net Operating Income	**$ -7,380.71**	**$3,700.00**	**$ -11,080.71**	**-199.48 %**
Net Income	**$ -7,380.71**	**$3,700.00**	**$ -11,080.71**	**-199.48 %**

6 Open and print the custom report you created in the last chapter called Transaction Detail by Account.

7 Export your Transactions Detail by Account report to Excel and save it with the file name: Student Name (replace with your name) Ch 08 Case 01 Transaction Detail by Account.xlsx.

8 Reconcile your company's checking account. No services charges were incurred or interest earned. The ending bank statement balance on 1/31/18 was $29,202.37.

9 After a review of the company's most recent bank statement and a comparison with the company's checking account, you discover some checks and payments recorded in the checking account that did not appear on the bank statement. Place a check next to all checks and payments <u>except</u> for check 1009 to Ben Franklin for 3,113.22 and check 1010 to Betsy Ross for 1,149.87, neither of which had cleared the bank.

10 After a review of the company's most recent bank statement and a comparison with the company's checking account, you discover some deposits and other credits recorded in the checking account that did not appear on the bank statement. Place a check next to all deposits and other credits <u>except</u> for a deposit on 1/8/18 from Blondie's Boards for 1,300.00, which had not cleared the bank.

11 Print the resulting Reconciliation Report.

12 Sign out of your company.

Case 2

Now it is time to create a budget and reconcile a bank account. Based on what you learned in the text using the Sample Company, you are to make the following changes to the Case 2 company you modified in Chapter 7:

1   Add an invoice on 1/30/19 to customer: Hagen's Toys, terms: Net 30, for 100 hours of custom painting.

2   Add an invoice on 1/31/19 to a new customer: Zack's RC, terms: Net 30, for 2 Seawind Carbon Sailboats and 2 Mystique RES.

3   Create a new budget titled "Budget 1." Be sure to select FY 2019 (Jan 2019–Dec 2019) from the Fiscal Year drop-down list in the new budget window. Enter the following budgeted amounts: sales: 10,000, services: 4,000, cost of goods sold: 5,000, advertising: 500, insurance: 425, interest expense: 300, meals and entertainment: 250, and payroll: 9,000. Amounts provided should be input for each month of 2019.

4   Create and customize, save customization as Budget Overview Budget 1, print, and export to Excel a Budget Overview report for the month of January 2019. Your report should look like Figure 8.18.

Figure 8.18

Budget Overview (January 2019)

Case 2
BUDGET OVERVIEW: BUDGET 1 - FY19 P&L
January 2019

	TOTAL
Income	
Sales	10,000.00
Services	4,000.00
Total Income	**$14,000.00**
Cost of Goods Sold	
Cost of Goods Sold	5,000.00
Total Cost of Goods Sold	**$5,000.00**
Gross Profit	**$9,000.00**
Expenses	
Advertising	500.00
Insurance	425.00
Interest Expense	300.00
Meals and Entertainment	250.00
Payroll	9,000.00
Total Expenses	**$10,475.00**
Net Operating Income	**$ -1,475.00**
Net Income	**$ -1,475.00**

5   Create and customize, save customization as Budget vs. Actuals Budget 1, print, and export to Excel a Budget vs. Actuals report for the month of January 2019. Your report should look like Figure 8.19.

Figure 8.19

Budget vs. Actuals (January 2019)

Case 2
BUDGET VS. ACTUALS: BUDGET 1 - FY19 P&L
January 2019

	ACTUAL	BUDGET	OVER BUDGET	% OF BUDGET
TOTAL				
Income				
Sales	9,000.00	10,000.00	−1,000.00	90.00 %
Services	4,725.00	4,000.00	725.00	118.13 %
Total Income	$13,725.00	$14,000.00	$ −275.00	98.04 %
Cost of Goods Sold				
Cost of Goods Sold	4,910.00	5,000.00	−90.00	98.20 %
Total Cost of Goods Sold	$4,910.00	$5,000.00	$ -90.00	98.20 %
Gross Profit	$8,815.00	$9,000.00	$ −185.00	97.94 %
Expenses				
Advertising	500.00	500.00	0.00	100.00 %
Insurance	400.00	425.00	−25.00	94.12 %
Interest Expense	300.00	300.00	0.00	100.00 %
Meals and Entertainment	240.00	250.00	−10.00	96.00 %
Payroll	9,224.26	9,000.00	224.26	102.49 %
Total Expenses	$10,664.26	$10,475.00	$189.26	101.81 %
Net Operating Income	$ −1,849.26	$ −1,475.00	$ −374.26	125.37 %
Net Income	$ −1,849.26	$ −1,475.00	$ −374.26	125.37 %

6 Open and print the custom report you created in the last chapter called Transaction Detail by Account.

7 Export your Transactions Detail by Account report to Excel and save it with the file name: Student Name (replace with your name) Ch 08 Case 02 Transaction Detail by Account.xlsx.

8 Reconcile your company's checking account. No service charges were incurred or interest earned. The ending bank statement balance on 1/31/19 was $30,693.47.

9 After a review of the company's most recent bank statement and a comparison with the company's checking account, you discover some checks and payments recorded in the checking account that did not appear on the bank statement. Place a check next to all checks and payments except for check 1009 to Frank Benjamin for 2,359.50 and check 1010 to Sara Juarez for 973.29, neither of which had cleared the bank.

10 After a review of the company's most recent bank statement and a comparison with the company's checking account, you discover a deposit and other credit recorded in the checking account that did not appear on the bank statement. Place a check next to all deposits and other credits except for a deposit on 1/7/19 from Benson's RC for 4,500.00, which had not cleared the bank.

11 Print the resulting Reconciliation Report.

12 Sign out of your company.

Case 3

Now it is time to create a budget and reconcile a bank account. Based on what you learned in the text using the Sample Company, you are to make the following changes to the Case 3 company you modified in Chapter 7:

1 Add the following bill and product received from Samsung, Inc. on 1/30/20, terms: Net 15, received 5 Samsung Galaxy 8 and 8 Samsung Note phones.

2 Add an invoice on 1/30/20 to a new taxable customer: Diamond Girl, Inc., terms: Net 30, for 4 Samsung Galaxy 8 and 5 Samsung Note phones and 6 hours of Phone Consulting. Remember to override the sales tax rate as you've done in previous chapters.

3 Add a payment received from GHO Marketing on 1/31/20 for $2,610, which was deposited the same day into the checking account.

4 Create a new budget titled "Budget 1." Be sure to select FY 2020 (Jan 2020–Dec 2020) from the Fiscal Year drop-down list in the new budget window. Enter the following budgeted amounts: sales of product income: 20,000, services: 1,000, cost of goods sold: 10,000, advertising: 1,000, insurance: 500, interest expense: 350, meals and entertainment: 250, and payroll: 7,000. Amounts provided should be input for each month of 2020.

5 Create and customize a Budget Overview report for January 2020 with no cents. Save customization as Budget Overview Budget 2, print, and export to Excel a Budget Overview report for the month of January 2020. Your report should look like Figure 8.20.

Figure 8.20

Budget Overview (January 2020)

BUDGET OVERVIEW: BUDGET 2 - FY20 P&L
January 2020

	TOTAL
▾ Income	
Sales of Product Income	20,000
Services	1,000
Total Income	**$21,000**
▾ Cost of Goods Sold	
Cost of Goods Sold	10,000
Total Cost of Goods Sold	**$10,000**
GROSS PROFIT	**$11,000**
▾ Expenses	
Advertising & Marketing	1,000
Insurance	500
Interest Expense	350
Meals & Entertainment	250
Payroll	7,000
Total Expenses	**$9,100**
NET OPERATING INCOME	**$1,900**
NET INCOME	**$1,900**

6 Create and customize, save customization as Budget vs. Actuals Budget 2, print, and export to Excel a Budget vs. Actuals report for the month of January 2020. Your report should look like Figure 8.21.

Figure 8.21

Budget vs. Actuals for January 2020

BUDGET VS. ACTUALS: BUDGET 2 - FY20 P&L
January 2020

	TOTAL			
	ACTUAL	BUDGET	OVER BUDGET	% OF BUDGET
▾ Income				
Sales of Product Income	12,800	20,000	-7,200	64.00 %
Services	450	1,000	-550	45.00 %
Total Income	**$13,250**	**$21,000**	**$ -7,750**	63.00 %
▾ Cost of Goods Sold				
Cost of Goods Sold	9,150	10,000	-850	92.00 %
Total Cost of Goods Sold	**$9,150**	**$10,000**	**$ -850**	92.00 %
GROSS PROFIT	**$4,100**	**$11,000**	**$ -6,900**	37.00 %
▾ Expenses				
Advertising & Marketing	1,300	1,000	300	130.00 %
Insurance	300	500	-200	60.00 %
Interest Expense	300	350	-50	86.00 %
Meals & Entertainment	123	250	-127	49.00 %
Payroll	6,960	7,000	-40	99.00 %
Total Expenses	**$8,983**	**$9,100**	**$ -117**	99.00 %
NET OPERATING INCOME	**$ -4,883**	**$1,900**	**$ -6,783**	-257.00 %
NET INCOME	**$ -4,883**	**$1,900**	**$ -6,783**	-257.00 %

7 Reconcile your company's checking account. No service charges were incurred or interest earned. The ending bank statement balance on 1/31/20 was $51,771.07.

8 After a review of the company's most recent statement and a comparison with the company's checking account you note that 1 check and 1 deposit that were recorded in the checking account did not appear on the bank statement. Place a check next to all checks and payments except for check 329 to Jedi Vu for 1,002.78 and the deposit from GHO Marketing for 2,610.00, which had not cleared the bank.

9 Print the resulting Reconciliation Report.

10 Sign out of your company.

Case 4

Now it is time to create a budget and reconcile a bank account. Based on what you learned in the text using the Sample Company, you are to make the following changes to the Case 4 company you modified in Chapter 7:

1 Create a new budget titled "Budget 1." Be sure to select FY 2021 (Jan 2021–Dec 2021) from the Fiscal Year drop-down list in the new budget window. Enter the following budgeted amounts for 2021: sales: 50,000, sales of product income: 4,000, cost of goods sold: 1,500, advertising & marketing: 2,400, insurance: 2,000, interest expense: 300, payroll: 15,000, and repairs & maintenance $500. Amounts provided should be input for each month of 2021.

2 Create, customize (save customization as Budget Overview), and print a Budget Overview report for the month of January 2021 without cents showing accounts vs. totals. Your report should look like Figure 8.22.

Figure 8.22

Budget Overview for January 2021

Case 04 - Student Name (ID Number)

BUDGET OVERVIEW: BUDGET 1 - FY21 P&L

January 2021

	TOTAL
▾ Income	
Sales	50,000
Sales of Product Income	4,000
Total Income	**$54,000**
▾ Cost of Goods Sold	
Cost of Goods Sold	1,500
Total Cost of Goods Sold	**$1,500**
GROSS PROFIT	$52,500
▾ Expenses	
Advertising & Marketing	2,400
Insurance	2,000
Interest Expense	300
Payroll	15,000
Repairs & Maintenance	500
Total Expenses	**$20,200**
NET OPERATING INCOME	$32,300
NET INCOME	$32,300

3 Create, customize (save customization as Budget vs. Actuals), and print a Budget vs. Actuals report for the month of January 2021 without cents showing accounts vs. totals. Your report should look like Figure 8.23.

Figure 8.23

Budget vs. Actuals for
January 2021

Case 04 - Student Name (ID Number)

BUDGET VS. ACTUALS: BUDGET 1 - FY21 P&L
January 2021

	TOTAL			
	ACTUAL	BUDGET	OVER BUDGET	% OF BUDGET
▼ Income				
Sales	48,400	50,000	-1,600	97.00 %
Sales of Product Income	3,570	4,000	-430	89.00 %
Total Income	**$51,970**	**$54,000**	**$ -2,030**	96.00 %
▼ Cost of Goods Sold				
Cost of Goods Sold	1,632	1,500	132	109.00 %
Total Cost of Goods Sold	**$1,632**	**$1,500**	**$132**	109.00 %
GROSS PROFIT	**$50,338**	**$52,500**	**$ -2,162**	96.00 %
▼ Expenses				
Advertising & Marketing	1,800	2,400	-600	75.00 %
Insurance	2,400	2,000	400	120.00 %
Interest Expense	120	300	-180	40.00 %
Payroll	14,680	15,000	-320	98.00 %
Repairs & Maintenance	750	500	250	150.00 %
Total Expenses	**$19,750**	**$20,200**	**$ -450**	98.00 %
NET OPERATING INCOME	**$30,588**	**$32,300**	**$ -1,712**	95.00 %
NET INCOME	**$30,588**	**$32,300**	**$ -1,712**	95.00 %

4   Reconcile your company's checking account. No service charges were incurred, or interest earned. The ending bank statement balance on 1/31/21 was $10,936.19.

5   After a review of the company's most recent statement and a comparison with the company's checking account you note that a $10,000 deposit on 1/26/21 and checks 25509 and 25510 (for $1,376.37 and $1,522.66 respectfully) had not cleared the bank.

6   Print the resulting Reconciliation Report.

7   Sign out of your company.

9

Adjusting Entries

Student Learning Outcomes

Upon completion of this chapter, the student will be able to do the following:

- Prepare an unadjusted trial balance
- Make adjusting entries for the following:
  - o Prepaid expenses
  - o Accrued expenses
  - o Unearned revenue
  - o Accrued revenue
  - o Depreciation

Overview

Intuit has provided a Sample Company online to let new users test drive its QBO product. In this chapter, you will open this Sample Company and practice adjusting entry activities in QBO. Prior to the creation of periodic financial statements, generally accepted accounting principles (GAAP) require that accounting records be adjusted to reflect accrual accounting. This process insures revenues are recorded in the period in which they are earned and that expenses are recorded in the period in which they were consumed. In the process, expenses will be matched in the same period to the revenues generated from incurring those expenses.

There are five types of adjusting entries. Expenses paid, prior to being consumed, should be deferred (such as supplies, rent, insurance, etc.) and recorded as assets (such as supplies asset, prepaid rent, prepaid insurance, etc.) until they are consumed. To defer is to postpone. Expenses incurred prior to being paid (payroll, rent, utilities, etc.) must be recorded and accrued as a liability. To accrue is to increase. Revenue collected prior to being earned must be deferred (such as sales, services, etc.) and recorded as liabilities (such as unearned revenue) until they are earned. Revenues earned prior to being collected (sales and services, etc.) must be recorded and accrued as a receivable. Lastly, fixed assets (buildings, furniture, equipment, vehicles, etc.) must be depreciated over their useful life to match costs with revenues.

Remember, if you stop in the middle of this work, none of your work will be saved. So, when you return, the same sample company, without your work, will appear. In some parts of the chapter, you will be asked to sign out of the Sample Company and sign back in so the Sample Company is reset to its original state. In the end of chapter work, you will be asked to perform the same tasks completed on the Sample Company on your Student Company. That work, of course, will be saved.

Throughout this text, figures illustrating bills, expenses, checks, purchase orders, and credit card transactions will have the title Account details not Category details and the column title as Account and not Category as shown on your QBO software.

Steps will also use the term Account when your QBO software will reflect the use of the term Category. Once again this change took place after this text was completed. See the Preface of this text for a complete discussion of the confusion this change created. However, journal entries, used extensively in this chapter, refer to accounts and not categories. Go figure.

Trial Balance

In this section, you will create a trial balance (before adjusting entries), which must be analyzed in light of end of the period business events to determine the required adjusting entries.

To create a trial balance for the Sample Company, do the following:

1 Open your Internet browser.

2 Type **https://qbo.intuit.com/redir/testdrive** into your browser's address text box and the press [**Enter**] to view the Sample Company Dashboard.

3 Click **Reports** from the navigation bar.

4 Type **Trial Balance** in the Find report by name search box and then select **Trial Balance** from the drop-down list provided..

5 Change the From: date to the first of the previous month and the To: date to the last day of the previous month (in this case **11/1/18** and **11/30/18**; your date will be different as will your amounts), then click **Run Report** to see a partial view of the trial balance shown in Figure 9.1.

Figure 9.1

Trial Balance report (partial view)

Craig's Design and Landscaping Services
TRIAL BALANCE
As of November 30, 2018

	DEBIT	CREDIT
Checking	1,201.00	
Savings	800.00	
Accounts Receivable (A/R)	5,281.52	
Inventory Asset	596.25	
Undeposited Funds	2,062.52	
Truck:Original Cost	13,495.00	
Accounts Payable (A/P)		1,602.67
Mastercard		123.72
Arizona Dept. of Revenue Payable		0.00
Board of Equalization Payable		370.94
Loan Payable		4,000.00
Notes Payable		25,000.00
Opening Balance Equity	9,337.50	
Design income		2,250.00
Discounts given	89.50	
Landscaping Services		1,477.50
Landscaping Services:Job Materials:Fountains and Garden Lighting		2,246.50
Landscaping Services:Job Materials:Plants and Soil		2,351.97
Landscaping Services:Job Materials:Sprinklers and Drip Systems		138.00
Landscaping Services:Labor:Installation		250.00
Landscaping Services:Labor:Maintenance and Repair		50.00
Pest Control Services		110.00
Sales of Product Income		912.75
Services		503.55

Adjusting Journal Entries: Prepaid Expenses

Further investigation of this trial balance and period end business activities indicates that $500 of supplies were recorded as a miscellaneous expense but should have been deferred as a supplies asset until consumed in some future period. Thus, an adjusting entry is necessary.

To record an adjusting entry for supplies in the Sample Company, do the following:

1   Continue from where you left off. If you closed the Sample Company, follow the steps to reopen it found at the beginning of this chapter.

2   Click the + icon, and click **Journal Entry**.

3   Type the last day of the previous month into the **Journal date** text box (in this case 11/30/18).

4   Type **Supplies Asset** on line 1 of the Account column, and click + **Add Supplies Asset** shown in Figure 9.2. (This is another way to add a new account in QBO.)

Figure 9.2

Journal entry (adding a new account)

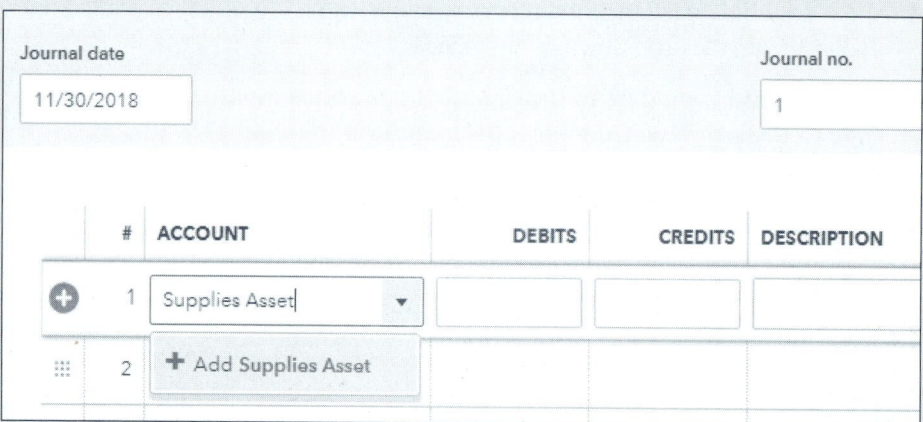

5   Select **Other Current Assets** from the drop-down list in the **Account Type** text box.

6   Select **Prepaid Expenses** from the drop-down list in the **Detail Type** text box.

7   Click **Save and close**.

8   Type **500** into the Debit column of line 1.

9   Select **Miscellaneous** from the drop-down list in line 2 of the Accounts column.

10   Accept **500** into the Credit column of line 2 to view the journal entry shown in Figure 9.3.

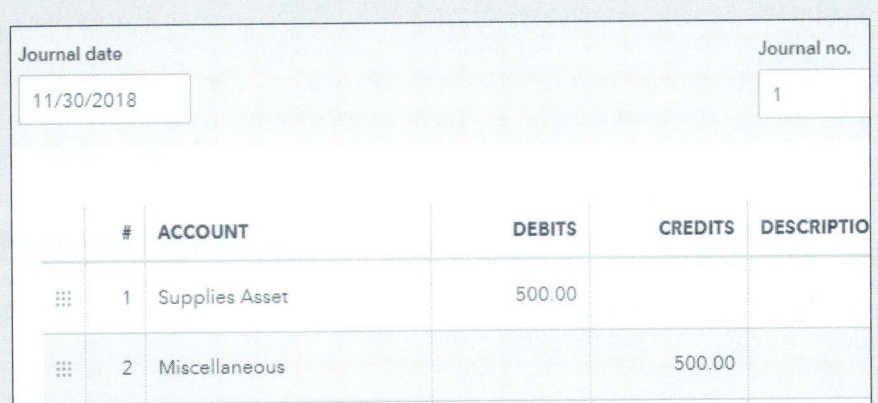

Figure 9.3

Journal Entry #1 (to defer supplies)

11 Click **Save and close**.

The same process could be used to defer a cost that had been recorded as an expense but should be deferred as an asset at period end. Examples might include insurance to be deferred as either prepaid insurance or prepaid expenses or as rent to be deferred as either prepaid rent or prepaid expenses.

Another example of this occurs when an expense is deferred in a prior period but is consumed in the current period. We will use the Supplies Asset created as an example assuming $100 of supplies were consumed in the month leaving $400 of supplies as an asset.

To record an adjusting journal entry to record the consumption of supplies, do the following:

1 Continue from where you left off. If you closed the Sample Company, follow the steps to reopen it found at the beginning of this chapter.

2 Click the + icon and then click **Journal Entry**.

3 Type the last day of the previous month into the **Journal date** text box (in this case 11/30/18).

4 Select **Supplies** from the drop-down list in line 1 of the Account column. (This is an expense account already in the Company's chart of accounts.)

5 Type **100** into the Debit column of line 1.

6 Select **Supplies Asset** from the drop-down list in line 2 of the Accounts column.

7 Accept **100** into the Credit column of line 2 to view the journal entry shown in Figure 9.4.

Figure 9.4

Journal entry (recording the consumption of supplies)

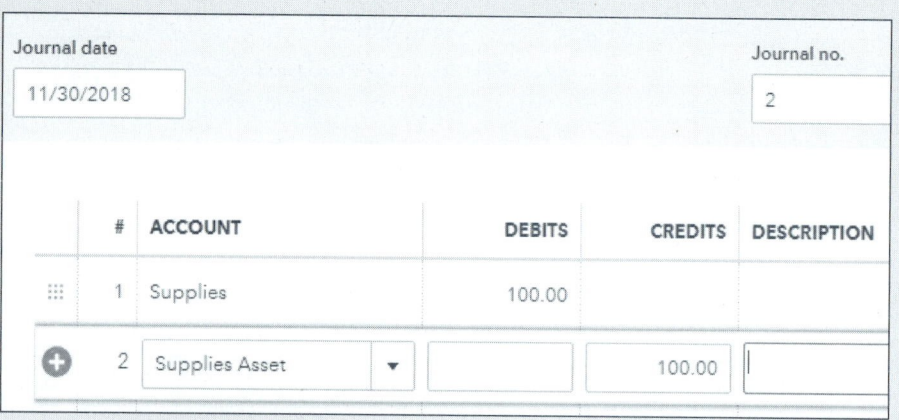

Journal date					Journal no.
11/30/2018					2

#	ACCOUNT		DEBITS	CREDITS	DESCRIPTION
1	Supplies		100.00		
2	Supplies Asset	▾		100.00	

8 Click **Save and close**.

9 Closing the journal entry should reveal the trial balance created before but updated to reflect the supplies asset account shown in Figure 9.5.

Figure 9.5

Trial Balance after supplies adjustments (partial view)

Craig's Design and Landscaping Services

TRIAL BALANCE
As of December 10, 2018

	DEBIT	CREDIT
Checking	1,201.00	
Savings	800.00	
Accounts Receivable (A/R)	5,281.52	
Inventory Asset	596.25	
Supplies Asset	400.00	
Undeposited Funds	2,062.52	
Truck:Original Cost	13,495.00	
Accounts Payable (A/P)		1,602.67

10 Click the Supplies Asset **400.00** amount, then (if necessary) adjust the report period like you've done previously, and then click **Run Report** to reveal a Transaction Report for the Supplies Asset account shown in Figure 9.6.

11 Click **Back to report summary** to return to the Trial Balance report.

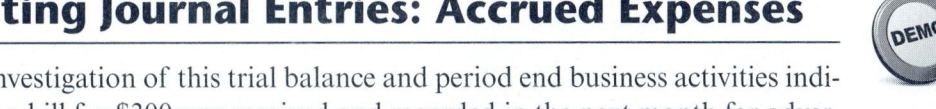

Figure 9.6

Transaction Report (for supplies asset)

DATE	TRANSACTION TYPE	NUM	NAME	MEMO/DESCRIPTION	ACCOUNT	SPLIT	AMOUNT	BALANCE
▾ Supplies Asset								
11/30/2018	Journal Entry	2			Supplies Asset	-Split-	-100.00	-100.00
11/30/2018	Journal Entry	1			Supplies Asset	-Split-	500.00	400.00
Total for Supplies Asset							$400.00	
TOTAL							$400.00	

Craig's Design and Landscaping Services

TRANSACTION REPORT

November 2018

The first entry deferred $500 from miscellaneous expense; the second entry recorded the consumption of supplies reducing the asset account.

Adjusting Journal Entries: Accrued Expenses

Further investigation of this trial balance and period end business activities indicates that a bill for $300 was received and recorded in the next month for advertising consumed in the current month. Thus, an adjusting journal entry needs to be made to accrue this expense. For our purposes, we will create a new accrued liabilities account to keep track of these accruals and keep them separate from accounts payable.

To record an adjusting journal entry to record the accrual of advertising expense, do the following:

1 Continue from where you left off. If you closed the Sample Company, follow the steps to reopen it found at the beginning of this chapter.

2 Click the + icon, and click **Journal Entry**.

3 Type the last day of the previous month into the Journal date text box (in this case 11/30/18).

4 Select **Advertising** from the drop-down list in line 1 of the Account column.

5 Type **300** into the Debits column of line 1.

6 Type **Accrued Liabilities** on line 2 of the Account column and then click **+ Add Accrued Liabilities**.

7 Select **Other Current Liabilities** from the drop-down list in the **Account Type** text box.

8 Select **Other Current Liabilities** from the drop-down list in the **Detail Type** text box.

9 Click **Save and close**.

10 Accept **300** into the Credits column of line 2 to view the journal entry shown in Figure 9.7.

Figure 9.7

Journal entry (accruing advertising expense)

Journal date					Journal no.
11/30/2018					3

	#	ACCOUNT	DEBITS	CREDITS	DESCRIPTION
:::	1	Advertising	300.00		
:::	2	Accrued Liabilities		300.00	

11 Click **Save and close**.

12 Closing the journal entry should reveal the trial balance created before but now updated to reflect the accrual of advertising expense to the accrued liabilities account.

13 Click the Accrued Liabilities **300.00** amount, then (if necessary) adjust the report period like you've done previously, and then click **Run Report** to reveal a Transaction Report.

14 Click **Back to report summary** to return to the Trial Balance report.

Adjusting Journal Entries: Unearned Revenue

Further investigation of this trial balance and period end business activities indicates that design income recorded on sales receipt #1003 for $337.50 to Dylan Sollfrank were never performed even though cash had been received. Thus, the revenue had not been earned. Work is expected to occur next month, thus this amount of revenue must be deferred and set up as an unearned revenue liability.

To record an adjusting journal entry to reflect earned revenue, do the following:

1 Continue from where you left off. If you closed the Sample Company, follow the steps to reopen it found at the beginning of this chapter.

2 Click the + icon and then click **Journal Entry**.

3 Type the last day of the previous month into the Journal date text box (in this case 11/30/18).

4 Select **Design Income** from the drop-down list in line 1 of the Account column.

5 Type **337.50** into the Debits column of line **1**.

6   Select **Dylan Sollfrank** from the drop-down list of customers in the Name column of line 1.

7   Type **Unearned Revenue** on line 2 of the Account column and then click + **Add Unearned Revenue**.

8   Select **Other Current Liabilities** from the drop-down list in the **Category Type** text box.

9   Select **Other Current Liabilities** from the drop-down list in the **Detail Type** text box.

10   Click **Save and close**.

11   Accept **337.50** into the Credits column of line 2 and then select **Dylan Sollfrank** from the drop-down list of customers in the Name column of line 2 to view the journal entry shown in Figure 9.8.

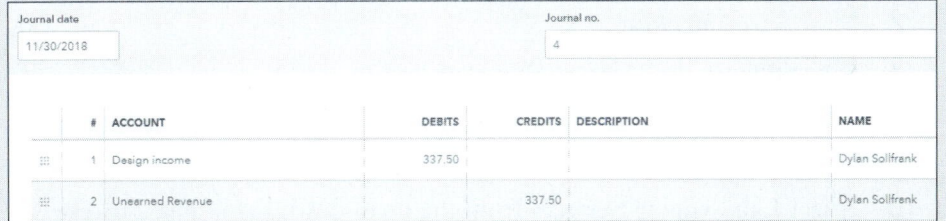

Figure 9.8

Journal entry (recording unearned revenue)

12   Click **Save and close**.

13   Closing the journal entry should reveal the trial balance created before but updated to reflect the deferral of revenue to the unearned revenue liability account.

14   Click the Unearned Revenue **337.50** amount, then (if necessary) adjust the report period like you've done previously, and then click **Run Report** to reveal a Transaction Report.

15   Click **Back to report summary** to return to the Trial Balance report.

Adjusting Journal Entries: Accruing Revenue

Further investigation of this trial balance and period end business activities indicates that some landscaping services of $500 were performed on the last day of the month for Diego Rodriguez but not invoiced to the customer or recorded into the accounting records until a few days into the next month. Thus, you will need to record an adjusting journal entry to accrue revenue and an accrued receivable.

To record an adjusting journal entry to reflect earned revenue, do the following:

1   Continue from where you left off. If you closed the Sample Company, follow the steps to reopen it found at the beginning of this chapter.

2   Click the **+** icon and then click **Journal Entry**.

3   Type the last day of the previous month into the **Journal date** text box (in this case 11/30/18).

4   Type **Accrued Receivable** on line 1 of the Account column and then click **+ Add Accrued Receivable**.

5   Select **Other Current Assets** from the drop-down list in the **Account Type** text box.

6   Select **Other Current Assets** from the drop-down list in the **Detail Type** text box.

7   Click **Save and close**.

8   Type **500** into the Debits column of line 1.

9   Select **Diego Rodriguez** from the drop-down list of customers in the Name column of line 1.

10   Select **Landscaping Services** from the drop-down list in line 2 of the Account column.

11   Accept **500** in the Credits column of line 2.

12   Select **Diego Rodriguez** from the drop-down list of customers in the Name column of line 2 to view the journal entry shown in Figure 9.9.

Figure 9.9

Journal entry (recording accrued revenue)

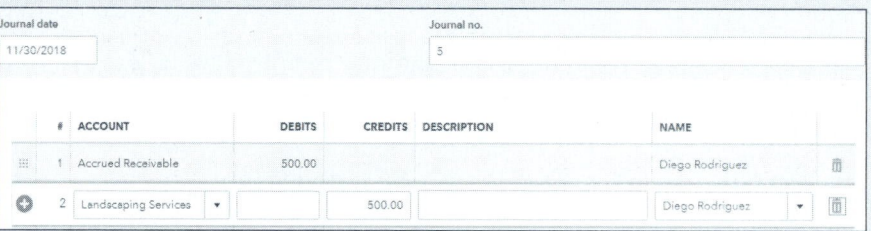

13   Click **Save and close**.

14   Closing the journal entry should reveal the trial balance created before but updated to reflect the accrual of revenue to the accrued receivable account.

15   Click the Accrued Receivable **500.00** amount, then (if necessary) adjust the report period like you've done previously, and then click **Run Report** to reveal a Transaction Report.

16   Click **Back to report summary** to return to the Trial Balance report.

Adjusting Journal Entries: Depreciation

Further investigation of this trial balance and period end business activities indicates the company's only fixed asset, a truck, needed to be depreciated for the month. Monthly depreciation is $1,000. Normally, the adjusting entry would debit depreciation expense and credit accumulated depreciation. However, the accounts set up in the Sample Company are both named depreciation. Thus, you decide to change the account names first and then record the depreciation adjusting journal entry.

To edit account names and then record an adjusting journal entry to record depreciation, do the following:

1 Continue from where you left off. If you closed the Sample Company, follow the steps to reopen it found at the beginning of this chapter.

2 Click the **Gear** icon, then click **Chart of Accounts**, and then click **See your Chart of Accounts**.

3 Click **Edit** from the drop-down arrow next to the words View Register on the Depreciation line listed under the Truck account.

4 Type **Accumulated** in front of Depreciation in the **Name** text box and then click **Save and close**.

5 Scroll down to the bottom of the chart of accounts and select **Edit** from the drop-down arrow next to the words Run report on the Depreciation line listed above Miscellaneous.

6 Type **Expense** after Depreciation in the **Name** text box and then click **Save and close**.

7 Click the + icon and then click **Journal Entry**.

8 Type the last day of the previous month into the Journal date text box (in this case 11/30/18).

9 Select **Depreciation Expense** from the drop-down list in line 1 of the Account column.

10 Type **1,000** into the Debits column of line 1.

11 Select **Truck:Accumulated Depreciation** from the drop-down list in line 2 of the Accounts column.

12 Accept **1,000.00** as the Credits column amount. Your screen should look like Figure 9.10.

Journal date				Journal no.	
11/30/2018				6	

	#	ACCOUNT	DEBITS	CREDITS	DESCRIPTION
⣿	1	Depreciation Expense	1,000.00		
⣿	2	Truck:Accumulated Depreciation		1,000.00	

Figure 9.10

Journal entry (recording depreciation)

13   Click **Save and close**.

14   Click **Reports** from the navigation bar and then type **Trial Balance** in the **Find report by name** text box and then select **Trial Balance** from the drop-down list to view the trial balance.

15   Change the To: and From: dates like you did earlier in this chapter and then click **Run report** to reveal a trial balance now updated to reflect the depreciation expense and accumulated depreciation just recorded.

16   Click the Truck:Accumulated Depreciation **1,000.00** amount, then (if necessary) adjust the report period like you've done previously, and then click **Run Report** to reveal a Transaction Report.

17   Click **Back to report summary** to return to the Trial Balance report. Your completed Trial Balance report should look like Figure 9.11.

Figure 9.11

Revised Trial Balance report (partial view)

Craig's Design and Landscaping Services

TRIAL BALANCE
As of November 30, 2018

	DEBIT	CREDIT
Checking	1,201.00	
Savings	800.00	
Accounts Receivable (A/R)	5,281.52	
Accrued Receivable	500.00	
Inventory Asset	596.25	
Supplies Asset	400.00	
Undeposited Funds	2,062.52	
Truck:Accumulated Depreciation		1,000.00
Truck:Original Cost	13,495.00	
Accounts Payable (A/P)		1,602.67
Mastercard		123.72
Accrued Liabilities		300.00
Arizona Dept. of Revenue Payable		0.00
Board of Equalization Payable		370.94
Loan Payable		4,000.00
Unearned Revenue		337.50
Notes Payable		25,000.00

End Note

In this chapter, you recorded adjusting entries to create accrual accounting based records. In the next chapter, you will create financial statements and useful reports.

practice

chapter 9

Chapter 9 Questions

1 What is an unadjusted trial balance?

2 What is an adjusted trial balance?

3 Why accrue an expense?

4 Why defer an expense?

5 Why accrue revenues?

6 Why defer revenues?

7 What QBO task is used to record accruals and deferrals?

8 Why depreciate a fixed asset?

9 Describe the new method you learned in this chapter to add a new account from within a journal entry.

10 Describe the method you learned in this chapter to add a customer to a transaction within a journal entry.

Chapter 9 Matching

a. Prepaid Expenses _____ Debit this account when recording depreciation

b. Accrue _____ Credit this account when accruing an expense

c. Unearned Revenue _____ Debit this account when accruing revenue

d. Defer _____ Supplies consumed

e. Depreciation Expense _____ Credit this account when recording depreciation

f. Supplies Asset _____ Expenses not yet consumed

g. Supplies Expense _____ Revenue not yet earned

h. Accrued Receivables _____ To increase

i. Accrued Liabilities _____ Supplies not yet consumed

j. Accumulate Depreciation _____ To postpone

Chapter 9 Cases

The following cases require you to open the company you updated in Chapter 8. Each of the following cases continues throughout the text in a sequential manner. For example, if you are assigned Case 1, you will use the file you modified in this chapter in all following chapters. Each of the following cases is similar in concepts assessed but differs in amounts and transactions.

To reopen your company, do the following:

1 Open your Internet browser.

2 Type **https://qbo.intuit.com** into your browser's address text box.

3 Type your User ID and Password into the text boxes as you've done before.

Case 1

Now it is time to make some adjusting journal entries. Based on what you learned in the text using the Sample Company, you are to make the following changes to the Case 1 company you modified in Chapter 8:

1   Open and review your previously customized report named Trial Balance 1/31/18.

2   Record the appropriate adjusting journal entries on 1/31/18 based on the following:

   a.   An inventory of supplies reveals that only $75 of supplies remain as of 1/31/18.

   b. $800 of prepaid expenses expired (representing prepaid rent) in the month of January.

   c.   A bill for $150 was received and recorded in the next month for repairs and maintenance consumed in the current month. Create a new liability account as you did earlier in the chapter.

   d.   Consulting services recorded on sales receipt #1004 for $2,500.00 to Surf Rider Foundation were never performed even though cash had been received. Thus, the revenue had not been earned. Create a new liability account as you did earlier in the chapter.

   e.   Consulting services of $8,500 were performed on the last day of the month for a new customer: Blazing Boards but not invoiced to the customer or recorded into the accounting records until a few days into the next month. Create a new asset account as you did earlier in the chapter.

   f.   Depreciation Expense of $575 ($75 and $500 for Equipment and Furniture & Fixtures, respectively) needed to be recorded for the month. Before recording this journal entry, edit the "Depreciation" expense account so that the new name is "Depreciation Expense." Also, change the account title for Furniture & Fixtures accumulated depreciation from "Depreciation" to "Accumulated Depreciation" as you did earlier in the chapter.

3   Open, print, and export to Excel your previously customized report named Trial Balance 1/31/18, which should now reflect your adjusting journal entries.

4   Open, print, and export to Excel your previously customized report named Transaction Detail by Account, which should now reflect your adjusting journal entries.

Case 2

Now it is time to make some adjusting journal entries. Based on what you learned in the text using the Sample Company, you are to make the following changes to the Case 2 company you modified in Chapter 8:

1   Open and review your previously customized report named Trial Balance 1/31/19.

2 Record the appropriate adjusting journal entries on 1/31/19 based on the following:

    a. An inventory of supplies reveals that only $200 of supplies remain as of 1/31/19.

    b. $1,800 of prepaid expenses expired (representing prepaid insurance) in the month of January.

    c. A bill for $750 was received and recorded in the next month for legal fees performed in the current month. Create a new liability account as you did earlier in the chapter.

    d. Custom painting services recorded on invoice #1003 for $4,500.00 to Hagen's toys were never performed even though invoiced. Thus, the revenue had not been earned. Create a new liability account as you did earlier in the chapter.

    e. Repair services of $6,298 were performed on the last day of the month for a new customer: Kelly's Awesome Copters but not invoiced to the customer or recorded into the accounting records until a few days into the next month. Create a new asset account as you did earlier in the chapter.

    f. Depreciation Expense of $1,000 ($375 and $625 for Furniture and Machinery & Equipment, respectively) needed to be recorded for the month. Before recording this journal entry edit the "Depreciation" expense account so the new name is "Depreciation Expense." Also, change the account title for Machinery & Equipment accumulated depreciation from "Depreciation" to "Accumulated Depreciation" like you did earlier in the chapter.

3 Open, print, and export to Excel your previously customized report named Trial Balance 1/31/19, which should reflect your adjusting journal entries.

4 Open, print, and export to Excel your previously customized report named Transaction Detail by Account, which should reflect your adjusting journal entries.

Case 3

Now it is time to make some adjusting journal entries. Based on what you learned in the text using the Sample Company, you are to make the following changes to the Case 3 company you modified in Chapter 8:

1 Open and review your previously customized report named Trial Balance 1/31/20.

2 Record the appropriate adjusting journal entries on 1/31/20 based on the following:

    a. An inventory of supplies reveals that only $200 of supplies remain as of 1/31/20. (You'll need to add a new Supplies account- Account Type Expenses, Detail Type: Supplies & Materials, Name: Supplies)

    b. $1,500 of prepaid expenses expired (representing prepaid insurance) in the month of January.

c. A bill for $350 was received and recorded in the next month from FixIt, Inc. for repairs performed in the current month. Create a new liability account like you did earlier in the chapter.

d. Phone Consulting services recorded on invoice #1003 for $210.00 to Diamond Girl, Inc. were never performed even though invoiced. Thus, the revenue had not been earned. Create a new liability account like you did earlier in the chapter.

e. Phone Consulting services of $1,800 were performed on the last day of the month for a new customer: Graham Engineering, Inc. but not invoiced to the customer or recorded into the accounting records until a few days into the next month. Create a new asset account like you did earlier in the chapter.

f. Depreciation Expense of $1,200 ($850 and $350 for Buildings and Machinery & Equipment respectively) needed to be recorded for the month. Before recording this journal entry, edit the "Depreciation" expense account so that the new name is "Depreciation Expense." Also change the account title for the Machinery & Equipment accumulated depreciation account from "Depreciation" to "Accumulated Depreciation" like you did earlier in the chapter. This also needs to be done for the Buildings accumulation depreciation account.

3 Open, print, and export to Excel your previously customized report named Trial Balance 1/31/20, which should now reflect your adjusting journal entries.

4 Open, print, and export to Excel your previously customized report named Transaction Detail by Account, which should now reflect your adjusting journal entries.

Case 4

Now it is time to make some adjusting journal entries. Based on what you learned in the text using the Sample Company, you are to make the following changes to the Case 4 company you modified in Chapter 8:

1 Open and review your previously customized report named Trial Balance 1/31/21.

2 Record the appropriate adjusting journal entries on 1/31/21 based on the following:

a. An inventory of supplies reveals that only $200 of supplies remain as of 1/31/21. You'll need to create a new Supplies Expense account (Account Type: Expenses, Detail Type: Supplies & Materials, Name: Supplies Expense).

b. $1,500 of prepaid expenses expired (representing prepaid insurance) in the month of January.

c. A bill for $675 was received and recorded in the next month from FixIt, Inc. for advertising placed in the current month. Create a new liability account like you did earlier in the chapter.

d. Training services recorded on invoice #1003 for $3,750 to Flyer Corporation were only partially performed even though invoiced. Thus, the $2,000 of sales had not been earned. Create a new liability account like you did earlier in the chapter.

e. Training services of $750 were performed on the last day of the month for a new customer: Jules, Inc. but not invoiced to the customer or recorded into the accounting records until a few days into the next month. Create a new asset account like you did earlier in the chapter and record additional sales.

f. Depreciation Expense of $1,500 ($500, $600, and $400 for Buildings, Furniture, and Machinery & Equipment, respectively) needed to be recorded for the month. Before recording this journal entry, edit the "Depreciation" expense account so that the new name is "Depreciation Expense." Also change the account title for the Buildings, Furniture, and Machinery & Equipment accumulated depreciation account from "Depreciation" to "Accumulated Depreciation" like you did earlier in the chapter.

3 Print your Trial Balance 1/31/21 report that should now reflect your adjusting journal entries.

Financial Statements and Reports

Upon completion of this chapter, the student will be able to do the following:

- Create an income statement
- Create a balance sheet
- Create a statement of cash flows
- Create an accounts receivable aging summary
- Create an accounts payable aging summary
- Create an inventory valuation summary
- Customize and save reports

Overview

Intuit has provided a Sample Company online to let new users test drive its QBO product. In this chapter, you will open this Sample Company and practice creating reports in QBO. Prior to the creation of periodic financial statements, generally accepted accounting principles (GAAP) require that accounting records be adjusted to reflect accrual accounting. You completed that process in the previous chapter.

Four standard reports exist in financial accounting: the income statement, the statement of stockholders' equity, the balance sheet, and the statement of cash flows. QBO does not have a report for stockholders' equity. It does have the others along with a host of other reports so you can understand the underlying business events that have occurred during a particular accounting period. You will be exploring the A/R Aging Summary, A/P Aging Summary, and Inventory Valuation Summary reports. You will also be customizing them by adding columns, removing cents.

Remember, if you stop in the middle of this work, none of your work will be saved. So, when you return, the same Sample Company, without your work, will appear. In some parts of the chapter, you will be asked to sign out of the Sample Company and sign back in so the Sample Company is reset to its original state. In the end of chapter work, you will be asked to perform the same tasks completed on the Sample Company on your Student Company. That work, of course, will be saved.

Throughout this text, figures illustrating bills, expenses, checks, purchase orders, and credit card transactions will have the title Account details not Category details and the column title as Account and not Category as shown on your QBO software. Steps will also use the term Account when your QBO software will reflect the use of the term Category. Once again this change took place after this text was completed. See the Preface of this text for a complete discussion of the confusion this change created.

Income Statement

In this section, you will create an income statement. Intuit decided years ago to call this report Profit and Loss rather than an Income Statement. Even though this may confuse the accounting professional and accounting student, it resonates with the small business user that uses QBO. This report is designed to communicate the revenues earned and expenses incurred for a business over a month, quarter, or year.

Intuit defines this report as follows: "Shows money you earned (income) and money you spent (expenses) so you can see how profitable you are." That is not exactly how an accounting professional or accounting student was taught but close enough. Accountants define the income statement as a report reflecting revenues less expenses to derive net income. Intuit is not about to change its wording to accommodate us, so we will accept it at face value. Thus, revenues are the same as income in the Profit and Loss report. For simplicity, we will refer to this as the Profit and Loss report.

To create a Profit and Loss report for the Sample Company, do the following:

1 Open your Internet browser.

2 Type **https://qbo.intuit.com/redir/testdrive** into your browser's address text box, and then press [**Enter**] to view the Sample Company Dashboard.

3 Click **Reports** from the navigation bar.

4 Type **Profit and Loss** in the Find report by name search box and then select the **Profit and Loss** text which appears below the search text box.

You recall that when using the Sample Company, dates change based upon the system date of Intuit's servers on which these data reside. The system date was 12/10/18 when this report was created; therefore, the default dates for this report were 1/1/18 to 12/10/18 as seen in the Report period text boxes at the top of Figure 10.1.

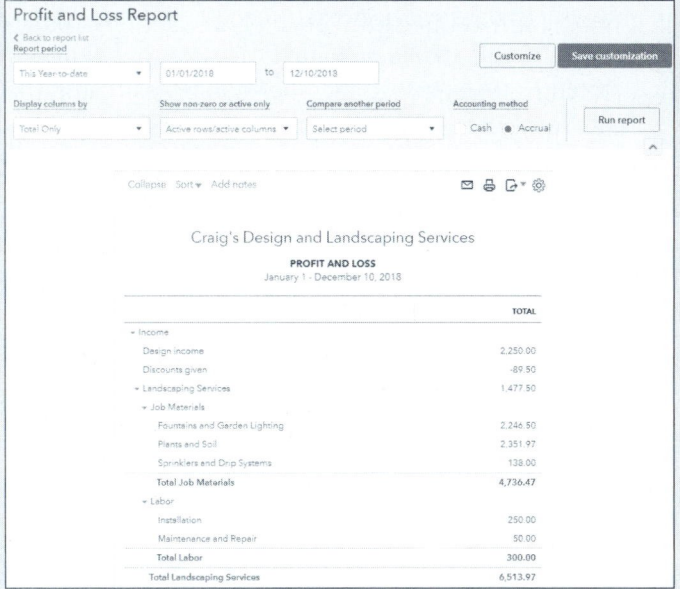

Figure 10.1

Profit and Loss report (collapsed and partial views)

5   Change the From: date to the first of the previous month and the To: date to the last day of the previous month and click **Run Report**. Since the system date was 12/10/18 when this report was created, the report shown in Figure 10.2 is for the period 11/1/18 to 11/30/18. Your report will have a different period than that shown next.

Figure 10.2

Profit and Loss report (partial view)

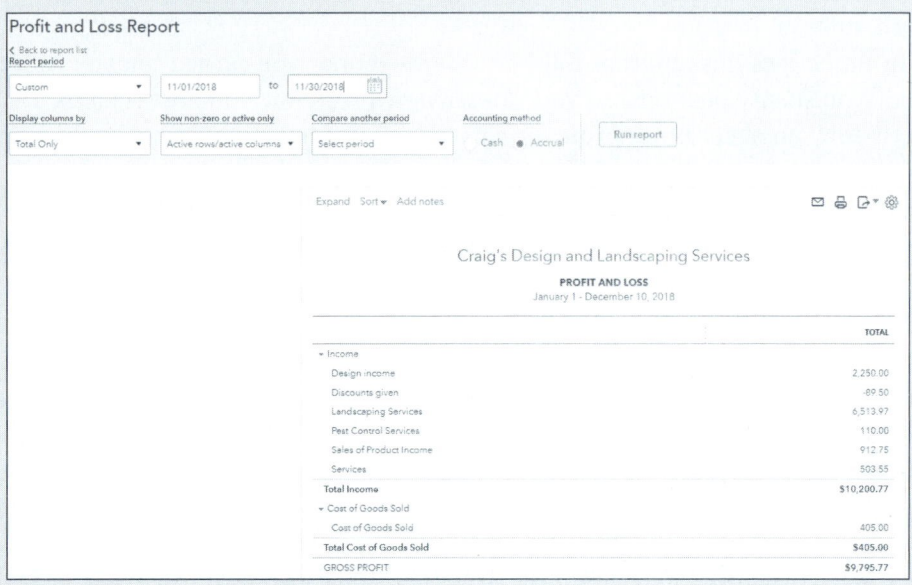

Trouble? If you are doing this work in a different year, 2019, for example, you may have to type a different year and a different month to view the data.

By defining the accounting period as I did earlier for the month of November 2018, the only events reported are those recorded during that period. All reports in QBO allow you to drill down to specific transactions recorded in that period. You drill down by clicking an account on a report. That reveals a transactions report for that account for that period. Double clicking a specific transaction in the transactions report reveals a specific source document, such as an invoice, sales receipt, cash receipt, bill, etc. Recall the **Trouble?** earlier. The amounts you are asked to investigate next will most likely be different than that stated in the steps. Remember you're just using the Sample Company to explore. You will not find these issues in the end-of-chapter case problems.

6   Click the **1,275.00** amount (or whatever amount is shown) next to the Design income account as shown in Figure 10.2 to view the Transaction report for the Design income account for the month of November shown in Figure 10.3, remembering that this figure illustrates the details behind the number you just clicked.

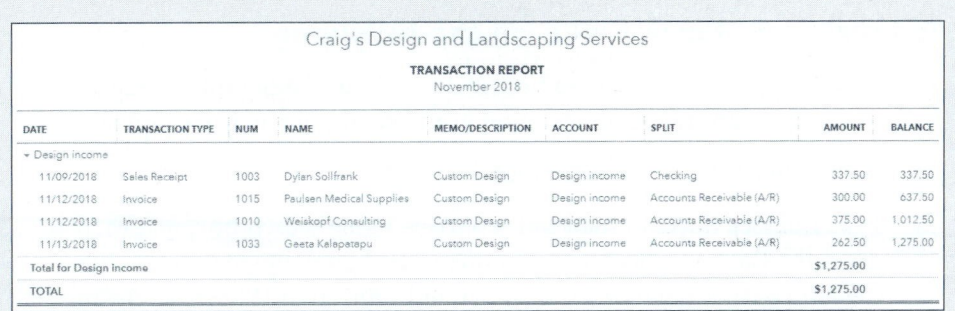

Figure 10.3

Transaction Report (for the design income account)

7 Click on the **Dylan Sollfrank** sales receipt to view Sales Receipt #1003 shown in Figure 10.4.

Figure 10.4

Sales Receipt #1003

8 Click **Cancel** to return to the transaction report, and click **Back to report summary** to return to the Profit and Loss report and then save this report as Profit and Loss Nov 2018 (your date will be different).

Balance Sheet

In this section, you will create a balance sheet that reports on your company's assets, liabilities, and stockholders' equity as of a specific date (not period). However, when creating this report, QBO provides you the ability to define the period in which underlying account balances will reflect in their transactions reports. QBO default is this Year-to-date. Recall the **Trouble?** earlier. The amounts you are asked to investigate next will most likely be different than that stated in the steps. Remember you're just using the Sample Company to explore. You will not find these issues in the end-of-chapter case problems.

To create a balance sheet, do the following:

1 Continue from where you left off. If you closed the Sample Company, follow the steps to reopen it found at the beginning of this chapter.

2 Click **Reports** from the navigation bar.

3 Type **Balance Sheet** in the Find report by name search box, and then select the **Balance Sheet** text which appears below the search text box to view the partial balance sheet shown in Figure 10.5. Alternatively, the Balance Sheet can be accessed in the Sample Company by clicking **Balance Sheet** from the list of Favorites in the **Reports** section.

Figure 10.5

Balance Sheet (partial view)

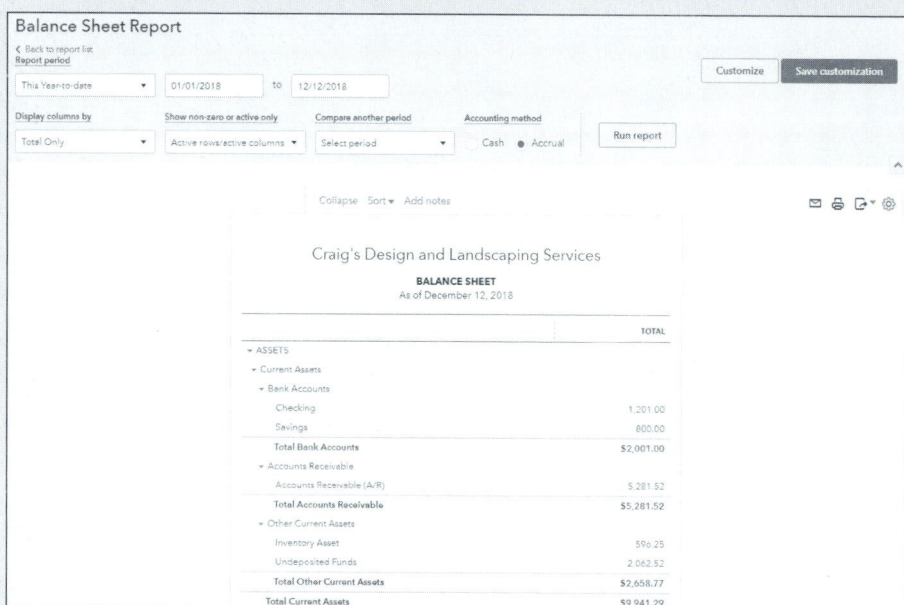

4 The system date was 12/12/18 when this report was created (yours will be your current system date); therefore, the default dates for this report were 1/1/18 to 12/12/18 as seen in the Report period text boxes at the top of Figure 10.5. Change the From: date to the first of the previous month and the To: date to the last day of the previous month like you did previously with the Profit and Loss statement and click **Run Report**. Since the system date was 12/12/18 when this report was created, the report shown in Figure 10.6 is for the period 11/1/18 to 11/30/18. Your report will have a different period than that shown next.

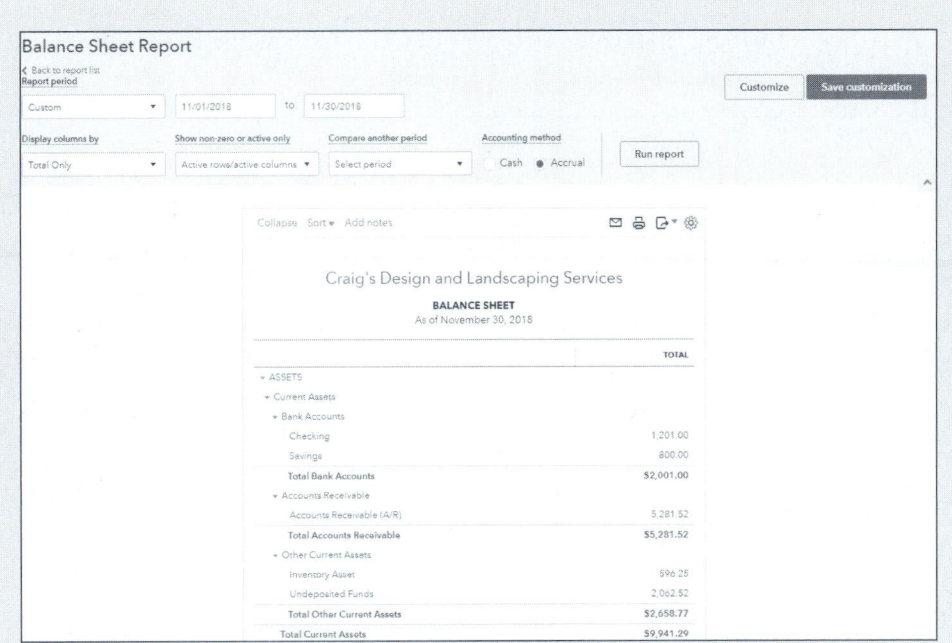

Figure 10.6

Balance Sheet (partial view)

5 Click the Accounts Receivable (A/R) balance that, as shown in Figure 10.6, is **5,281.52** (or whatever balance is shown for Accounts Receivable) to view a transaction report for Accounts Receivable (A/R) for the month you specified shown in Figure 10.7. (Your balance may differ.)

Figure 10.7

Transaction Report (for Accounts Receivable (A/R): partial view)

Craig's Design and Landscaping Services

TRANSACTION REPORT
November 2018

DATE	TRANSACTION	NUM	NAME	MEMO/DESCRIPT	ACCOUNT	SPLIT	AMOUNT	BALANCE
▾ Accounts Receivable (A/R)								
Beginning Balance								2,154.00
11/02/2018	Invoice	1012	Shara Barnett:Barnett Design		Accounts Receivable (A/R)	-Split-	274.50	2,428.50
11/04/2018	Invoice	1013	Travis Waldron		Accounts Receivable (A/R)	-Split-	81.00	2,509.50
11/04/2018	Invoice	1004	Cool Cars		Accounts Receivable (A/R)	-Split-	2,369.52	4,879.02
11/07/2018	Invoice	1005	Freeman Sporting Goods:55 T...		Accounts Receivable (A/R)	-Split-	54.00	4,933.02
11/07/2018	Invoice	1018	Sushi by Katsuyuki		Accounts Receivable (A/R)	Landscaping Services	80.00	5,013.02
11/09/2018	Payment	1886	Cool Cars		Accounts Receivable (A/R)	Checking	-694.00	4,319.02
11/12/2018	Payment		Sushi by Katsuyuki		Accounts Receivable (A/R)	Undeposited Funds	-80.00	4,239.02
11/13/2018	Invoice	1001	Amy's Bird Sanctuary	Front yard, ...	Accounts Receivable (A/R)	-Split-	108.00	4,347.02
11/13/2018	Invoice	1009	Travis Waldron		Accounts Receivable (A/R)	Services	103.55	4,450.57
11/13/2018	Invoice	1032	Travis Waldron		Accounts Receivable (A/R)	-Split-	414.72	4,865.29
11/14/2018	Payment		Freeman Sporting Goods:55 T...		Accounts Receivable (A/R)	Checking	-50.00	4,815.29

6 Scroll to the end of this report to view the ending balance of 5,281.52 (or whatever balance you have), which matches the Balance Sheet report shown in Figure 10.8.

11/14/2018	Invoice	1015	Paulsen Medical Supplies		Accounts Receivable (A/R)	-Split-	954.75	5,887.04
11/14/2018	Payment	2064	Travis Waldron		Accounts Receivable (A/R)	Checking	-103.55	5,783.49
11/15/2018	Invoice	1034	Rondonuwu Fruit and Vegi		Accounts Receivable (A/R)	-Split-	78.60	5,862.09
11/15/2018	Invoice	1033	Geeta Kalapatapu		Accounts Receivable (A/R)	-Split-	629.10	6,491.19
11/15/2018	Payment		Amy's Bird Sanctuary		Accounts Receivable (A/R)	Undeposited Funds	-220.00	6,271.19
11/15/2018	Payment		Travis Waldron		Accounts Receivable (A/R)	Undeposited Funds	-81.00	6,190.19
11/16/2018	Invoice	1035	Mark Cho		Accounts Receivable (A/R)	-Split-	314.28	6,504.47
11/16/2018	Payment		Cool Cars		Accounts Receivable (A/R)	Undeposited Funds	-1,675.52	4,828.95
11/16/2018	Payment		Freeman Sporting Goods:096...		Accounts Receivable (A/R)	Undeposited Funds	-387.00	4,441.95
11/16/2018	Invoice	1037	Sonnenschein Family Store		Accounts Receivable (A/R)	-Split-	362.07	4,804.02
11/16/2018	Invoice	1036	Freeman Sporting Goods:096...		Accounts Receivable (A/R)	-Split-	477.50	5,281.52
Total for Accounts Receivable (A/R)							$3,127.52	
TOTAL							$3,127.52	

Figure 10.8

Transaction Report end (for Accounts Receivable)

7 Click **–1.675.52** (a payment from Cool Cars) to view the receive payment window shown in Figure 10.9.

Figure 10.9

Payment Received (from Cool Cars)

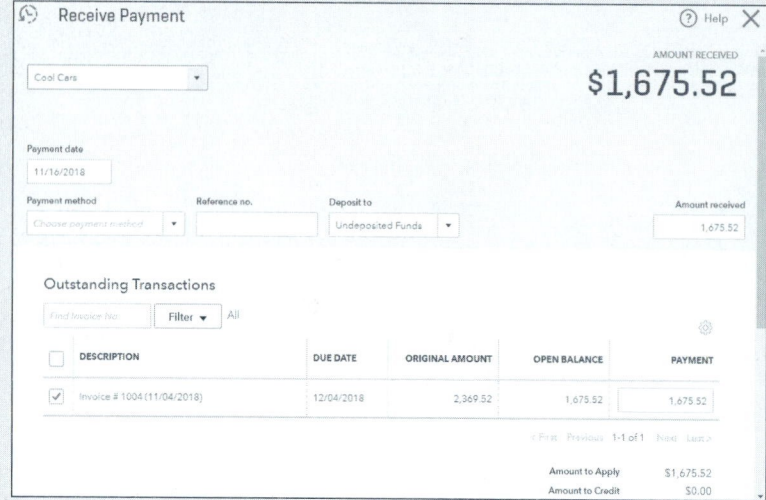

8 Click **Cancel** to return to the transaction report, and click **Back to report summary** to return to the Balance Sheet.

Statement of Cash Flows

In this section, you will create a statement of cash flows, which reports on a company's operating, investing, and financing activities. Recall the **Trouble?** earlier. The amounts you are asked to investigate next will most likely be different than that stated in the steps. Remember you're just using the Sample Company to explore. You will not find these issues in the end-of-chapter case problems.

To create a statement of cash flows, do the following:

1 Continue from where you left off. If you closed the Sample Company, follow the steps to reopen it found at the beginning of this chapter.

2 Click **Reports** from the navigation bar.

3 Type **Statement of Cash Flows** in the Find a report by name search box, and then select the **Statement of Cash Flows** text which appears below the search text box to view the partial statement of cash flows shown in Figure 10.10.

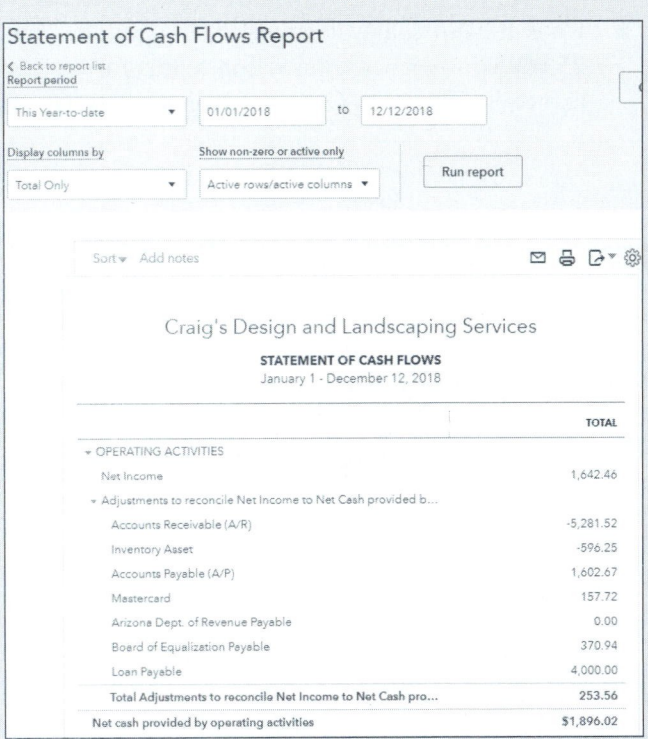

Figure 10.10

Statement of Cash Flows (partial view)

4 The system date was 12/12/18 when this report was created; therefore, the default dates for this report were 1/1/18 to 12/12/18 as seen in the Report period text boxes at the top of Figure 10.10. Change the From: date to the first of the previous month and the To: date to the last day of the previous month like you did previously with the balance sheet and click **Run Report**. Since the system date was 12/12/18 when this report was created, the report shown in Figure 10.11 is for the period 11/1/18 to 11/30/18. Your report will have a different period than that shown next.

Craig's Design and Landscaping Services
STATEMENT OF CASH FLOWS
November 2018

	TOTAL
▾ OPERATING ACTIVITIES	
Net Income	949.78
▾ Adjustments to reconcile Net Income to Net Cash provided by ...	
Accounts Receivable (A/R)	-3,127.52
Inventory Asset	-596.25
Accounts Payable (A/P)	371.28
Mastercard	-34.36
Board of Equalization Payable	324.54
Loan Payable	4,000.00
Total Adjustments to reconcile Net Income to Net Cash provi...	937.69
Net cash provided by operating activities	$1,887.47
▾ FINANCING ACTIVITIES	
Notes Payable	25,000.00
Opening Balance Equity	-27,832.50
Net cash provided by financing activities	$ -2,832.50
NET CASH INCREASE FOR PERIOD	$ -945.03
Cash at beginning of period	5,008.55
CASH AT END OF PERIOD	$4,063.52

Figure 10.11

Statement of Cash Flows (partial view)

5 Click the Notes Payable balance that, as shown in Figure 10.11, is **25,000.00** to view a transaction report for Notes Payable for November shown in Figure 10.12. (Your balance and dates will differ.)

Figure 10.12

Transaction Report (for notes payable)

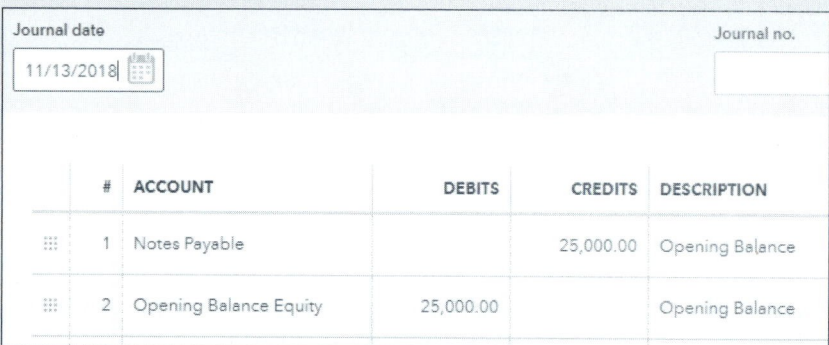

DATE	TRANSACTION TYPE	NUM	NAME	MEMO/DESCRIPTION	ACCOUNT	SPLIT	AMOUNT	BALANCE
▾ Notes Payable								
11/13/2018	Journal Entry			Opening Balance	Notes Payable	-Split-	25,000.00	25,000.00
Total for Notes Payable							$25,000.00	
TOTAL							$25,000.00	

6 Click **25,000.00** to view the journal entry shown in Figure 10.13.

Figure 10.13

Journal date (entry to record the notes payable opening balance)

Journal date   Journal no.

11/13/2018

#	ACCOUNT	DEBITS	CREDITS	DESCRIPTION
1	Notes Payable		25,000.00	Opening Balance
2	Opening Balance Equity	25,000.00		Opening Balance

7 Click **Cancel** to return to the transaction report, and click **Back to report summary** to return to the Statement of Cash Flows.

Accounts Receivable Aging Summary

In this section, you will create an accounts receivable aging summary, which reflects unpaid invoices for the current period and for the last 30, 60, and 90+ days as of a specific date. Aging summaries help find customers who may be delinquent in their payments and help a company estimate the need for an allowance for uncollectible accounts. Aging information must take into consideration the company's normal terms for a customer. For example, it would not be an issue if many customers are in the 60+ category, but the normal terms for those customers are net 60. However, it would be an issue if the normal terms are net 30 and the same situation existed. Recall the **Trouble?** earlier. The amounts you are asked to investigate next will most likely be different than that stated in the steps. Remember you're just using the Sample Company to explore. You will not find these issues in the end-of-chapter case problems.

To create an accounts receivable aging summary report, do the following:

1 Continue from where you left off. If you closed the Sample Company, follow the steps to reopen it found at the beginning of this chapter.

2 Click **Reports** from the navigation bar.

3 Type **Accounts receivable aging summary** in the Find a report by name search box, and then select the **Accounts receivable aging summary** text, which appears below the search text box to view the accounts receivable (A/R) aging report. Change the "as of" date to the end of the month prior to your system date. In this case, since the system date was 12/12/18, the "as of" date was changed to 11/30/18. Then click **Run Report** to view the report shown in Figure 10.14.

Craig's Design and Landscaping Services
A/R AGING SUMMARY
As of November 30, 2018

	CURRENT	1 - 30	31 - 60	61 - 90	91 AND OVER	TOTAL
Amy's Bird Sanctuary		239.00				$239.00
Bill's Windsurf Shop			85.00			$85.00
▾ Freeman Sporting Goods						$0.00
0969 Ocean View Road	477.50					$477.50
55 Twin Lane	4.00		81.00			$85.00
Total Freeman Sporting Goods	481.50		81.00			$562.50

Figure 10.14

Accounts Receivable (A/R) Aging Summary (partial view)

4 Click on the **85.00** owed by Bill's Windsurf Shop shown in Figure 10.14 to view A/R Aging Detail report shown in Figure 10.15.

Craig's Design and Landscaping Services
A/R AGING DETAIL
As of November 30, 2018

DATE	TRANSACTION TYPE	NUM	CUSTOMER	DUE DATE	AMOUNT	OPEN BALANCE
▾ 31 - 60 days past due						
09/29/2018	Invoice	1027	Bill's Windsurf Shop	10/29/2018	85.00	85.00
Total for 31 - 60 days past due					$85.00	$85.00
TOTAL					$85.00	$85.00

Figure 10.15

Accounts Receivable (A/R) Aging Detail Report (partial view)

5   Click **85.00** to view invoice #1027 shown in Figure 10.16.

Figure 10.16

Invoice #1027 (to Bill's Windsurf Shop)

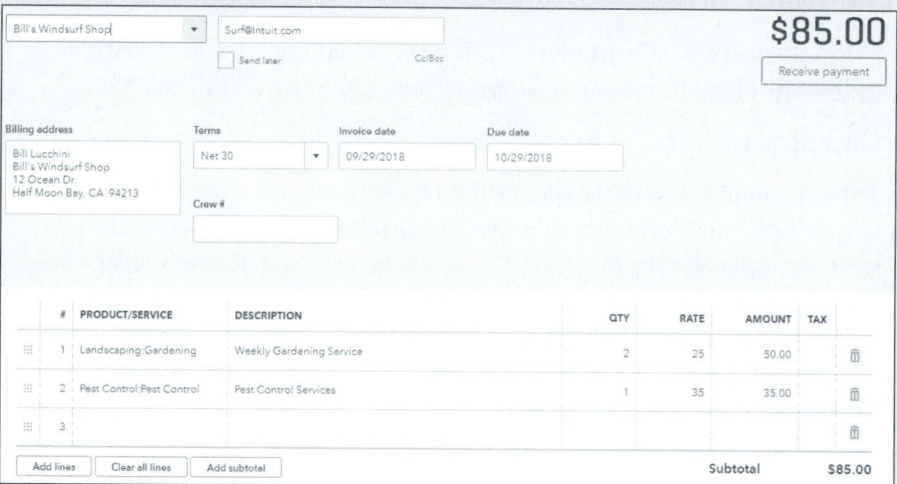

6   Call Bill to find out when he is planning to pay you. Actually, no, do not do that. Instead, click **Cancel** to return to the detail report, and click **Back to report summary** to return to the A/R Aging Summary report.

Accounts Payable Aging Summary

In this section, you will create an accounts payable aging summary, which reflects unpaid bills for the current period and for the last 30, 60, and 90+ days as of a specific date. Aging summaries help prioritize the payment of bills. Aging information must take into consideration the company's normal terms from a vendor. For example, it would not be an issue if a large amount of vendors bills are in the 60+ category, but the normal terms for those vendors are net 60. However, it would be an issue if the normal terms are net 30, and the same situation existed. Recall the **Trouble?** earlier. The amounts you are asked to investigate next will most likely be different than that stated in the steps. Remember you're just using the Sample Company to explore. You will not find these issues in the end-of-chapter case problems.

To create an accounts payable aging summary report, do the following:

1 Continue from where you left off. If you closed the Sample Company, follow the steps to reopen it found at the beginning of this chapter.

2 Click **Reports** from the navigation bar.

3 Type **Accounts payable aging summary** in the Find a report by name search box, and then select the **Accounts payable aging summary** text which appears below the search text box to view the accounts payable aging report. Change the "as of" date to the end of the month prior to your system date. In this case, since the system date was 12/12/18, the "as of" date was changed to 11/30/18. Then click **Run Report** to view the report shown in Figure 10.17.

Craig's Design and Landscaping Services

A/P AGING SUMMARY
As of November 30, 2018

	CURRENT	1 - 30	31 - 60	61 - 90	91 AND OVER	TOTAL
Brosnahan Insurance Agency		241.23				$241.23
Diego's Road Warrior Bodyshop	755.00					$755.00
Norton Lumber and Building ...		205.00				$205.00
PG&E		86.44				$86.44
Robertson & Associates		315.00				$315.00
TOTAL	$755.00	$847.67	$0.00	$0.00	$0.00	$1,602.67

Figure 10.17

Accounts Payable (A/P) Aging Summary

4 Click on the **86.44** owed to PG&E shown in Figure 10.17 to view A/P Aging Detail report shown in Figure 10.18.

Craig's Design and Landscaping Services

A/P AGING DETAIL
As of November 30, 2018

DATE	TRANSACTION TYPE	NUM	VENDOR	DUE DATE	PAST DUE	AMOUNT	OPEN BALANCE
▾ 1 - 30 days past due							
10/02/2018	Bill		PG&E	11/01/2018	41	86.44	86.44
Total for 1 - 30 days past due						$86.44	$86.44
TOTAL						$86.44	$86.44

Figure 10.18

Accounts Payable (A/P) Aging Detail Report

5 Click **86.44** to view the bill shown in Figure 10.19.

Figure 10.19

Bill (from PG&E)

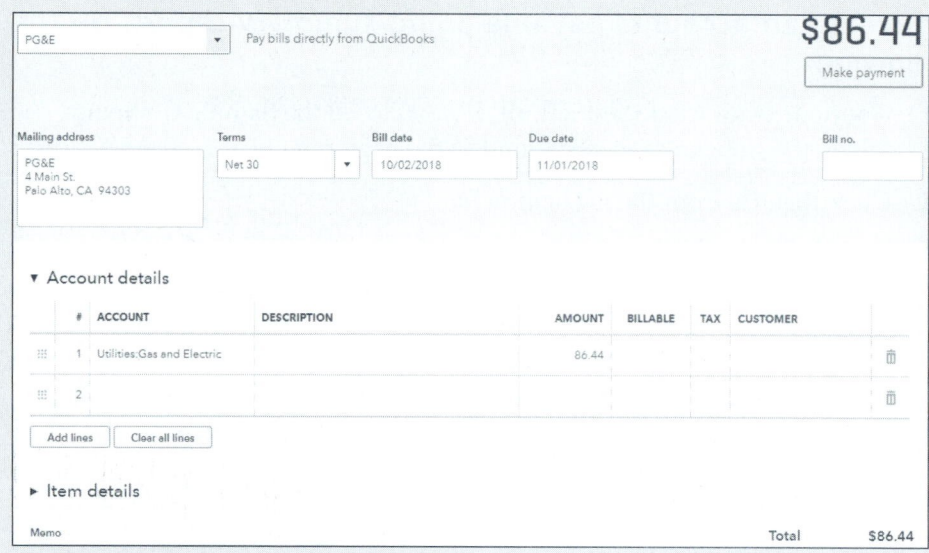

6　Write a check to PG&E before the power gets cut off. Actually, no, do not do that. Instead, click **Cancel** to return to the detail report, and click **Back to report summary** to return to the A/P Aging Summary report.

Inventory Valuation Summary

In this section, you will create an inventory valuation summary that reflects each inventory item's quantity on hand, its average cost, and the resulting valuation as of a specific date. Recall the **Trouble?** earlier. The amounts you are asked to investigate next will most likely be different than that stated in the steps. Remember you're just using the Sample Company to explore. You will not find these issues in the end-of-chapter case problems.

To create an inventory valuation summary report, do the following:

1　Continue from where you left off. If you closed the Sample Company, follow the steps to reopen it found at the beginning of this chapter.

2　Click **Reports** from the navigation bar.

3　Type **Inventory** in the Find a report by name search box, and then select the **Inventory Valuation Summary** text which appears with other inventory reports below the search text box to view the inventory valuation summary report. Change the "as of" date to the end of the month prior to your system date. In this case, since the system date was 12/12/18, the "as of" date was changed to 11/30/18. Then click **Run Report** to view the report shown in Figure 10.20.

Craig's Design and Landscaping Services

INVENTORY VALUATION SUMMARY
As of November 30, 2018

	SKU	QTY	ASSET VALUE	CALC. AVG
▼ Design				
▼ Fountains				
Pump	P461-17	25.00	250.00	10.00
Rock Fountain	R154-88	2.00	250.00	125.00
Total Fountains			500.00	
Total Design			500.00	
▼ Landscaping				
▼ Sprinklers				
Sprinkler Heads	S867-56	25.00	18.75	0.75
Sprinkler Pipes	S867-62	31.00	77.50	2.50
Total Sprinklers			96.25	
Total Landscaping			96.25	
TOTAL			$596.25	

Figure 10.20

Inventory Valuation Summary

4   Click on the **25** representing the number of pumps on hand shown in Figure 10.20 to view an Inventory Valuation Detail report shown in Figure 10.21.

Craig's Design and Landscaping Services

INVENTORY VALUATION DETAIL
As of November 30, 2018

DATE	TRANSACTION TYPE	NUM	NAME	QTY	RATE	FIFO COST	QTY ON HAND	ASSET VALUE
▼ Design								
▼ Fountains								
▼ Pump								
11/16/2018	Inventory Qty Adjust	START		16.00	10.00	160.00	16.00	160.00
11/16/2018	Check	75	Hicks Hardware	3.00	10.00	30.00	19.00	190.00
11/16/2018	Bill		Norton Lumber and Building...	8.00	10.00	80.00	27.00	270.00
11/16/2018	Invoice	1036	Freeman Sporting Goods:09...	-1.00	10.00	-10.00	26.00	260.00
11/16/2018	Invoice	1037	Sonnenschein Family Store	-1.00	10.00	-10.00	25.00	250.00
Total for Pump				25.00		$250.00	25.00	$250.00
Total for Fountains				25.00		$250.00	25.00	$250.00
Total for Design				25.00		$250.00	25.00	$250.00

Figure 10.21

Inventory Valuation Detail

5   Click **Bill** reflecting the purchase of eight pumps shown in Figure 10.21 to view the bill shown in Figure 10.22.

Figure 10.22

Bill (from Norton Lumber for the purchase of eight pumps)

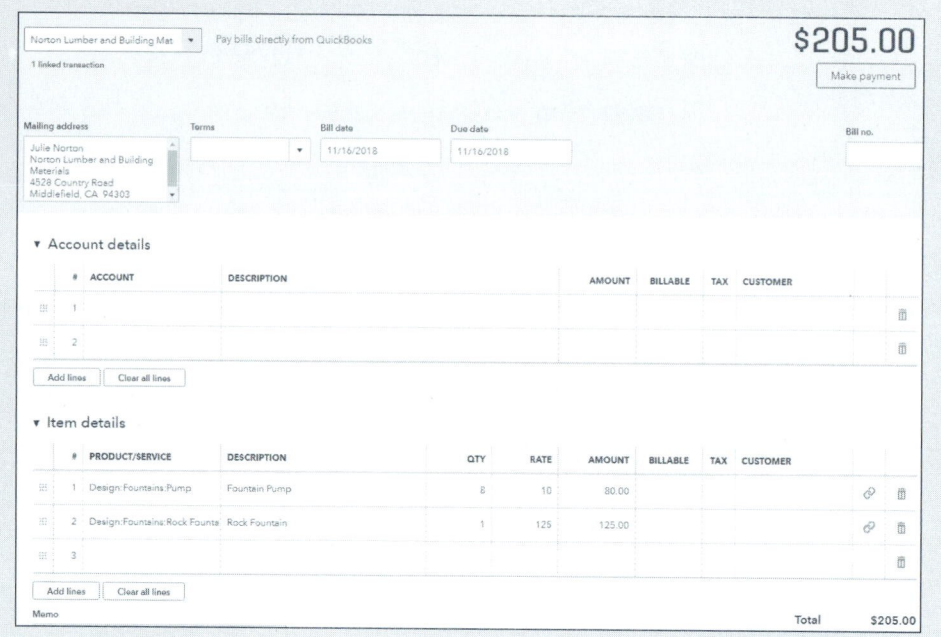

6 Click **Cancel** to return to the detail report, and click **Back to report summary** to return to the A/P Aging Summary report.

Customizing and Saving Reports

All of the reports available in QBO can be customized in some fashion and saved for later use. In this section, you will customize a Profit and Loss report as an example. Recall the **Trouble?** earlier. The amounts you are asked to investigate next will most likely be different than that stated in the steps. Remember you're just using the Sample Company to explore. You will not find these issues in the end-of-chapter case problems.

To customize and save a Profit and Loss report, do the following:

1 Continue from where you left off. If you closed the Sample Company, follow the steps to reopen it found at the beginning of this chapter.

2 Click **Reports** from the navigation bar.

3 Type **Profit** in the Find a report by name search box and then select the **Profit and Loss** text which appears below the search text box.

4 Click **Collapse**.

5 Change the From: date to the first of the month 3 months prior to your system date and the To: date to the end of the month prior to your system date. In this case, since the system date was 12/12/18, the From: date was changed to 9/1/18 and the To: date was changed to 11/30/18. Then click **Run Report** to view the report shown in Figure 10.23.

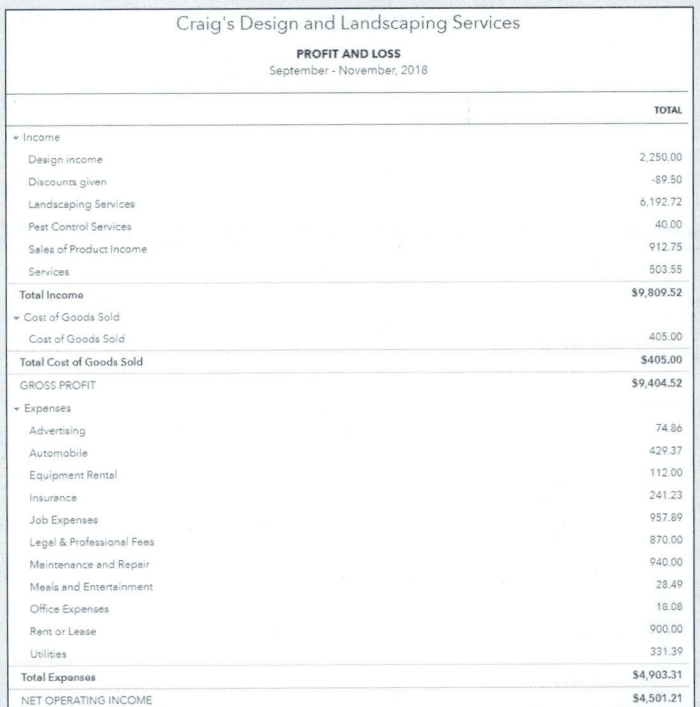

Figure 10.23

Profit and Loss report
(partial view)

6   Click **Customize**, click **Rows/Columns**, and then select **Months** from the
Columns drop-down list in the **Rows/Columns** section of the Customize
Profit and Loss window shown in Figure 10.24.

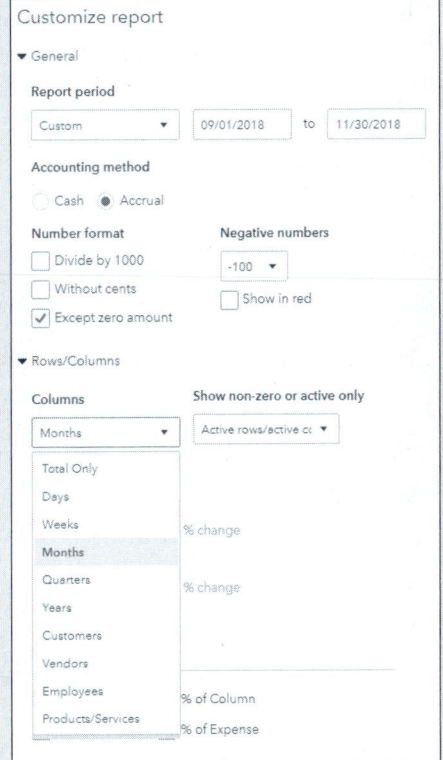

Figure 10.24

Customize Profit and Loss report

7   Scroll down the Customize Profit and Loss window, and place a check in
the **% of Income** check box.

8 Click **Run Report** to view the customized Profit and Loss report shown in Figure 10.25.

Craig's Design and Landscaping Services
PROFIT AND LOSS
September - November, 2018

	SEP 2018		OCT 2018		NOV 2018		TOTAL	
	CURRENT	% OF INCOME	CURRENT	% OF INCOME	CURRENT	% OF INCOME	CURRENT	% OF INCOME
▾ Income								
Design income			975.00	64.54 %	1,275.00	18.44 %	$2,250.00	22.94 %
Discounts given					-89.50	-1.29 %	$ -89.50	-0.91 %
Landscaping Services	1,313.00	94.94 %	635.64	42.08 %	4,244.08	61.37 %	$6,192.72	63.13 %
Pest Control Services	70.00	5.06 %	-100.00	-6.62 %	70.00	1.01 %	$40.00	0.41 %
Sales of Product Income					912.75	13.20 %	$912.75	9.30 %
Services					503.55	7.28 %	$503.55	5.13 %
Total Income	$1,383.00	100.00 %	$1,510.64	100.00 %	$6,915.88	100.00 %	$9,809.52	100.00 %
▾ Cost of Goods Sold								
Cost of Goods Sold					405.00	5.86 %	$405.00	4.13 %
Total Cost of Goods Sold	$0.00	0.00%	$0.00	0.00%	$405.00	5.86 %	$405.00	4.13 %
GROSS PROFIT	$1,383.00	100.00 %	$1,510.64	100.00 %	$6,510.88	94.14 %	$9,404.52	95.87 %

9 Click **Save Customization**.

10 Type **Profit and Loss Comparison** as the new name for this report and then click **Save**.

End Note

In this chapter, you did not add business events, but you did create the basic financial statement reports: profit and loss, balance sheet, and statement of cash flows. In addition, you drilled down beyond those reports to transaction detail reports and to source documents like payments, invoices, bills, etc. You created some analytical reports to learn more about accounts receivable, accounts payable, and inventory. Lastly, you learned how to customize reports and save those reports for later use.

Chapter 10 Questions

View the sample company QBO file to answer these questions by creating reports:

1   Invoice 1015 was created for which customer?

2   What was the first item sold on invoice 1015?

3   What was the last item sold that was categorized as sales of product income?

4   Who sent a bill for $315.00 in accounting fees?

5   How many sprinkler heads are currently on hand?

6   What is the average cost per unit of sprinkler heads?

7   Who is the most delinquent customer?

8   What is the total amount of receivables that are current?

9   What amount of payables are 1–30 days past due?

10   What amount of cash was provided by financing activities?

Chapter 10 Matching

a. Income statement	_____	Click on an event in any transaction report
b. Balance sheet	_____	Click an account on any report
c. Statement of cash flows	_____	Click to add a new column in a report
d. AR aging report	_____	Reflects unpaid bills for the current period
e. AP aging report	_____	Reports revenues and expenses
f. Inventory valuation report	_____	Includes operating, investing, and financing activities
g. Profit and Loss report	_____	Reports inventory quantities on hand
h. To view a transaction report	_____	Reports assets, liabilities, and equities
i. To view a source document	_____	Another name for the income statement
j. % of income check box	_____	Reflects unpaid invoices for the current period

Chapter 10 Cases

The following cases require you to open the company you updated in Chapter 9. Each of the following cases continues throughout the text in a sequential manner. Each of the following cases is similar in concepts assessed but differ in amounts and transactions.

To reopen your company, do the following:

1 Open your Internet browser.

2 Type **https://qbo.intuit.com** into your browser's address text box.

3 Type your User ID and Password into the text boxes as you have earlier.

Case 1

Now it is time to create, customize, and print some new reports. Based on what you learned in the text using the Sample Company, you are to make the following changes to the Case 1 company you modified in Chapter 9:

1 Create, print, and export to Excel a Profit and Loss report for January 2018. Customize this report by adding a percent of income column and saving and by sharing your customization as Profit and Loss Jan 2018.

2 Using the Profit and Loss report created above, drill down to a Transactions Report for the Sales account. Print and export this report to Excel. Save and share this report as a Sales Transaction Report.

3 Create, print, and export to Excel a Balance Sheet report as of 1/31/18. Customize this report by adding a percent of column and saving and sharing your customization as Balance Sheet Jan 2018.

4 Using the Balance Sheet report created above, drill down to a Transactions Report for the Checking account. Print and export this report to Excel. Save and share this report as Checking Report.

5 Create, print, and export to Excel a Statement of Cash Flows report as of 1/31/18. Save and share your customization as Statement of Cash Flows Jan 2018.

6 Using the Statement of Cash Flows report created above, drill down to a Transactions Report for the Accounts Receivable account. Print and export this report to Excel. Save and share this report as an A/R SCF Report.

7 Create, print, and export to Excel an A/R Aging Summary report for the month of January 2018. Save and share your customization as A/R Aging Summary Jan 2018.

8 Create, print, and export to Excel an A/P Aging Summary report for the month of January 2018. Save and share your customization as A/P Aging Summary Jan 2018.

9 Create, print, and export to Excel an Inventory Valuation Summary report for the month of January 2018. Save and share your customization as an Inventory Valuation Summary Jan 2018.

Case 2

Now it is time to create, customize, and print some new reports. Based on what you learned in the text using the Sample Company, you are to make the following changes to the Case 2 company you modified in Chapter 9:

1 Create, print, and export to Excel a Profit and Loss report for January 2019. Customize this report by adding a percent of income column. Save and share your customization as Profit and Loss Jan 2019.

2 Using the Profit and Loss report created above, drill down to a Transactions Report for the Insurance account. Print and export this report to Excel. Save and share this report as an Insurance Transaction Report.

3 Create, print, and export to Excel a Balance Sheet report as of 1/31/19. Customize this report by adding a percent of column. Save and share your customization as Balance Sheet Jan 2019.

4 Using the Balance Sheet report created above, drill down to a Transactions Report for the Inventory Asset account. Print and export this report to Excel. Save and share this report as Inventory Report.

5 Create, print, and export to Excel a Statement of Cash Flows report as of 1/31/19. Save and share your customization as Statement of Cash Flows Jan 2019.

6 Using the Statement of Cash Flows report created above, drill down to a Transactions Report for the Prepaid Expenses account. Print and export this report to Excel. Save and share this report as PPE SCF Report.

7 Create, print, and export to Excel an A/R Aging Summary report for the month of January 2019. Save and share your customization as an A/R Aging Summary Jan 2019.

8 Create, print, and export to Excel an A/P Aging Summary report for the month of January 2019. Save and share your customization as an A/P Aging Summary Jan 2019.

9 Create, print, and export to Excel an Inventory Valuation Summary report for January 2018. Save and share your customization as Inventory Valuation Summary Jan 2018.

Case 3

Now it is time to create, customize, and print some new reports. Based on what you learned in the text using the Sample Company, you are to make the following changes to the Case 3 company you modified in Chapter 9:

1 Create, print, and export to Excel a Profit and Loss report for the month of January 2020. Customize this report by adding a percent of income column and saving and sharing your customization as Profit and Loss Jan 2020.

2 Using the Profit and Loss report created earlier, drill down to a Transactions Report for the Advertising & Marketing account. Print and export this report to Excel. Save and share this report as Advertising & Marketing Transaction Report.

3   Create, print, and export to Excel a Balance Sheet report as of 1/31/20. Customize this report by adding a percent of row column and saving and sharing your customization as Balance Sheet Jan 2020.

4   Using the Balance Sheet report created earlier, drill down to a Transactions Report for the Accounts Receivable (A/R) account. Print and export this report to Excel. Save and share this report as AR Report.

5   Create, print, and export to Excel a Statement of Cash Flows report as of 1/31/20. Save and share your customization as Statement of Cash Flows Jan 2020.

6   Using the Statement of Cash Flows report created earlier, drill down to a Transactions Report for the Payroll Tax Payable account. Print and export this report to Excel. Save and share this report as Payroll Tax SCF Report.

7   Create, print, and export to Excel an A/R Aging Summary report for the month of January 2020. Save and share your customization as A/R Aging Summary Jan 2020.

8   Create, print, and export to Excel an A/P Aging Summary report for the month of January 2020. Save and share your customization as A/P Aging Summary Jan 2020.

9   Create, print, and export to Excel an Inventory Valuation Summary report for the month of January 2020. Save and share your customization as Inventory Valuation Summary Jan 2020.

Case 4

Now it is time to create, customize and print some new reports. Based on what you learned in the text using the Sample Company, you are to make the following changes to the Case 4 company you modified in Chapter 9:

1   Create and print a Profit and Loss report for the month of January 2021. Customize this report by adding a percent of income column and saving your customization as Profit and Loss Jan 2021.

2   Using the Profit and Loss report you just created, drill down to a Transactions report for the Advertising & Marketing account. Print and save this report as Advertising Transaction Report.

3   Create and print a Balance Sheet report as of 1/31/21. Customize this report by adding a percent of row column. Collapse, print, and save this report as Balance Sheet Jan 2021.

4   Using the Balance Sheet report you just created, drill down to a Transactions Report for the Accounts Receivable (A/R) account. Print and save this report as AR Report.

5   Create and print a Statement of Cash Flows report as of 1/31/21. Save your customization as Statement of Cash Flows Jan 2021.

6   Using the Statement of Cash Flows report you just created, drill down to a Transactions Report for the Payroll Tax Payable account. Print and save this report as Payroll Tax SCF Report.

7   Create and print an Accounts receivable aging summary report for the month of January 2021. Save your customization as A/R Aging Summary Jan 2021.

8   Create and print an Accounts payable aging summary report for the month of January 2021. Save your customization as A/P Aging Summary Jan 2021.

9   Create and print an Inventory Valuation Summary report for the month of January 2021. Save your customization as Inventory Valuation Summary Jan 2021.

Sales Tax

Some companies are required to collect sales tax from customers depending on the state(s) in which they do business. Sales tax in QuickBooks Online has gotten getting easier! Through the New Automated Sales Tax experience, you just need to answer a few simple questions and QuickBooks Online will know what taxes apply to your business, set them up, and automatically track your sales taxes.

This means you no longer need to select a tax rate when you create an invoice or other transaction. As long as your Sales Tax Center and all applicable tax agencies are set up, the system will automatically do it for you!

Be advised that end of chapter Cases 1 & 2 do not require the collection of sales tax. Case 3 does require sales taxes be collected, however, the sales tax rate is overridden to a flat rate. Case 4 does require the collection of sales tax using the new Automated Sales Tax system.

The following are steps to set up the new Automated Sales Tax system.

To set up a company's sales tax:

1 Click **Taxes** from the navigation bar.

2 Click **Set up sales tax** button (assuming you've already entered your company's address during the set up process), then click **Looks good** to confirm the company address, and then click **Next**. Click **No** when asked if you need to collect sales tax out of California. Now view the window shown in Figure A.1.

Figure A.1

Sales Tax Center

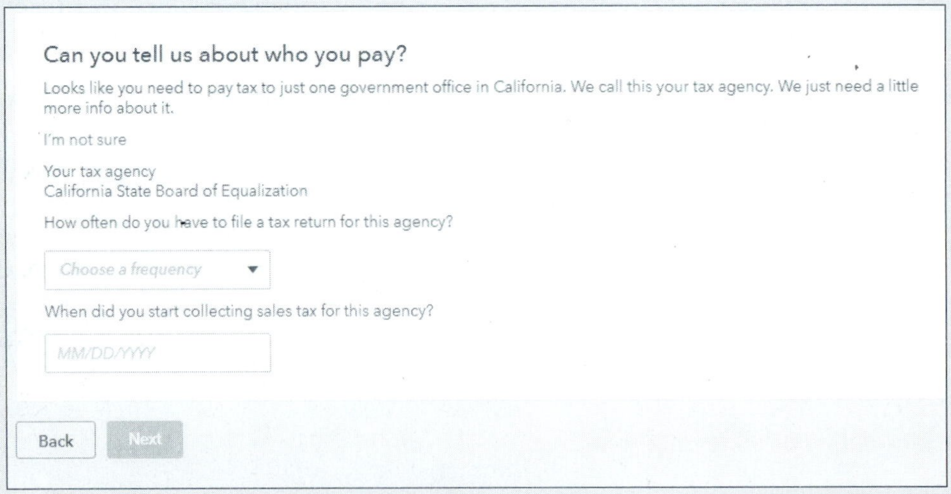

Can you tell us about who you pay?

Looks like you need to pay tax to just one government office in California. We call this your tax agency. We just need a little more info about it.

I'm not sure

Your tax agency
California State Board of Equalization

How often do you have to file a tax return for this agency?

Choose a frequency ▼

When did you start collecting sales tax for this agency?

MM/DD/YYYY

Back   Next

3 Select **Yearly** in the Filing frequency drop-down text box, then type **01/01/2020** in the Start date text box, and then click **Next**.

4 Click **Got it** to complete your sales tax setup.

Comprehensive Case Problems

Your instructor may assign you these comprehensive case problems after you complete all 10 chapters of the text. These are an *extension* of the cases assigned at the end of Chapters 3–10 of the *QuickBooks Online for Accounting 3e* text. To be explicit, Case 1 can be used by students only if they have *successfully completed* Case 1 through Chapter 10, Case 2 can be used by students only if they have *successfully completed* Case 2 through Chapter 10, Case 3 can be used by students only if they have *successfully completed* Case 3 through Chapter 10, and Case 4 can be used by students only if they have *successfully completed* Case 4 through Chapter 10. This is because QBO only allows you access to one company.

Case 1 Comprehensive Problem

Case 1, which begins in Chapter 3, is a company which distributes surfboards and is in La Jolla, California. Business events in Case 1 occurred from 12/31/17 to 1/31/18 when presented in Chapters 3–10. The following is a description of business events that occurred in the month of February 2018.

Date	Description of Event	Chapter	Event
2/1/2018	Add a new product	4	Add a new product with quantity tracked – Biscuit Bonzer, initial quantity on hand: 0, as of date 2/1/2018, price: $1,000.00, cost: $675.00, income account: Sales, expense account: Cost of Goods Sold. Vendor: Channel Islands.
2/1/2018	Edit the chart of accounts	3	Change the name of the account Notes Payable to Notes Payable – Bank of CA.
2/1/2018	Add a new service	4	Add a new service – Repairs, Rate: $85.00, income account: Services.
2/1/2018	Modify budget	8	Modify the following monthly budgeted amounts (Budget 1) for February 2018 through December 2018 as follows: sales: $35,000, services: $2,000, cost of goods sold: $21,500, interest expense: $800, payroll: $13,000, rent or lease: $2,500, travel: $500, utilities: $300.
2/1/2018	Add new employee	7	Add a new employee: Jane Price, 65 Ocean View Lane, La Jolla, CA 92037, Employee ID No. 555-15-3537.
2/1/2018	Add a new customer	4	Add a new customer – Awesome Surf, 501 Boardwalk Place, Santa Cruz, CA 95060.
2/5/2018	Add a sales receipt	4	Add a new sales receipt 1005 for $2,810 – Customer: Awesome Surf, payment method: Check, reference no.: 984 deposits to: Undeposited Funds, product: The Water Hog, quantity: 1 and Rook 15, quantity 3.
2/6/2018	Add a new invoice	4	Add a new invoice 1006 for $820 – Custemer: Surf Rider Foundation, terms: Net 30, service: Repairs, quantity: 2, product: Rook 15, quantity: 1.
2/7/2018	Add a cash receipt	4	Add a new cash receipt – Customer: Blondie's Boards, payment method: Check, reference 1003, deposit to: Undeposited Funds, amount received: $8,000.00, applied to Invoice # 1003.
2/8/2018	Make a bank deposit	4	Add a bank deposit to the checking account in the amount of $15,810.00 which represents payments from Blondie's Boards for $5,000 and $8,000 and Awesome Surf for $2,810.
2/9/2018	Add a new vendor	5	Add a new vendor – BoardsWest, 36 Anacapa St., Santa Barbara, CA 93101, terms: Net 30.

2/9/2018	Add a new product	5	Add a new product with quantity tracked – Wiley One, initial quantity on hand: 0, as of date 2/9/2018, price: $4,000.00, cost: $2,400.00, income account: Sales, expense account: Cost of Goods Sold. Vendor: BoardsWest.
2/9/2018	Add a new account	3	Add a new account – Category type: Other Current Assets, detail type: Other Current Assets, name: Employee Loans.
2/9/2018	Add a new purchase order	5	Add a new purchase order 1003 for $9,600 to purchase 4 Wiley One boards from vendor BoardsWest.
2/10/2018	Use credit card	5	Add a credit card charge, vendor: Village Travel, using credit card: VISA, account: Travel, amount: $775.00.
2/11/2018	Record a check	5	Add check 1013, vendor: Office Depot, amount: $575.00, account: Supplies Asset.
2/11/2018	Add a new purchase order	5	Add a new purchase order 1004 for $12,400 – Vendor: Channel Islands ordered 10 Fred Rubbles, 6 Rook 15, and 8 The Water Hog boards.
2/12/2018	Add a new bill	5	Add a new bill based on a purchase order 1002 for $4,700 – Vendor: Stewart Surfboards, terms: Net 30. All items ordered were received.
2/13/2018	Add a new bill	5	Add a new bill without a purchase order – San Diego Gas & Electric, terms: Net 15, account: Utilities, amount $150.00.
2/14/2018	Add a new bill	5	Add a new bill without a purchase order – Prime Properties, terms: Net 15, account: Rent or Lease, amount: $2,500.00.
2/14/2018	Pay a bill with a check	5	Pay bill $7,500 due to Prime Properties using check no. 1012.
2/15/2018	Add new fixed asset accounts	6	Create four new fixed asset accounts: category type: Fixed Assets, detail type: Buildings and Accumulated Depreciation (where appropriate), account names: Original Cost (a sub-account of Building) and Accumulated Depreciation (a sub-account of Building) and Land with category type: Fixed Asset, detail type: Land.
2/15/2018	Purchase land and building	6	Add the purchase of land and a warehouse building from Prime Properties, check: 1014, amount: $2,000, as a down payment on land $5,000 and a building $15,000. The balance was paid by signing a long-term note for $18,000 (create a new account called Notes Payable – Chase, a Category Type: Long-Term Liabilities, Detail Type: Notes Payable.)
2/19/2018	Sell common stock	6	Add the sale of common stock to Shareholders as a deposit of a $15,000 check.
2/19/2018	Pay dividends	6	Add the payment of dividends to Shareholders on 2/19/18, check 1015, in the amount of $500.
2/20/2018	Make a loan payment	6	Add the payment of $339.68 to Chase Bank (a new vendor) as an installment on the land and building purchase made on 2/15/18 which included interest expense of $75.00 and principal amount of $264.68 using check 1016.
2/20/2018	Make a loan payment	6	Record the payment of 1,132.27 to Bank of CA on 2/20/18 (as an installment on a loan received last month) which included interest expense of 250.00 and principal amount of 882.27 using check 1017.
2/20/2018	Pay first payroll	7	Add payroll (as you did in the chapter) based on the information shown in Figure 1. (This payroll covers work through 2/15/18 but wasn't paid until 2/20/18.)
2/27/2018	Add a new bill	6	Add a new bill based on purchase order 1003 on 2/9/18 – Vendor: BoardsWest, terms: Net 30. All items ordered were received.
2/27/2018	Add a new invoice	4	Add invoice 1007 for $12,000 to Blazing Boards, terms: Net 30, for 3 Wiley One boards.
2/28/2018	Pay second payroll	7	Add payroll (as you did in the chapter) based on the information shown in Figure 2 below.
2/28/2018	Add a new bill	5	Add a new bill based on purchase order 1004 for $12,400 – Vendor: Channel Islands, terms: Net 15. All items ordered were received. (Hint: First clear all lines in the Item details section of the bill which are left over from a previous bill from Channel Islands.)
2/28/2018	Add a new invoice	4	Add an invoice 1008 for $12,990 to Blondie's Boards, terms: Net 30, for 8 Fred Rubble, 3 Rook 15, and 4 The Water Hog boards.

2/28/2018	Add a sales receipt	4	Add a sales receipt 1009 for Sarah Hay at Hey Hays Surf for $12,210 to record their check 988 which was deposited to the checking account for 1 California Nose Rider, 3 Fred Rubble, 1 Wiley One, 1 Water Hog, and 2 Rook 15 boards.
2/28/2018	Reconcile bank account	4	Reconcile your company's checking account. No service charges or interest were incurred or earned. The ending bank statement balance on 2/28/18 was $39,896.91. All checks cleared the bank except checks 1021, 1022, and 1023. All deposits cleared the bank except a check from Sarah Hay for $12,210.
2/28/2018	Adjust supplies	9	$250 of supplies were used in February. Use journal entry 10.
2/28/2018	Adjust prepaid rent	9	$800 of prepaid expenses expired (representing prepaid rent) in the month of February. Use journal entry 11.
2/28/2018	Accrue expenses	9	A bill for $450 was received and recorded in the next month for travel consumed in the current month. Use journal entry 12. In January, you accrued $150 in maintenance costs which remains unpaid. No adjustment necessary but payment needs to be made next month.
2/28/2018	Defer revenue	9	Consulting services recorded on invoice #1004 for $2,500.00 to Surf Rider Foundation were unearned as of 1/31/18 but were performed in February 2018. Thus, the revenue was earned. This requires the reversal of journal entry 7 recorded on 1/31/18. (Hint: look at journal entry 7 and use journal entry 13 to reverse it on 2/28/18.)
2/28/2018	Accrue revenue	9	Consulting services of $8,500 (340 hours) were performed as of 1/31/18 for Blazing Boards but not invoiced to the customer or recorded into the accounting records. Revenue was accrued using journal entry 8. Add invoice 1010 to bill Blazing Boards for this service. This also requires reversal of journal entry 8 recorded on 1/31/18. (Hint: look at journal entry 8 and use journal entry 14 to reverse it on 2/28/18.)
2/28/2018	Accrue depreciation	9	Depreciation Expense of $675 ($100, $75, and $500 for Building, Equipment, and Furniture & Fixtures, respectively) needs to be recorded for the month. Use journal entry 15 to record this depreciation.
2/28/2018	Accrue revenue	9	Consulting services of $10,200 were performed on 2/28/18 for a new customer Kyle Hain but not invoiced or recorded into the accounting records. Use journal entry 16 to accrue this revenue.

Pay/Tax/Withholding	Ben	Betsy	Jane	Total
Hours if applicable	n/a	62	60	
Annual salary or hourly rate	95,000	21.50	20.00	
Gross pay	3,958.33	1,333.00	1,200.00	5,291.33
Federal withholding	542.29	182.62	164.40	724.91
Social security employee (6.2%)	245.42	82.65	74.40	328.07
Medicare employee (1.45%)	57.40	19.33	17.40	76.73
Employee withholding	845.11	284.60	256.20	1,129.71
Social security employer (6.2%)	245.42	82.65	74.40	328.07
Medicare employer (1.45%)	57.40	19.33	17.40	76.73
Employer payroll tax expense	302.82	101.98	91.80	404.80
Net Check amount	3,113.22	1,048.40	943.80	5,105.42
Check number	1018	1019	1020	

Figure 1

1st Semi-monthly Payroll

Figure 2

2nd Semi-monthly Payroll

Pay/Tax/Withholding	Ben	Betsy	Jane	Total
Hours if applicable	n/a	52	45	
Annual salary or hourly rate	95,000	21.50	20.00	
Gross pay	**3,958.33**	**1,118.00**	**900.00**	**5,076.33**
Federal withholding	542.29	153.17	123.30	**695.46**
Social security employee (6.2%)	245.42	69.32	55.80	**314.74**
Medicare employee (1.45%)	57.40	16.21	13.05	**73.61**
Employee withholding	**845.11**	**238.70**	**192.15**	**1,083.81**
Social security employer (6.2%)	245.42	69.32	55.80	**314.74**
Medicare employer (1.45%)	57.40	16.21	13.05	**73.61**
Employer payroll tax expense	**302.82**	**85.53**	**68.85**	**388.35**
Net Check amount	3,113.22	879.30	707.85	**3,992.52**
Check number	**1021**	**1022**	**1023**	

Requirements:

1 Create, save, and print a Profit and Loss report for February 2018.

2 Create, save, and print a Sales Transaction report for February 2018.

3 Create, save, and print a Balance Sheet report for February 28, 2018.

4 Create, save, and print a Checking report for February 2018.

5 Create, save, and print a Statement of Cash Flows report for February 2018.

6 Create, save, and print an A/R Aging Summary report for February 2018.

7 Create, save, and print an A/P Aging Summary report for February 2018.

8 Create, save, and print an Inventory Valuation Summary report for February 2018.

9 Create, save, and print a transactions list by date report for February 2018.

10 Create, save, and print a Budget vs. Actuals report for February 2018.

Case 2 Comprehensive Problem

Case 2, which begins in Chapter 3, is a company which distributes remote control toys and is in La Jolla, California. Business events in Case 2 occurred from 12/31/18 to 1/31/19 when presented in Chapters 3–10. The following is a description of business events that occurred in the month of February 2019.

Date	Description of Event	Chapter	Event
2/1/2019	Add a new product	4	Add a new product – Speedy Whit, initial quantity on hand: 0, as of date 2/1/2019, price: $1,500.00, cost: $925.00, income account: Sales, expense account: Cost of Goods Sold.

2/1/2019	Add a new vendor	5	Add a new vendor – 3D Robotics, 36 Anacapa St., Santa Barbara, CA 93101, terms: Net 30.
2/1/2019	Edit the chart of accounts	3	Change the name of the account Notes Payable to Notes Payable – Bank of San Diego.
2/1/2019	Add a new service	4	Add a new service – Consulting, Rate: $105.00, income account: Services.
2/1/2019	Modify budget	8	Modify the following monthly budgeted amounts (Budget 1) for February 2019 through December 2019 as follows: sales: $22,000, services: $4,800, cost of goods sold: $11,000, interest expense: $400, payroll: $10,000, rent or lease: $2,500, travel: $500, utilities: $300. All other accounts remain the same.
2/1/2019	Add new employee	7	Add a new employee: Juan Perez, 65 Ocean View Lane, La Jolla, CA 92037, Employee ID No.: 555-15-3537.
2/1/2019	Add a new customer	4	Add a new customer – Briggs Construction, 501 Boardwalk Place, Santa Cruz, CA 95060.
2/5/2019	Add a sales receipt	4	Add a new sales receipt 1005 for $3,300 – Customer: Briggs Construction, payment method: Check, reference no.: 984 deposits to: Undeposited Funds, product: Broon F830 Ride, quantity: 1 and Sport Cub S, quantity 3.
2/6/2019	Add a new invoice	4	Add a new invoice 1006 for $2,250 – Customer: Hagen's Toys, terms: Net 30, service: Consulting, quantity: 10, product: Sport Cub S, quantity: 2.
2/7/2019	Add a cash receipt	4	Add a new cash receipt – Customer: Hagen's Toys, payment method: Check, reference 5841, deposit to: Undeposited Funds, amount received: $1,425. (related to invoice # 1002)
2/8/2019	Make a bank deposit	4	Add a bank deposit to the checking account in the amount of $5,650. (Benson's RC $925, Brigg's Const. $3,300, and Hagen's Toys $1,425)
2/9/2019	Add a new product	4	Add a new product – Pro View, initial quantity on hand: 0, as of date 2/9/2019, price: $2,500, cost: $1,200, income account: Sales, expense account: Cost of Goods Sold.
2/9/2019	Add a new account	3	Add a new account – Category type: Other Current Assets, detail type: Other Current Assets, name: Security Deposits.
2/9/2019	Add a new purchase order	5	Add a new purchase order 1003 for $11,550 to purchase 6 Speedy Whit and 5 Pro View drones from vendor 3D Robotics.
2/9/2019	Use credit card	5	Add a credit card charge, new vendor: Village Travel, using credit card: AMEX, account: Travel, amount: $1,800.
2/11/2019	Record a check	5	Add check 1011, vendor: Staples, amount: $750, account: Supplies Asset.
2/11/2019	Add a new purchase order	5	Add a new purchase order 1004 for $3,695 – Vendor: E-flite for 5 Sport Cub S and 4 Mystique RES drones.
2/12/2019	Add a new bill	5	Add a new bill based on a purchase order 1002 for $8,820 – Vendor: Kyosho, terms: Net 30. All items ordered were received.
2/13/2019	Add a new bill	5	Add a new bill without a purchase order – San Diego Gas & Electric (a new vendor), terms: Net 15, account: Utilities, amount $150.00.
2/13/2019	Add a new bill	5	Add a new bill without a purchase order – Deluxe Properties (a new vendor), terms: Net 15, account: Rent or Lease, amount: $3,500.00.
2/13/2019	Add new fixed asset accounts	6	Create four new fixed asset accounts: category type: Fixed Assets, detail type: Buildings and Accumulated Depreciation (where appropriate), account names: Original Cost (a sub-account of Building) and Accumulated Depreciation (a sub-account of Building) and Land with category type: Fixed Asset, detail type: Land.
2/13/2019	Purchase land and building	6	Add the purchase of land and a warehouse building from Deluxe Properties, check: 1012, amount: $10,000, as a down payment on land $15,000 and a building $35,000. The balance was paid by signing a long-term note for $40,000 to the Bank of San Diego (a new vendor).

2/15/2019	Pay first payroll	7	Add payroll (as you did in the chapter) based on the information shown in Figure 1.
2/19/2019	Sell common stock	6	Add the sale of common stock to Shareholders as a deposit of a $10,000 check #3009.
2/19/2019	Pay dividends	6	Add the payment of dividends to Shareholders on 2/19/19, check 1016, in the amount of $500.
2/20/2019	Make a loan payment	6	Add the payment of $1,216.88 to the Bank of San Diego as an installment on the land and building purchase made on 2/15/19 which included interest expense of $200 and principal amount of $1,016.88 using check 1017.
2/22/2019	Add a new bill	5	Add a new bill based on a purchase order 1003 – Vendor: 3D Robotics, terms: Net 30, amount: $11,550. All items ordered were received.
2/25/2019	Add a new invoice	4	Add invoice 1007 for $10,500 to Kelly's Awesome Copters terms: Net 30, for 4 Speedy Whit and 3 Broon F830 Ride drones.
2/25/2019	Pay a bill with a check	5	Pay bill $3,500 due to Deluxe Properties using check no. 1018.
2/26/2019	Receive payment	4	Receive payment on account from Hagen's Toys of $4,500 from Invoice 1003 using check #938.
2/27/2019	Add a new invoice	4	Add an invoice 1008 for $4,755 to A+ Engineering (a new customer) terms: Net 30, for 15 hours of consulting, 2 Speedy Whit drones, and 4 hours of custom painting.
2/27/2019	Add a new bill	5	Add a new bill based on purchase order 1004 for $3,695 – Vendor: E-flite, terms: Net 15. All items ordered were received. (Hint: First clear all lines in the Item details section of the bill which are left over from a previous bill from E-flite.)
2/27/2019	Add a sales receipt	4	Add a sales receipt 1009 for Fly by Night (a new customer) for $2,700 to record cash received which was deposited to the checking account for 3 Sport Cub S and 2 Mystique RES drones.
2/27/2019	Make a deposit	4	Deposited Hagen's Toys check for $4,500 into the checking account.
2/28/2019	Add a new invoice	4	Add invoice 1010 to record repair services performed for Kelly's Awesome Copters. This transaction had been accrued on 1/31/2019 via journal entry #8. (A variety of rates were used on this repair, thus just enter $6,298 as the RATE for this invoice and 1 as the QTY.)
2/28/2019	Add a bill	5	Add a bill for legal services rendered by Galas & Associates (new vendor) for $750. This had been accrued on 1/31/2019 using journal entry 6.
2/28/2019	Pay second payroll	7	Add payroll (as you did in the chapter) based on the information shown in Figure 2 below.
2/28/2019	Reconcile bank account	8	Reconcile you company's checking account. No service charges or interest were incurred or earned. The ending back statement balance on 2/28/19 was $29,835.47. All checks cleared the bank except checks 1019, 1020, and 1021. All deposits cleared the bank except a deposit from Hagen's Toys for $4,500.
2/28/2019	Adjust supplies	9	$250 of supplies were used in February. Use journal entry 10.
2/28/2019	Adjust prepaids	9	$1,800 of prepaid expenses expired (representing prepaid insurance) in the month of February. Use journal entry 11.
2/28/2019	Accrue expenses	9	A bill for $850 was received and recorded in the next month for travel consumed in the current month. Use journal entry 12.
2/28/2019	Reverse accrual	9	Legal fees accrued on 1/31/2019 for $750 via journal entry 6 were properly recorded in February. Use journal entry 13 to reverse it.
2/28/2019	Defer revenue	9	Consulting services recorded on invoice #1008 for $1,575 to A+ Engineering were not yet performed and thus were unearned as of 2/28/19. Use journal entry 14 to defer this revenue.
2/28/2019	Accrue depreciation	9	Depreciation Expense of $1,125 ($125, $375 and $625 for Building, Furniture, and Machinery & Equipment, respectively) needed to be recorded for the month. Use journal entry 15 to record this depreciation.

| 2/28/2019 | Reverse accrual | 9 | $6,298 of revenue had been accrued on 1/31/2019 via journal entry #8 for services rendered but not yet invoiced. These were then invoiced using invoice 1010 to Kelly's Awesome Copters. (Hint – reverse journal entry 8 via a new journal entry 16.) |
| 2/28/2019 | Accrue revenue | 9 | Consulting services of $15,000 were performed on 2/28/19 for a new customer Wesley Ray but not invoiced or recorded into the accounting records. Use journal entry 17 to accrue this revenue. |

Pay/Tax/Withholding	Frank	Sara	Juan	Total
Hours if applicable	n/a	80	65	
Annual salary or hourly rate	72,000	18.75	17.00	
Gross pay	**3,000.00**	**1,500.00**	**1,105.00**	**4,500.00**
Federal withholding	411.00	205.50	151.39	616.50
Social security employee (6.2%)	186.00	93.00	68.51	279.00
Medicare employee (1.45%)	43.50	21.75	16.02	65.25
Employee withholding	**640.50**	**320.25**	**235.92**	**960.75**
Social security employer (6.2%)	186.00	93.00	68.51	279.00
Medicare employer (1.45%)	43.50	21.75	16.02	65.25
Employer payroll tax expense	**229.50**	**114.75**	**84.53**	**344.25**
Net Check amount	2,359.50	1,179.75	869.08	3,539.25
Check number	**1013**	**1014**	**1015**	

Figure 1

1st Semi-monthly Payroll

Pay/Tax/Withholding	Frank	Sara	Juan	Total
Hours if applicable	n/a	75	70	
Annual salary or hourly rate	72,000	18.75	17.00	
Gross pay	**3,000.00**	**1,406.25**	**1,190.00**	**4,406.25**
Federal withholding	411.00	192.66	163.03	603.66
Social security employee (6.2%)	186.00	87.19	73.78	273.19
Medicare employee (1.45%)	43.50	20.39	17.26	63.89
Employee withholding	**640.50**	**300.24**	**254.07**	**940.74**
Social security employer (6.2%)	186.00	87.19	73.78	273.19
Medicare employer (1.45%)	43.50	20.39	17.26	63.89
Employer payroll tax expense	**229.50**	**107.58**	**91.04**	**337.08**
Net Check amount	2,359.50	1,106.01	935.93	3,465.51
Check number	**1019**	**1020**	**1021**	

Figure 2

2nd Semi-monthly Payroll

Requirements:

1 Create, save, and print a Profit and Loss report for February 2019.

2 Create, save, and print a Total Income Transaction report for February 2019. (Hint: click the Total Income amount in the Profit and Loss report for February 2019.)

3 Create, save, and print a Balance Sheet report for February 28, 2019.

4 Create, save, and print a Checking report for February 2019.

5 Create, save, and print a Statement of Cash Flows report for February 2019.

6 Create, save, and print an A/R Aging Summary report for February 2019.

7 Create, save, and print an A/P Aging Summary report for February 2019.

8 Create, save, and print an Inventory Valuation Summary report for February 2019.

9 Create, save, and print a Transactions List by Date report for February 2019.

10 Create, save, and print a Budget vs. Actuals report for February 2019.

Case 3 Comprehensive Problem

Case 3, which begins in Chapter 3, is a company which sells and services cell phones to consumers (retail business) and is in La Jolla, California. Business events in Case 3 occurred from 12/31/19 to 1/31/20 when presented in Chapters 3–10. The following is a description of business events that occurred in the month of February 2020.

Date	Description of Event	Chapter	Event
2/2/2020	Add new products	4	Add two new taxable products –iPhone 8, initial quantity on hand: 0, as of date 2/1/2020, Inventory asset account: Inventory Asset, price: $850.00, cost: $650.00, income account: Sales of Product Income, expense account: Cost of Goods Sold (taxable) and iPhone 8 Plus, initial quantity on hand: 0, as of date 2/1/2020, Inventory asset account: Inventory Asset, price: $1,050.00, cost: $850.00, income account: Sales of Product Income, expense account: Cost of Goods Sold (taxable).
2/2/2020	Change the name of a product	4	Change the name of the Apple iPhone 7 to iPhone 7.
2/2/2020	Add a new vendor	5	Add a new vendor – LG Baker Distributing Company, 36 Sequoia St., Redlands, CA 92374, terms: Net 30.
2/2/2020	Add a new product	4	Add a new taxable product – LG V30, initial quantity on hand: 0, as of date 2/2/2020, Inventory asset account: Inventory Asset, price: $830.00, cost: $600.00, income account: Sales of Product Income, expense account: Cost of Goods Sold (taxable).
2/3/2020	Add a new service	4	Add a new service – LG Repairs, Rate: $95.00, income account: Services (not taxable).
2/3/2020	Modify budget	8	Modify the following monthly budgeted amounts (Budget 2) for February 2020 through December 2020 as follows: sales of product income: $25,000, services: $9,000, cost of goods sold: $18,000, advertising & marketing: $2,000, insurance: $750, interest expense: $200, meals and entertainment: $0, payroll: $11,000, utilities: $300.
2/3/2020	Add new employee	7	Add a new employee: Obi-Wan Kenobi, 65 Ocean View Lane, La Jolla, CA 92037, Employee ID No.: 555-22-9741.

2/3/2020	Add a bill	5	Add a bill from FixIt, Inc. (a new vendor) terms: Net 15, for repairs made last month for $350. This bill was accrued as of 1/31/2020. You will reverse this accrual at the end of this month.
2/4/2020	Add a new customer	4	Add a new customer – United Air, 598 Terrace View, Santa Cruz, CA 95060.
2/5/2020	Add a sales receipt	4	Add a new sales receipt 1004 for $1,320 – Customer: GHO Marketing, payment method: Check, reference no.: 1641, deposits to: Undeposited Funds, product: iPhone 7, quantity: 1 and Samsung Galaxy 8, quantity 1. (Be sure to override the sales tax to a flat 10% of taxable products.)
2/6/2020	Add a new purchase order	5	Add a new purchase order 1003 for $16,700 to purchase 10 iPhone 8 and 12 iPhone 8 Plus phones from vendor Apple Computer, Inc.
2/7/2020	Add a new purchase order	5	Add a new purchase order 1004 for $9,000 to purchase 15 LG V30 phones from vendor LG Baker Distributing Company.
2/10/2020	Add a new invoice	4	Add a new invoice 1005 for $9,955 – Customer: United Air, terms: Net 30, Product: Pixel, quantity: 10 and Samsung Note, quantity: 3. (Be sure to override the sales tax to a flat 10% of taxable products.)
2/10/2020	Add a new invoice	4	Add a new invoice 1006 for $1,800 – Customer: Graham Engineering, Inc., terms: Net 30, Service: Phone Consulting. Use 1 as the QTY and $1,800 as the rate. (Not taxable.)
2/11/2020	Add a cash receipt	4	Add a new cash receipt – Customer: Diamond Girl, Inc., payment method: Check, reference 7419, deposit to: Undeposited Funds, amount received: $6,865 (related to invoice # 1003).
2/11/2020	Pay bills	5	Pay $8,900 in bills from Hathaway Insurance, Google, Inc. and the News-Press, using check numbers 330, 331, and 332.
2/11/2020	Make a bank deposit	4	Add a bank deposit to the checking account in the amount of $8,185 to deposit previously received payments from GHO Marketing ($1,320) and Diamond Girl, Inc. ($6,865).
2/11/2020	Modify chart of accounts	3	Change the name of the Inventory Asset account to Inventory.
2/12/2020	Record a credit card purchase	5	Purchase supplies from Staples using the AMEX credit card $800. (Be sure to use the Supplies Asset account.)
2/12/2020	Record a check	5	Add check 333 to Etrade for $15,000 in additional investments.
2/12/2020	Record a check	5	Add check 334 to Property, Inc. (a new vendor) for $12,000 to prepay 1-year rent on a storage facility.
2/12/2020	Add a new purchase order	5	Add a new purchase order 1005 for $16,500 – Vendor: Samsung, Inc. for 10 Samsung Galaxy 8 and 20 Samsung Note phones.
2/13/2020	Add a new bill	5	Add a new bill based on a purchase order 1004 for $9,000 – Vendor: LG Baker Distributing Company., terms: Net 30. All items ordered were received.
2/14/2020	Add a new bill	5	Add a new bill based on a purchase order 1003 for $16,700 – Vendor: Apple Computer, Inc., terms: Net 30. All items ordered were received.
2/14/2020	Add a new bill	5	Add a new bill without a purchase order – San Diego Gas & Electric (a new vendor), terms: Net 15, account: Utilities, amount $300.00.
2/15/2020	Add new fixed asset accounts	6	Create a new fixed asset account: category type: Fixed Assets, detail type: Furniture & Fixtures, name: Furniture & Fixtures. Track depreciation of this asset.
2/15/2020	Record a credit card purchase and bank loan using a journal entry.	6	Add the purchase of $25,000 in furniture from Staples, Inc. $5,000 was charged to the AMEX credit card and the $20,000 balance was paid by signing a note payable using journal entry 10. (Be sure to indicate Rabobank in the name section of the notes payable entry and to record the purchase in the original cost sub-account of Furniture & Fixtures.)
2/15/2020	Pay first payroll	7	Add payroll (as you did in the chapter) based on the information shown in Figure 1. (Use checks 335 – 337)

2/17/2020	Sell common stock	6	Add the sale of common stock as a deposit of a $10,000 check #283 from Shareholders.
2/17/2020	Pay dividends	6	Add the payment of dividends to Shareholders, check 338, in the amount of $200.
2/18/2020	Make a loan payment	6	Add the payment of $590.38 made to Rabobank as an installment on the furniture purchased on 2/15/2020 which included interest expense of $66.67 and principal amount of $523.71 using check 339.
2/19/2020	Make a loan payment	6	Add the payment of $944.77 to Chase Bank as an installment on the note payable on 1/16/20 which includes interest expense of $106.67 and principal amount of $838.10 using check 340.
2/20/2020	Add a new bill	5	Add a new bill of $16,500 based on a purchase order 1005 – Vendor: Samsung, Inc., terms: Net 30. All items ordered were received. (Hint: First clear all lines in the Item details section of the bill which are left over from a previous bill from Samsung, Inc.)
2/25/2020	Pay bills	5	Pay bills from Samsung, Inc. ($6,950) and Apple Computer, Inc. ($16,700) using checks 341 and 342.
2/25/2020	Add a new invoice	4	Add invoice 1007 for $17,160 to Surfer Sales, terms: Net 30, for 10 iPhone 8 Plus and 6 iPhone 8 phones plus tax. (Be sure to override the sales tax to a flat 10% of taxable products.)
2/25/2020	Receive payment	4	Receive payment on account from Graham Engineering, Inc. of $1,800 from Invoice 1006 using check #1641 into the Undeposited Funds account.
2/27/2020	Add a new invoice	4	Add an invoice 1008 for $14,025 to Diamond Girl, Inc., terms: Net 30, Product: Samsung Note, Quantity: 15 (Be sure to override the sales tax to a flat 10% of taxable products.)
2/27/2020	Add a new invoice		Add an invoice 1009 for $875 to Rooney Enterprises (a new customer), for 25 hours of Phone Consulting @ $35/hour, terms: Net 30.
2/27/2020	Make a deposit	4	Deposited Graham Engineering, Inc.'s check for $1,800 into the checking account.
2/29/2020	Pay second payroll	7	Add payroll (as you did in the chapter) based on the information shown in Figure 2 below. (Use checks 343 – 345)
2/29/2020	Reconcile bank account	8	Reconcile your company's checking account. No service charges or interest were incurred or earned. The ending bank statement balance on 2/29/2020 was $6,358.23. All checks cleared the bank except checks 343, 344, and 345. All deposits cleared the bank except a deposit from Graham Engineering, Inc. for $1,800.
2/29/2020	Adjust supplies	9	$700 of supplies were used in February. Use journal entry 11.
2/29/2020	Adjust prepaids	9	$2,800 of prepaid expenses expired the month of February ($1,800 related to insurance expense and $1,000 related to rent.) Use journal entry 12.
2/29/2020	Accrue expenses	9	A bill for $2,550 was received and recorded in the next month for legal fees consumed in the current month. Use journal entry 13.
2/29/2020	Reverse accrual	9	Repair fees accrued on 1/31/2020 for $350 via journal entry 6 were properly recorded in February. Use journal entry 14 to reverse this accrual.
2/29/2020	Defer revenue	9	Phone Consulting services recorded on invoice 1009 for $875 for Rooney Enterprises, were deemed unearned as of 2/28/20. Use journal entry 15 to defer this revenue.
2/29/2020	Reverse deferral	9	Phone Consulting services deferred in the prior month of $210 were earned in February. Use journal entry 16 to reverse journal entry 7 recorded on 1/31/2020.
2/29/2020	Accrue depreciation	9	Depreciation Expense of $1,700 ($850, $500, and $350 for Building, Furniture, and Machinery & Equipment, respectively). Use journal entry 17 to record this depreciation.
2/29/2020	Accrue revenue	9	Phone Consulting services of $3,500 were performed on 2/28/2020 for a new customer Rigel Works but not invoiced or recorded into the accounting records. Use journal entry 18 to accrue this revenue.

Pay/Tax/Withholding	Kira	Jedi	Obi-Wan	Total
Hours if applicable	n/a	72	80	
Annual salary or hourly rate	48,000.00	17.00	22.00	
Gross pay	**2,000.00**	**1,224.00**	**1,760.00**	**4,984.00**
Federal withholding	274.00	167.69	241.12	**682.81**
Social security employee (6.2%)	124.00	75.89	109.12	**309.01**
Medicare employee (1.45%)	29.00	17.75	25.52	**72.27**
Employee withholding	**427.00**	**261.33**	**375.76**	**1,064.09**
Social security employer (6.2%)	124.00	75.89	109.12	**309.01**
Medicare company employer (1.45%)	29.00	17.75	25.52	**72.27**
Employer payroll tax expense	**153.00**	**93.64**	**134.64**	**381.28**
Net Check amount	1,573.00	962.67	1,384.24	**3,919.91**

Figure 1

1st Semi-monthly Payroll

Pay/Tax/Withholding	Kira	Jedi	Obi-Wan	Total
Hours if applicable	n/a	65	85	
Annual salary or hourly rate	48,000.00	17.00	22.00	
Gross pay	**2,000.00**	**1,105.00**	**1,870.00**	**4,975.00**
Federal withholding	274.00	151.39	256.19	**681.58**
Social security employee (6.2%)	124.00	68.51	115.94	**308.45**
Medicare employee (1.45%)	29.00	16.02	27.12	**72.14**
Employee withholding	**427.00**	**235.92**	**399.25**	**1,062.17**
Social security employer (6.2%)	124.00	68.51	115.94	**308.45**
Medicare company employer (1.45%)	29.00	16.02	27.12	**72.14**
Employer payroll tax expense	**153.00**	**84.53**	**143.06**	**380.59**
Net Check amount	1,573.00	869.08	1,470.75	**3,912.83**

Figure 2

2nd Semi-monthly Payroll

Requirements:

1 Create, save, and print a Profit and Loss report for February 2020 which includes a % of income column.

2 Create, save, and print a Total Income Transaction report for February 2020.

3 Create, save, and print a Balance Sheet report for February 29, 2020.

4 Create, save, and print a Checking report for February 2020.

5 Create, save, and print a Statement of Cash Flows report for February 2020.

6 Create, save, and print an A/R Aging Summary report for February 2020.

7 Create, save, and print an A/P Aging Summary report for February 2020.

8 Create, save, and print an Inventory Valuation Summary report for February 2020.

9 Create, save, and print a Transactions List by Date report for February 2020.

10 Create, save, and print a Budget vs. Actuals report for February 2020.

Case 4 Comprehensive Problem

Case 4, which begins in Chapter 3, is a Sports Gym which sells month to month memberships and related merchandise.. Business events in Case 4 occurred from 12/31/20 to 1/31/21 when presented in Chapters 3–10. The following is a description of business events that occurred in the month of February 2021.

Date	Description of Event	Chapter	Event
2/2/2021	Add new product	4	Add a new taxable product –Bowflex Xtreme Home Gym, initial quantity on hand: 0, as of date 2/1/2021, Inventory asset account: Inventory Asset, price: $1,199.00, cost: $700.00, income account: Sales of Product Income, expense account: Cost of Goods Sold (taxable)
2/2/2021	Change the name of a product	4	Change the name of the Yoga pants to Xtreme Yoga Pants.
2/2/2021	Add a new vendor	5	Add a new vendor – Sole Fitness LLC,1844 Raven Rd., Diana, TX 75640, terms: Net 30.
2/2/2021	Add a new product	4	Add a new taxable product – Sole E98 Elliptical, initial quantity on hand: 0, as of date 2/2/2021, Inventory asset account: Inventory Asset, price: $2,300.00, cost: $1,500.00, income account: Sales of Product Income, expense account: Cost of Goods Sold (taxable).
2/3/2021	Add a new service	4	Add a new service – Annual Fee - Individual, Rate: $1,620.00, income account: Sales (not taxable).
2/3/2021	Modify budget	8	Modify the following monthly budgeted amounts (Budget 1) for February 2021 through December 2021 as follows: sales of product income: $6,000, sales: $60,000, cost of goods sold: $3,000, advertising & marketing: $3,000, insurance: $2,100, interest expense: $325, payroll: $16,000, repairs & maintenance: $700.
2/3/2021	Add new employee	7	Add a new employee: Sammy Watkins, 300 Westwood Blvd., Westwood, CA 90037, Employee ID No.: 555-22-9741.
2/3/2021	Add a bill	5	Add a bill from Supreme Marketing, terms: Net 15, for advertising performed last month for $675. This bill was accrued as of 1/31/2021. You will reverse this accrual at the end of this month.
2/4/2021	Add a new customer	4	Add a new customer – Fox Broadcasting Company, 10201 West Pico Blvd., Los Angeles, CA 90064, terms: Net 30.

2/5/2021	Add a sales receipt	4	Add a new sales receipt 1005 for $6,480 – New Customer: Harrison Ford, payment method: Check, reference no.: 1987, deposit to: Undeposited Funds, service: Annual Fee - Individual, quantity: 4.
2/5/2021	Add a new purchase order	5	Add a new purchase order 1003 for $2,100 to purchase 3 Bowflex Xtreme Home Gyms from vendor Bowflex, Inc.
2/5/2021	Add a new purchase order	5	Add a new purchase order 1004 for $7,500 to purchase 5 Sole E98 Elliptical machines from vendor Sole Fitness LLC.
2/8/2021	Add a new invoice	4	Add a new invoice 1006 for $29,453.10– Customer: Fox Broadcasting Company, terms: Net 30, Service: Monthly Fee – Corporate Membership 50 Employees, quantity: 4 and Bowflex Dumbbells, quantity: 20.
2/9/2021	Add a new invoice	4	Add a new invoice 1007 for $12,000 – Customer: ABC Studios, terms: Net 30, Service: Monthly Fee – Corporate Membership 50 Employees Quantity - 2
2/11/2021	Receive payment	4	Receive payment – Customer: ABC Studios, payment method: Check, reference 98745, deposit to: Undeposited Funds, amount received: $7,368.75 (related to invoice # 1002).
2/11/2021	Pay bills	5	Pay $6,800 in bills from Bowflex Inc. and Supreme Marketing, using check numbers 25511and 25512.
2/11/2021	Make a bank deposit	4	Add a bank deposit to the checking account in the amount of $13,848.75to deposit previously received payments from ABC Studios ($7,368.75) and Harrison Ford ($6,480.00).
2/11/2021	Modify chart of accounts	3	Change the name of the Inventory Asset account to Inventory.
2/12/2021	Record a credit card purchase	5	Purchase supplies from Wal-Mart (a new vendor) using the VISA credit card $1,800. (Be sure to use the Supplies asset account.)
2/12/2021	Record a check	5	Add check 25513 to Barber Investments, Inc. for $10,000 in additional investments.
2/12/2021	Record a check	5	Add check 25514 to Leaseco, Inc. (a new vendor) for $6,000 to prepay 1-year rent on a storage facility. (Prepaid Expenses)
2/12/2021	Add a new purchase order	5	Add a new purchase order 1005 for $25,000 – Vendor: NordicTrack, Inc. for 5 new treadmills for use in the facility not for resale (Equipment).
2/15/2021	Add a new bill	5	Add a new bill based on a purchase order 1003 for $2,100 – Vendor: Bowflex Inc., terms: Net 15. All items ordered were received.
2/15/2021	Add a new bill	5	Add a new bill without a purchase order – LADWP (a new vendor), terms: Net 15, account: Utilities, amount $900.00.
2/15/2021	Add new fixed asset accounts	6	Create new fixed asset accounts: category type: Fixed Assets, detail type: Fixed Asset Computers, name: Computers. Track depreciation of this asset. Be sure to change the name of the Computer accumulated depreciation account from Depreciation to Accumulated Depreciation.
2/15/2021	Record a credit card purchase and bank loan using a journal entry.	6	Add the purchase of $45,000.00 in computers from Best Buy (a new vendor) $10,000.00 was charged to the VISA credit card and the $35,000.00 balance was paid by signing a note payable using journal entry 10. (Be sure to indicate Coast Bank in the name section of the notes payable entry and to record the purchase in the original cost sub-account of Computers.)
2/15/2021	Pay first payroll	7	Using recurring transactions (as you did in the chapter) pay Graham, Beckett, and Allegra based on the information shown in Figure 1. Using the Check function pay Sammy based on the information shown in Figure 1. Be sure to indicate that Sammy's check is a recurring transaction. (Use checks 25515 – 25518)
2/17/2021	Sell common stock	6	Add the sale of common stock as a deposit of a $25,000.00 check #1974 from Shareholders.
2/17/2021	Pay dividends	6	Add the payment of dividends to Shareholders, check 25519, in the amount of $1,000.00.

2/18/2021	Make a loan payment	6	Add the payment of $2,000.00 made to Coast Bank as an installment on notes payable which included interest expense of $300.00 and principal amount of $1,700.00 using check 25520.
2/19/2021	Add a new bill	5	Add a new bill of $2,985.00 based on a purchase order 1002 – Vendor: Precor., terms: Net 30. All items ordered were received.
2/25/2021	Pay bills	5	Pay bills from LADWP ($900.00) and Supreme Marketing ($675.00) using checks 25521 and 25522.
2/26/2021	Add a bill	5	Add a new bill of $7,500 based on purchase order 1004 – Vendor: Sole Fitness LLC, Terms: net 30.
2/27/2021	Add a new invoice	4	Add invoice 1008 for $7,555.50 to Jules, Inc., terms: Net 30, for 3 Sole E98 Elliptical machines plus tax.
2/27/2021	Receive payment	4	Receive payment on account from ABC Studios. of $12,000.00 from Invoice 1007 using check #19981 into the Undeposited Funds account.
2/27/2021	Add a new bill	5	Add a new bill of $25,000.00 based on purchase order 1005 – Vendor: NordicTrack Inc., Terms: net 30.
2/27/2021	Add a sales receipt	4	Add a new sales receipt 1009 for $3,280.62 to Tayor Swift (a new customer), Product: Bowflex Xtreme Home Gym, Quantity: 2 and Product: Power Block Elite Dumbbells, Quantity: 2, deposited to Undeposited Funds, plus sales tax.
2/27/2021	Make a deposit	4	Deposited ABC Studios check for $12,000.00 into the checking account.
2/28/2021	Pay second payroll	7	Add payroll (as you did in the chapter) based on the information shown in Figure 2 below. (Use checks 25523 – 25526)
2/28/2021	Reconcile bank account	8	Reconcile your company's checking account. No service charges or interest were incurred or earned. The ending bank statement balance on 2/28/2021 was $19,173.16. All checks cleared the bank except checks 25524 and 25526 for $1,671.31 and $1,275.70 respectively. All deposits cleared the bank except a deposit from ABC Studios for $12,000.00.
2/28/2021	Adjust supplies	9	$1,700 of supplies were used in February. Use journal entry 11.
2/28/2021	Adjust prepaids	9	$3,000.00 of prepaid expenses expired the month of February ($2,000.00 related to insurance and $1,000 related to rent & lease.) Use journal entry 12.
2/28/2021	Reverse accrual	9	Reverse journal entry 6 made on 1/31/2021 to accrue advertising & marketing expenses of $675 to Supreme Marketing using journal entry 13.
2/28/2021	Accrue expenses	9	A bill for $1,300.00 was received and recorded in the next month for legal & professional services consumed in the current month. Use journal entry 14.
2/28/2021	Reverse accrual	9	Sales accrued on 1/31/2021 for $750.00 via journal entry 8 were properly recorded in February. Use journal entry 15 to reverse this accrual.
2/28/2021	Defer revenue	9	Sales of product income recorded on sales receipt 1009 for $3,280.62 to Taylor Swift, were deemed unearned as of 2/28/21. Use journal entry 16 to defer this revenue and reduce sales tax payable You'll need to review this sales receipt to determine amounts by account.
2/28/2021	Reverse deferral	9	Training services recorded on invoice #1003 for $3,750 to Flyer Corporation were only partially performed even though invoiced. $2,000 of sales had not been earned. and thus were deferred in the prior month. Use journal entry 17 to reverse journal entry 7 recorded on 1/31/2021.
2/28/2021	Accrue depreciation	9	Record Depreciation Expense of $1,600 ($500, $600, $400 and $100 for Building, Furniture, Machinery & Equipment, and Computer respectively). Use journal entry 18 to record this depreciation.
2/28/2021	Accrue revenue	9	Training (Sales) of $2,500 were performed on 2/28/2021for but not invoiced or recorded into the accounting records. Use journal entry 19 to accrue this revenue.

Pay/Tax/Withholding	Graham	Allegra	Beckett	Sammy	Total
Hours if applicable	n/a	70	80	90	
Annual salary or hourly rate	$ 75,000	$ 25.00	$ 22.00	$ 20.00	
Gross pay	**3,125.00**	**1,750.00**	**1,760.00**	**1,800.00**	**8.435.00**
Federal withholding	428.13	239.75	241.12	246.60	**1,155.60**
Social security employee (6.2%)	193.75	108.50	109.12	111.60	**522.97**
Medicare employee (1.45%)	45.31	25.38	25.52	26.10	**122.31**
Employee withholding	**667.19**	**373.63**	**375.76**	**384.30**	**1,800.87**
Social security employer (6.2%)	193.75	108.50	109.12	111.60	**522.97**
Medicare company employer (1.45%)	45.34	25.38	25.52	26.10	**122.34**
Employer payroll tax expense	**239.09**	**133.88**	**134.64**	**137.70**	**645.31**
Net Check amount	2,457.81	1,376.37	1,384.24	1,415.70	**5,218.42**

Figure 1

1st Semi-monthly Payroll

Pay/Tax/Withholding	Graham	Allegra	Beckett	Sammy	Total
Hours if applicable	n/a	85	72	83	
Annual salary or hourly rate	$ 75,000	$ 25.00	$ 22.00	$ 20.00	
Gross pay	**3,125.00**	**2,125.00**	**1,584.00**	**1,660.00**	**8,494.00**
Federal withholding	428.13	291.13	217.01	246.60	**1,182.86**
Social security employee (6.2%)	193.75	131.75	98.21	111.60	**535.31**
Medicare employee (1.45%)	45.31	30.81	22.97	26.10	**125.19**
Employee withholding	**667.19**	**453.69**	**338.18**	**384.30**	**1,843.36**
Social security employer (6.2%)	193.75	131.75	98.12	111.60	**535.31**
Medicare company employer (1.45%)	45.34	30.81	22.97	26.10	**125.22**
Employer payroll tax expense	**239.09**	**162.56**	**121.18**	**137.70**	**660.53**
Net Check amount	2,457.81	1,671.31	1,245.81	1,275.70	**5,374.93**

Figure 2

2nd Semi-monthly Payroll

Requirements:

1. Create, save, and print a Trial Balance report for February 2021.
2. Create, save, and print a Profit and Loss report for February 2021.
3. Create, save, and print a Total Income Transaction report for February 2021.
4. Create, save, and print a Balance Sheet report for February 28, 2021.
5. Create, save, and print a Checking report for February 2021.
6. Create, save, and print a Statement of Cash Flows report for February 2021.
7. Create, save, and print an A/R Aging Summary report for February 2021.
8. Create, save, and print an A/P Aging Summary report for February 2021.
9. Create, save, and print an Inventory Valuation Summary report for February 2021.
10. Create, save, and print a Transactions List by Date report for February 2021.
11. Create, save, and print a Budget vs. Actuals report for February 2021.

Overview – Do I Need to Become QuickBooks Online Certified?

There are two schools of thought here. The first is that becoming certified provides employers/clients independent confirmation of an individual's skill and proficiency in using QuickBooks Online. Thus, certification is a good resume builder. The second is that any employer/client that relies solely on certification to assure competency in using QuickBooks Online will eventually find themselves looking for a new QuickBooks Online professional.

Does it hurt? No. Does it help? Maybe. Is it necessary? No. What is important is the knowledge, skill, and proficiency in using QuickBooks as a tool to help businesses better understand the financial implications of their decisions.

In the author's opinion, certification takes a back seat to accounting education and experience. Thus, it is in the student's best interest to gain accounting knowledge (the more the better) through courses at accredited institutions in the topics of bookkeeping, financial accounting, managerial accounting, cost accounting, tax accounting, and the application of QuickBooks to different business situations. The next step is to gain experience through internships or part-time jobs working under a QuickBooks/Accounting professional. Add that to certification and you're ready for gainful employment.

The following is a summary overview of the QuickBooks certified user online exam objectives made available:

QuickBooks Certified User Online Exam Objectives

1 QuickBooks Setup and Maintenance (14%) – A student should know:

   a. What information QuickBooks does and does NOT require when creating a new QuickBooks account

   b. What lists can be imported and the basic steps to do so (including what is NOT imported)

   c. How to modify/change basic elements after setting up (e.g., accounts and company address)

   d. How to set up users including a basic knowledge of the access rights available for different user types

   e. How to navigate or move around QuickBooks:
   i) What info and functionality is found in the three key access points – navigation bar, global create, and company settings
   ii) What's located on the Dashboard and how to control what is or isn't seen
   iii) What each button (e.g., save and more) does on major forms (e.g., invoice and bill)

2 List Management (12%) – A student should know:

a. The names of the major lists in QuickBooks and what type of information is tracked on each

b. How to manage lists (Customers, Chart of Accounts, Products and Services, etc.). This includes:
   i) Who should appear on which names list (e.g., employees or customers) and how to handle situations where the same person company should be on more than one list
   ii) Adding new list entries
   iii) Removing list entries (including what QuickBooks does if an entry has a balance)
   iv) Editing list entries
   v) Merging list entries (including the basic rules of what can and can't be merged)

c. Which names MUST appear on which forms (i.e., which names are required on specific transactions otherwise QuickBooks will NOT save the transaction)

3 Sales/Money-In (20%) – A student should know:

a. How to set up a Product or Service

b. How this setup allows QuickBooks to perform the appropriate accounting behind the scenes to correctly impact Financial Statements

c. How to set up Customers including how to specify when payment is due (terms) and track multiple projects/jobs for a single customer (sub-customers)

d. How to record sales/revenue. This includes
   i) Knowing the advantages of using built in sales forms (e.g., invoice) over other methods (e.g., Bank Deposit or Journal Entry)
   ii) Completing the Invoicing (A/R) and Sales Receipt (no A/R) workflow from sale to bank deposit
   iii) How QuickBooks impacts and uses the Undeposited Funds, Accounts Receivable, and the bank accounts in the invoicing cycle
   iv) How to invoice for billable expenses (includes how to turn this feature on and record expenses to begin the process)
   v) How and why to record a customer credit

e. How and why to use Estimates, Delayed Charges, and Credit Memos and how these transactions affect customer balances

4 Purchases/Money-Out (18%) – A student should know:

a. How to set up a Product or Service to be used on purchase Forms and when this is appropriate and how this setup allows QuickBooks to perform the appropriate accounting behind the scenes to correctly impact Financial Statements

b. How to set up Vendors

c. When to use the following transactions/workflows. This includes knowing the steps to record them in QuickBooks when the company does NOT have connected bank accounts (online banking). And how each affects the Vendor's Balance
    i)   Purchase Orders
    ii) Entering and paying bills (A/P)
    iii) Recording Checks (hand written or printed)
    iv) Recording Credit and Debit Card transactions
    v)   Recording EFT's, online payments, wire transfers, etc.
    vi) Vendor Credits

d. When and how to void vs. delete a check

e. How to use the Vendor page and reports to identify how much your company owes, and when payment is due

5 Basic Accounting (10%) – A student should know:

a. What the basic financial statements are and have a basic understanding of their sections and what they mean

b. The difference between cash and accrual reports

c. How and why to set a closing date

d. How to enter a Journal Entry if asked to do so by an accountant

e. How to use the Audit Log to determine changes made by specific users

6 Reports (8%) – A student should know:

a. How to customize a report and run customized reports later

b. How to set up QuickBooks to automatically email reports

c. How and why to collapse and expand reports

d. How and why to export reports to Excel and any limitations on exporting the report back into QuickBooks

7 Customization/Saving Time (18%) – A student should know:

a. How to set up QuickBooks to track income and expenses for multiple locations, or to separate transactions by class (e.g., department and profit center)

b. How to create custom fields on invoices

c. How and why to make transactions recurring, including which transactions can be made recurring

d. Which forms can be customized and the steps to customize a sales form

e. How to use a keyboard shortcut to find a list of keyboard shortcuts

f. The time saving benefits of using QuickBooks online including:
    i)   Using QuickBooks on phones and tablets (IOS and Android). Students just need to be familiar with basic functionality and understand that QuickBooks mobile can use a mobile device's camera, phone, and GPS to save time

ii) Connecting Apps to expand what QuickBooks does including knowing where to find apps and know that apps expand what QuickBooks does and automatically synch data with QuickBooks

iii) The ability to have users/employees with different operating systems (e.g., Mac vs. P.C.) and web browsers (e.g., Chrome vs. Safari) still access the same data

iv) Not needing to backup, and no IT issues (e.g., reinstalling software in cases of crashes or new computer purchases) usually associated with desktop software

Links to QuickBooks Certification Information

https://certiport.pearsonvue.com/Certifications/QuickBooks/Certified-User/Overview

https://quickbooks.intuit.com/accountants/training-certification/certifications/

Index

A

account(s). *See also* charts of accounts
Accounts Payable
 establishing beginning
  balance, 41–42
 journalizing, 41–42
Accounts Receivable
 establishing beginning
  balance, 41–42
 journalizing, 41–42
 reports, 30
creating, 3–4
Inventory Asset, 96
Opening Balance Equity, 43–45
Payroll (expense), 128
Payroll Tax Payable (liability),
 128
Account Quickreport, 27
Accounts Payable (A/P) account
 establishing beginning balance,
  41–42
 journalizing, 41–42
 Transaction Report, 96
Accounts Payable (A/P) Aging Detail
 Report, 195
Accounts Payable (A/P) Aging
 Summary report, 194–196
Accounts Payable (A/P) Register
 page, 26
Accounts Receivable (A/R) account
 establishing beginning balance,
  41–42
 journalizing, 41–42
 reports, 30
 Transaction reports, 189
Accounts Receivable (A/R) Aging
 Detail Report, 193
Accounts Receivable (A/R) Aging
 Summary reports, 192–194
accrued expenses, 173–174
accruing revenue, 175–176
adjusting entries, 168–178
 accrued expenses, 173–174
 accruing revenue, 175–176
 creating trial balance, 169
 depreciation, 176–178
 overview, 168–169
 prepaid expenses
  deferring supplies as asset,
   170–171
  recording consumption of
   supplies, 171–173
 types of, 168
 unearned revenue, 174–175
Advanced settings, 32
aging summaries
 Accounts Payable Aging
  Summary report, 194–196
 Accounts Receivable Aging
  Summary reports, 192–194
A/P account. *See* Accounts Payable
 (A/P) account
A/P (Accounts Payable) Aging Detail
 Report, 195
A/P (Accounts Payable) Aging
 Summary report, 194–196
A/P (Accounts Payable) Register
 page, 26

A/R account. *See* Accounts Receivable
 (A/R) account
A/R (Accounts Receivable) Aging
 Detail Report, 193
A/R (Accounts Receivable) Aging
 Summary reports, 192–194

B

balance sheet, creating, 43–45, 188–190
Balance Sheet page, 44
Balance Sheet reports, 29
Bank and Credit Cards page, 22
bank deposit, inputting, 70
banking transactions, viewing, 21–23
bank reconciliations, 155–158
 creating, 156–158
 overview, 155
 Summary Reconciliation
  reports, 158
Basic Info window, 5
bill(s). *See also* invoices
 adding purchase order
  information, 89
 after adding purchase order
  information, 89
 credit card, 93–94
 entering, 88
 paying, 91–94
 for prepaid expenses, 91
 for services, 90
 from vendors for receipt of
  products or services, 87–91
budget(s)
 Budget Overview reports, 152–154
 Budget *vs.* Actual reports, 154–155
 creating, 149–151
 reports, 151–155
Budgeting window, 150
Budget Overview reports, 152–154
Budget *vs.* Actual reports, 154–155
Business Overview reports, 28

C

Case studies
 adjusting entries, 180–183
 budgets and bank reconciliations,
  160–167
 financial statements and reports,
  202–205
 investing and financing activities,
  118–125
 operating activities, purchases
  and cash payments, 98–107
 operating activities, sales and
  cash receipts, 73–82
 payroll, 137–148
 setting up company, 48–59
cash receipts, 67–70
charts of accounts. *See also* account(s)
 modifying, 37–42
  adding additional accounts,
   40–41
  adding checking accounts,
   37–38
  adding products and services, 38–40
 viewing, 25–27

check payments, 94
common stock
 definition of, 112
 recording deposit of funds from
  sale of, 113
companies
 closing Opening Balance Equity
  account, 43–45
 establishing beginning balances,
  36–42
 modifying chart of accounts,
  36–42
 setting for, 35–36
Company Info window, 5–6
Company settings, 31
Create (+) menu, 7–8
Create window, 64, 66, 68, 70, 85, 92
Credit Card Charge, 94
credit card payment, 93–94
customer
 accessing information about,
  17–18
 adding, 63–64
Customer Information window, 63
Customers window, 6, 8

D

deferring, definition of, 168
Deposit window, 70
depreciation, 108–109, 176–178
dividends
 definition of, 112
 payment of, 113

E

employees
 accessing information about,
  20–21
 adding, 126–127
 paying, 129–135
  recording payment,
   129–135
  Recurring Transactions,
   132
  semi-monthly payroll
   information, 129,
   133
  Transaction Report, 131,
   134
  Trial Balance, 131, 134
Employees window, 6, 9
Expenses settings, 32
expense transactions, viewing, 23–25
Expense window, 25

F

financial statements
 balance sheet, 188–190
 income statements
  creating, 185–187
  definition of, 185
  Profit and Loss Report,
   185–186
  Sales Receipt, 187
  Transaction Report, 187
 overview, 184

Statement of Cash Flows, 190–192
financing activities. *See* investing and
 financing activities
fixed assets
 acquisition of in exchange for
  longterm debt, 115–116
 definition of, 108
 depreciation, 108–109
 recording purchase of, 109–110

G

Gear window, 10
generally accepted accounting principles (GAAP), 168

H

Help feature
 accessing, 11–12
 built-in resources, 11–12
 QuickBooks Community, 11–12
Help window, 12
Home page, 6–10

I

income statements
 creating, 185–187
 definition of, 185
 Profit and Loss Report, 185–186
 Sales Receipt, 187
 Transaction Report, 187
Inventory Asset Account, 96
Inventory Valuation Detail, 197
Inventory Valuation Summary report,
 196–198
investing and financing activities
 acquisition of fixed assets in
  exchange for long-term
  debt, 115–116
 common stock and dividends,
  112–113
 fixed assets, 108–110
 long-term debt, 114–116
 long-term investments, 111
invoices
 Accounts Receivable Aging Summary, 195
 adding, 66–67
 sales, 64–67

J

journalizing
 Accounts Payable (A/P) account,
  41–42
 Accounts Receivable (A/R)
  account, 41–42

L

lists
 of products and services, 61
 in QBO, 27–28
 viewing
  list of lists, 27
  list of terms, 28

long-term debt, 114–116
    acquisition of fixed assets in exchange for, 115–116
    recording receipt of funds from borrowing, 114–115
    repayment with interest, 115
long-term investments
    definition of, 111
    recording purchase of, 111

M

Manage Users window, 11

O

Opening Balance Equity account, 43–45
operating activities
    paying bills, 91–94
    purchases and cash payments, 83–97
        adding vendors, 83–84
        purchase orders, 84–87
        recording bills, 87–91
        recording check payments, 94
        recording credit card payments, 93–94
        trial balance, 94–97
    sales and cash receipts, 60–71
        adding services, products, and customers, 60–64
        recording cash receipts, 67–70
        sales invoices, 64–67
        sales receipts, 64–67
        Transaction Detail by Account reports, 70–71

P

payments
    check, 94
    credit card, 93–94
    receipts of, 67–70
    recording, 129–135
payroll
    adding employees, 126–127
    adding payroll-related accounts, 128–129
    paying employees, 129–135
        recording payments, 129–135
        recurring transactions, 132
        semi-monthly payroll information, 129, 133
        Transaction Report, 131, 134
        Trial Balance, 131, 134
Payroll (expense) account, 128
Payroll Tax Payable (liability) account, 128
Plus (+) icon button, 7–8

prepaid expenses
    bills for, 91
    deferring supplies as asset, 170–171
    recording consumption of supplies, 171–173
products
    adding, 62–63, 84–87
    lists of, 61
    Purchase Order, 85, 87
    recording bills from vendors for receipt of, 87–91
Product/Service information window, 39
Profit and Loss budget, 149–151
Profit and Loss report, 29.
    See also income statements
    creating, 185–187
    customizing, 198–200
    saving, 198–200
Purchase of Equipment, 110
Purchase Order, 85, 87
purchases and cash payments, 83–97
    adding vendors, 83–84
    paying bills, 91–94
    purchase orders, 84–87
    recording bills, 87–91
    recording check payments, 94
    recording credit card payments, 93–94
    trial balance, 94–97

Q

QuickBooks Accountant (QBDT), 2
QuickBooks Online Plus (QBO)
    assigning instructor as company "accountant", 10–11
    choosing options in, 5
    creating accounts, 3–4
    definition, 1
    versus desktop version of QuickBooks, 2–3
    Help feature, 11–12
    navigating within, 6–10
    providing user information, 4–6

R

receipts of payment (cash receipts), 67–70. *See also* sales and cash receipts
Receive Payment window, 68
Reconcile - Checking form, 157–158
Reconcile window, 156
reconciliation process, 156
Recurring Transactions, 132
report(s)
    Accounts Payable Aging Detail, 195
    Accounts Payable Aging Summary, 194–196
    accounts receivable, 30
    Accounts Receivable Aging Detail Report, 193

Accounts Receivable Aging Summary, 192–194
Balance Sheet, 29
Business Overview, 28
Inventory Valuation Summary, 196–198
Profit and Loss, 185–187
Profit and Loss report, 29
Statement of Cash Flows, 30
Transaction
    for Accounts Payable account, 96
    for Accounts Receivable (A/R), 189
    for checking account, 96
    income statements, 187
    for Inventory Asset Account, 96
    for supplies asset, 173
Transaction Detail by Account
    creating, 45–46, 70–71
    exporting, 45–46, 70–71
    printing, 45–46, 70–71
revenue
    accruing, 175–176
    unearned, 174–175

S

sales and cash receipts, 60–71
    adding services, products, and customers, 60–64
    recording cash receipts, 67–70
    sales invoices, 64–67
    sales receipts
        adding, 64–67
        definition of, 64
    Transaction Detail by Account reports, 70–71
Sales Receipt after Sales Tax, 65
Sales Receipt before Sales Tax, 65
sales receipts
    adding, 64–67
    definition of, 64
    income statements, 187
Sales settings, 31
sales transactions, viewing, 23–25
Sample Company
    accessing customer information, 17–18
    accessing employee information, 20–21
    accessing vendor information, 18–20
    adding customers, 63–64
    adding new services, 60–62
    adding products, 62–63
    adding sales invoices, 64–67
    banking transactions, viewing, 21–23
    cash receipts, 67–70
    chart of accounts, viewing, 25–27
    expense transactions, viewing, 23–25
    list of lists, viewing, 27

list of terms, viewing, 28
    receipts of payment, 67–70
    recording purchase of long-term investment, 111
    sales transactions, viewing, 23–25
    settings management
        Advanced settings, 32
        Company settings, 31
        Expenses settings, 32
        Sales settings, 31
Sample Company Home page, 15–16
semi-monthly payroll information, 129, 133
services
    adding, 60–62
    lists of, 61
    paying bills for, 90
    recording bills from vendors for receipt of, 87–91
    settings management
        Advanced settings, 32
        Company settings, 31
        Expenses settings, 32
        Sales settings, 31
Set Up Your Account window, 3–4
Sign In Window, 48
Statement of Cash Flows, 30, 190–192
Summary Reconciliation reports, 158

T

Transaction Detail by Account
    creating, 45–46, 70–71
    exporting, 45–46, 70–71
    printing, 45–46, 70–71
Transaction reports
    for Accounts Payable account, 96
    for Accounts Receivable (A/R), 189
    for checking account, 96
    income statements, 187
    for Inventory Asset Account, 96
    for notes payable, 192
    for supplies asset, 173
trial balance
    creating, 94–97, 169
    investigating, 94–97

U

unearned revenue, 174–175
user information, 4–6
Users window, 10

V

Vendor Information window, 83–84
vendors
    accessing information about, 18–20
    adding, 83–84
    recording bills for receipt of products or services, 87–91
Vendors window, 6, 9